WHEN MONEY
SPEAKS

The *McCUTCHEON* DECISION,
CAMPAIGN FINANCE LAWS and the FIRST AMENDMENT

RONALD COLLINS
&
DAVID SKOVER

SCOTUS *BOOKS-in-BRIEF*

an imprint of

Top Five Books
OAK PARK, ILLINOIS

A SCOTUS Book-in-Brief

Published by Top Five Books, LLC
521 Home Avenue
Oak Park, Illinois 60304
www.top-five-books.com

ISBN: 978-1-938938-15-3 (Paperback)
ISBN: 978-1-938938-14-6 (eBook)

Cover image courtesy of Veer. Bobby Burchfield photo courtesy of McDermott Will & Emery LLP. Donald Verrilli photo courtesy of the U.S. Department of Justice. All other images courtesy of Ronald Collins.

May 19, 2014
Seattle, WA

To Annette —

O Captain! my Captain!
May you steer the ship
of state safely, courageously,
and wisely!
With great appreciation,

David

To
NADINE STROSSEN
The First Lady of Liberty

Contents

We know that money talks, but that is the problem, not the answer.
—Anthony Lewis (1976)

To me, [many of these campaign finance laws are] nothing less than outright suppression of speech of the most odious nature.
—Floyd Abrams (2005)

Prologue

HIS PROBLEM STARTED when he tried to give away money. Shaun McCutcheon believes in giving to charities like Feed the Children. He also believes in giving to political causes and campaigns; he thinks it will make America a better place. But if he acted as he wanted to on his political beliefs, he could find himself behind bars. The threat of a five-year penalty for contributing his own money to a political cause struck him as un-American. So he went to the Federal Election Commission and then to court. The federal campaign law, he argued, abridged his First Amendment rights.

The Arkansas-born and Alabama-raised electrical engineer makes a good living. Though rich, McCutcheon cannot be counted among the super-rich. "I do not come from a political family, and I do not come from a rich family," McCutcheon told *Politico*. "I understand that Republican politics is a lot of family business, but I'm not that." He is the CEO of Coalmont Electrical Development, which has twenty full-time employees. McCutcheon promotes commerce—he began Coalmont in 1996 and has built it up since then—and believes that government should be fiscally responsible. Perhaps that explains why he chose to serve as the finance director of the Jefferson County Republican Executive Committee. He is also the chairman of the Conservative Action Fund, a political action committee (PAC) that advances the messages and goals of conservative Republicans. In 2012 he lost his bid to become an Alabama delegate at the Republican National Convention for Mitt Romney. But that in no way dampened his commitment to conservatism.

At forty-six, Shaun McCutcheon is no status-quo man. "He wants change," Chris Brown, an Alabama Republican political consultant, told *USA Today*. "He wants guys who are going to shake it up." Much to the same effect, he described himself to the *Washington Post* as "just another political activist trying to change the world." To that end, the politically active bachelor contributed almost $384,000 to federal candidates, committees, and parties in the 2011–2012 election cycle, according to the Center for Responsive Politics. But McCutcheon wanted to do even more. Acting as an individual (and not a corporation), he aimed to give *more* of his personal money to the Republican National Committee (RNC), the National Republican Senatorial Committee (NRSC), and the National Republican Congressional Committee (NRCC), as well as to conservative candidates and PACs.

The problem? A federal campaign law, known as the Bipartisan Campaign Reform Act (BCRA), barred him from giving as much money as he would like, both to different PACS and in the aggregate. Governed by the Federal Election Commission (FEC), the law limits an individual to $48,600 in contributions to candidates and $74,600 in contributions to political parties, with an aggregate cap of $123,200. McCutcheon wanted to donate to twenty-seven candidates, most of whom were challengers, but could not because of the aggregate limits imposed by BCRA. With patriotic fervor, he doled out a number of checks in $1,776 increments. He contributed $33,088 to fifteen candidates during the 2012 election cycle, though he wanted to contribute more. During that cycle, he wanted to donate an additional $75,000 to party committees and $21,312 to candidates. For the 2013–2014 election cycle, he hoped to contribute a total of more than $60,000 to candidates, plus $75,000 to three Republican national party committees. Such contributions for both cycles would have exceeded federal limits. If he were to violate those limits, he would be guilty of a felony. (Though his lawyers challenged only the *aggregate* contribution limits and not the *individual* ones, the Center for Public Integrity revealed that McCutcheon had "made an excessive contribution to the Alabama Republican Party's federal political committee" in 2012. In response, Dan Backer, McCutcheon's lead lawyer, explained that they would contact the Alabama GOP to "advise them to re-designate or refund.")

The idea of being criminally penalized for supporting a cause or campaign with his money did not set well with McCutcheon. "It's a freedom of speech case about your right to spend your money on as many candidates as you choose," he told an Alabama reporter. Or as he was quoted in *USA Today*: "If the government tells you that you can't spend your money where you want, there should be a real, real good reason."

Was there a "good reason" to abridge the First Amendment right asserted by Shaun McCutcheon? When he broached the matter in a "conversation with conservative election lawyer Dan Backer," reported Paul Blumenthal, the lawyer responded with a resounding "no." (The day before, at a 2012 Conservative Political Action Conference in Washington, D.C., Backer urged his conservative allies to challenge campaign contribution laws.)

A three-judge federal trial court sitting in the District of Columbia, however, saw that matter differently. On September 28, 2012, the tribunal ruled against McCutcheon's challenge to the federal law. "It is not the judicial role to parse legislative judgment about what limits to impose," the judges concluded. Writing for the court, Judge Janice Rogers Brown nonetheless conceded that "the constitutional line between political speech and political contributions grows increasingly difficult to discern." Hoping that appellate jurists would act more favorably on this concession, McCutcheon took his case to the highest court in the land. On February 19, 2013, the Supreme Court agreed to hear *McCutcheon v. Federal Election Commission*. Oral arguments in the case were set for October 8. When the *McCutcheon* case was filed in the Supreme Court, nine states had laws restricting aggregate contributions, though the state laws were not at issue here.

Against that backdrop, Shaun McCutcheon found himself in the eye of a political storm over money and elections—a tempest that had been building momentum ever since the Supreme Court decided in 1976 that "money is speech." The hurricane raged with even greater force when in 2010 the justices held that the First Amendment protected corporations and labor unions in making independent campaign expenditures. That was the controversial *Citizens United* decision.

Jeffrey Toobin, writing in the *New Yorker*, was troubled by that decision and what might follow: "Think the Supreme Court's decision in *Citizens United* was bad? A worse one may be on the horizon." Fred Wertheimer, a campaign finance reformer and president of Democracy 21, agreed: "As damaging as *Citizens United* has been to our political system, the Supreme Court would make a bad situation far worse if it strikes down the overall contribution limits [required by federal campaign finance laws]." David Savage of the *Los Angeles Times* couched it this way: "In what may be Act 2 in the decline and fall of campaign funding laws, the Supreme Court appears poised to lift the lid on the total amount the wealthy can give directly to all candidates and political parties." The case "on the horizon," the "Act 2" case to which they were all referring, was *McCutcheon v. Federal Election Commission.*

In the early days of it all, Shaun McCutcheon loved the public attention that came his way. On September 19, 2013, his photograph appeared above the fold on the front page of *USA Today.* The banner read: "Brown. Roe. Miranda. McCutcheon?" Overnight, he became a national persona. A week or so later, the *Business Insider* blog tagged him as a "Conservative hero." He liked the appellation. "A lot of people know me," he told reporter Richard Wolf. "I never expected to be here," he added. "The whole thing has been an adventure." And so the adventure began, though how it would ultimately play out was still uncertain in the days before the justices resolved the matter. Even so, one thing seemed likely: the case would produce much of the same kind of division that accompanied the Roberts Court's 2012 health care ruling (*National Federation of Independent Business v. Sebelius*). By that measure, the *McCutcheon* decision promised to be "an adventure."

Campaign Spending—Political Crisis or Protected Communication?

There is a crisis in American politics, says one side. And money is the root cause of that crisis. It is a truism of our times: money talks, money matters, money buys elections. People with more money buy more political speech. By the same token, those seeking to enter the political conversation as candidates face a formidable barrier if they lack the large amount of money needed to wage a successful media campaign. In other words, it is necessary to either have great wealth or appeal to those who have great wealth. The issue, however, is not just the corrupting influence of money on our electoral system. A greater problem is the electorate's ostensible indifference to it. Citizens appear to have become weary. They seem to have accepted the "rules of the game," which allow the vicious cycle of money making more money—money buying media, media influencing polls, polls swaying elections, elections fostering candidates beholden to special interests, and elected officials looking for the next financial fix to buy the next election. As such, American democracy is in decline. This is our fate; this is our crisis.

The First Amendment is more than mere words, spoken or printed. It is about *expression* in the most magnificent sense, says the other side. That expression can be symbolic, artistic, or any peaceful form of manifesting one's sense of self. But when a man prints a pamphlet, he must first *pay* for it. When a woman posts lawn signs, she must first *purchase* them. Similarly, when citizens gather in a home at a fundraiser to support a candidate, they express themselves by the monetary contributions they make: "I believe in you enough to support you with my money." Mindful of that, recall the lofty words of the Declaration of Independence: "we mutually pledge to each other our lives, our *fortunes* and our sacred honor." Thus, money can be both the medium *and* the message. Admittedly, money is not all of who we are. Then again, neither is it something that can be easily divorced from how we express ourselves. For example, when we give to a homeless shelter, we make a statement. When a protest group places a paid ad in a newspaper, it makes a statement. By that logic, capitalism is the handmaiden of communication. That is the American way.

But is it?

No, argue the defenders of campaign finance laws. The "money race" has corrupted our political process. The demand for more and more "campaign cash" from the rich few is what defines the agenda for any candidate who hopes to win. Between 1974 and 2010, the total money spent by all federal candidates running in the House and Senate increased a whopping 525 percent, from $77 million to $1.8 billion. In 2012 the top ten individual donors (mostly Republicans) flexed their monetary muscles to the tune of $121 million in campaign money. And in that same year, President Barack Obama raised in excess of $715 million. Translated: politicians have become dependent on *big money*. Worse still, were McCutcheon to prevail in his First Amendment challenge, we would be left with "a system of legalized bribery in this country," as Fred Wertheimer told the *New York Times*.

Is that indeed true? Has our electoral process been corrupted? Is legalized bribery soon to become the norm?

Quite the contrary, reply the opponents of campaign finance laws, our system of electing political candidates has been fortified and made more robust because of money in politics. Political speech, they argue, is at the heart of the First Amendment, and spending money on political campaigns is central to freedom of expression. As John Bolton (who worked on the famed *Buckley v. Valeo* case) put it during a December 1997 C-SPAN program: "Campaign financing is probably the single best issue that defines…where you stand in the debate between the liberty of the individual on the one hand, and the power and authority of the government on the other."

Whether it be the Sierra Club, the American Federation of Teachers, or George Soros (who has spent some $20 million to back progressive candidates), associations and individuals spend large amounts of money to express their political views. According to a November 5, 2013, *New York Times* story, liberals are not immune from handing out big money to influence the outcomes of elections. "Democrats and unions, fearful that a landslide victory by Governor Chris Christie will reshape New Jersey's political landscape, have poured tens of millions of dollars into a record-breaking outside spending campaign that has transformed the state's election season." The *Times* story added, "according to the state's election law enforcement board, outside spending for candidates had topped $35 million, twice the amount spent when Mr. Christie, a Republican, was elected in 2009 and the highest recorded by any state except California."

While citizens vote *at* the voting booth, they vote *with* their dollars. Moreover, some argue that there is no proof that the kind of aggregate limits challenged in *McCutcheon* actually prevent electoral corruption or even the appearance of it. "If there is any evidence that these aggregate contribution limits provide any public benefits," says Paul Sherman of the

Institute for Justice, "the proponents of the laws haven't pointed to it. The vast majority of states have no comparable limits for contributions in state elections, and there is not the slightest evidence that those states are any more corrupt or less well governed than states that do."

Which was it: corrupting influence or not? In time, six men and three women would decide that question.

Enter the Court and the Constitution

The fight over money—over its corruptive influence or its speech-enhancing potential—has not been confined to the political arena. A contentious struggle has been waged in the revered chambers of the United States Supreme Court. In a series of twenty-nine cases decided between 1948 and 2013, the justices have gone back and forth as to when and under what circumstances lawmakers can slow the flood of money funneled into elections. In all of those First Amendment cases where opinions were rendered, the Court acted unanimously only twice, once in 1948 and then again in 1982.

Undaunted by a maze of confusing constitutional doctrines, the justices have rendered a total of eighty-nine individual opinions (per curiam, majority, concurring, and dissenting). Since Chief Justice John Roberts took his seat on the Court in 2005, six campaign-finance cases have been decided (two by 5–4 splits, two by 6–3, and one each by 6–2 and 7–2 margins). And all of this was *before* the Court agreed to hear *McCutcheon v. Federal Election Commission.*

Given that Congress and state lawmakers have often been unwilling in recent times to enact meaningful legislation to monitor the race for campaign cash, and given that a slim majority of the Supreme Court has often struck down whatever laws were enacted in this area, many Americans are calling for an amendment to the Constitution or a constitutional convention to rectify what they see as the ruin of our electoral process. Sixteen states have already passed resolutions calling for a constitutional amendment, and resolutions are pending in many others states as well. A grassroots movement is also underway to do what Congress and the courts refuse to do. It is time, they maintain, that We the People take action.

Meanwhile, ranks of highly talented First Amendment lawyers (from individual-rights groups to big law firms) work busily to preserve a core political free speech right and to prevent its frustration by constitutional amendment. Never in almost 225 years, they argue, has our First Amendment been amended, despite many attempts to do so. After the tirades passed, our First Amendment freedoms survived. And, they warn, that is how it should remain.

The Past, Present, and Future

This book is about Shaun McCutcheon and the case and cause he took to the Supreme Court as the lead plaintiff. It is likewise about the controversy (at once political and constitutional) swirling around the question of money and politics. There is also the law and its doctrines, which confuse even the initiated. In that respect, we have tried to present this story of the law in a way that is at once accurate and intelligible, duly mindful that some measure of insider nuance must be sacrificed along the way.

That said, it is well to remember that controversies do not exist in a vacuum—they involve people and the passions that fuel them. Hence, we have profiled the people—lawyers, judges, professors, and political activists—central to our story. In addition, there is that part of our narrative that weaves into the story of this case other stories from the past—some quite surprising—about those who championed or opposed campaign finance laws. And then there is the Supreme Court's new ruling on April 2, 2014, in the McCutcheon case, striking down aggregate limits on contributions to political candidates, parties, and committees—a ruling destined to shape the future of our First Amendment law and our electoral system. To supplement our story, we offer a few examples likely to be heard by the Court after the *McCutcheon* ruling.

Thirty years ago, Fred Friendly and Martha Elliott asked, "[Is] spending in elections the equivalent of political speech?" What follows is the story of how that question was answered in our times … and what, in light of *McCutcheon v. FEC*, that answer portends for future generations.

1. The Problem

No one in the history of American politics has ever won or lost a campaign on the subject of campaign finance reform.
—Senator Mitch McConnell (February 27, 1998)

Our politics are a disgrace and money is the root of the problem.
—Ronald Dworkin (1999)

MONEY CORRUPTS. It is an age-old problem. By biblical accounts, that was the problem of the Temple in the battle between Jesus and the moneychangers. Confronting them, Jesus overturned their tables and spilled their coins, adding: "Take these things away; do not make my Father's house a house of trade." Much the same gospel was preached, though in a secular vein, by George Mason in June 1787: "If we do not provide against corruption," he warned, "our government will soon be at an end." And so it has been since then, in both sacred and secular houses.

Turn the clock to 1973, when Senator Hubert Humphrey registered a stern warning to his colleagues about the impact of money on elections: "If it doesn't stop, there are going to be good men in this hall right here today who are going down the drain."

Now move forward to 2013 and consider what Senator Olympia Snowe had to say about that same problem, the problem of money in politics. "The current, seemingly singular preoccupation with fundraising of most senators and members of Congress," she stressed, "has become a major distraction from conducting normal business in Washington."

For the former Republican senator from Maine, this distraction is nothing less than a "twenty-four/seven scramble to raise money," which has turned politics into a "perpetual campaign cycle." And this preoccupation with raising money "unduly influences agendas and the issues on which legislators deliberate, but also contributes to an alarming reduction in the number of days actually spent legislating."

In a 2012 talk at the University of Chicago Law School, Judge Richard Posner was openly critical of the Supreme Court and its campaign finance jurisprudence. Speaking to a group of foreign scholars, the jurist who sits on the U.S. Court of Appeals for the Seventh Circuit told his audience, "Our political system is pervasively corrupt due to our Supreme Court taking away campaign [expenditure] restrictions on the basis of the First Amendment."

For others, like Bill Moyers, the problem is even more earth-shattering. "We are close to losing our democracy to the mercenary class," he said. "It is as if we are leaning way over the Grand Canyon and all that is needed is a swift kick in the pants—look out below! The predators in Washington are [very] close to monopoly control over our government." By his lights, moneyed interests and special interest groups have "bought the political system, lock, stock, and pork barrel, making change from within impossible." In other words, the system is corrupt to the point that it is in need of radical repair.

Has Humphrey's dire prediction come true? Is Snowe's assessment unduly pessimistic? Is Moyers' cynicism warranted? Does money corrupt the electoral process? If so, how *exactly* does it corrupt? Concentrated wealth and the power that comes with it are one of the mainstays of American capitalism. Such power, some say, helps to make our country great and ensures a robust spectrum of viewpoints. For others, however, it is exactly the opposite. Election money is the root cause of corruption in government.

So, which is it? Does money—political party money, PAC money, corporate money, and money from the wealthy few—improve or debase the electoral process? Before getting to that precise question, it may be helpful to shed a little historical light on the subject.

Nothing New under the Electoral Sun

Before and after the American Revolution, there have been cries against the undue influence of moneyed interests. At any pinpoint in time, there has always been some controversy over wealth and governance. For example, soon after the nation was formed, a battle ensued over money and politics in the 1816 controversy over chartering the United States Second Bank. When it was to be rechartered in 1832, President Andrew Jackson complained that the "rich and powerful too often bend the acts of government to their selfish purposes." Five years later, the first bill to ban campaign-related political assessments from government employees was introduced in Congress.

After the Civil War, the movement to do something about the corrosive effects of money on government began to take shape, though in modest form at the outset. Thus in 1867, Congress passed a campaign finance law to prohibit federal officials from soliciting contributions from navy yard workers. To much the same effect, in 1874 the Supreme Court expressed its disapproval of contingency contracts for lobbyists. And then in 1883, Congress enacted the Pendleton Civil Service Reform Act, which prohibited political contributions in exchange for appointment to any federal government position. The Act also barred solicitation of campaign donations on federal government property.

By 1907, the reformist movement gained political traction with passage of the Tillman Act. This was the first statute in the United States that prohibited corporations and national banks from making monetary contributions to federal candidates. A few years later, progressives again prevailed when the Federal Corrupt Practices Act became the law of the land. It established campaign-spending limits for political parties in House general elections, and later in those for the Senate. In the years following the Teapot Dome Scandal (1920–1923), Congress enacted amendments to the Federal Corrupt Practices Act. The amendments included disclosure requirements and certain limits on campaign contributions and spending. Those provisions survived judicial scrutiny when in 1934 the Supreme Court upheld the financial disclosure and reporting requirements of the Act.

Following World War II, efforts to curb the effects of money on politics continued by way of the Taft-Hartley Act, which placed limits on unions' spending in federal elections along with restrictions on direct campaign contributions by corporations and interstate banks. The law also barred them all from expending money to influence federal elections. The early 1970s saw the passage of the Federal Election Campaign Act, which was first used by the Nixon Administration against its political foes but then tapped by Nixon's adversaries to help unseat the president. Reform measures, at the federal and state levels, continued in various forms until 2002, when Congress ushered in the Bipartisan Campaign Reform Act. President George W. Bush signed the bill into law on March 27, 2002.

The Campaign from Democracy to "Dollarocracy"

To say that money can corrupt government is, in one sense, a truism. No one—idealistic progressive, pragmatic conservative, or wild-eyed libertarian—would grant that bribery should be allowed. While bribery is the rule in corrupt governments in places like Guatemala and Uganda, we take pride in vigorously prohibiting it here in America. But what if *before* an elected official takes office, he is enticed to vote a certain way because of huge campaign contributions from special interests who stand to benefit from his vote? Is that a form of bribery? Is that an example of corruption? Is that a way of doing indirectly what cannot be done directly? Or is it rather an example of voters (albeit well-to-do ones) doing what they have always done—offering strong support for those candidates who share their views? Such support may manifest itself in walking door-to-door for a candidate, or purchasing and placing lawn signs for a candidate, or paying for a billboard favoring a candidate, or giving to a group that supports the candidate and purchases televisions ads to endorse him. Is that a problem? Should we tolerate that? Is it corruption? Or is it not instead an example of our constitutional democracy at work, permitting Americans to express their election views by way of their time, efforts, and money? All of this is to ask a basic question: what is the relation of money to politics?

Some, like Senator Tom Coburn (R-OK), firmly maintain that there is a connection between what legislators do and what is given to them by way of political contributions or expenditures. "Thousands of instances," Coburn wrote in the *Wall Street Journal*, "exist where appropriations are leveraged for fundraising dollars or political capital." Many Americans agree. According to a 2011 Global Group Strategy survey, some 75 percent of those polled believe that "campaign contributions buy results in Congress." Still others, like former FEC Chairman Bradley Smith hold otherwise. "The evidence is pretty overwhelming," he has said, that "money does not play much of a role in what goes on in terms of legislative behavior."

For yet others, like Harvard's Lawrence Lessig, the matter is more complex. The real problem is not so much corruption as it is lawmakers' ever-increasing *dependence* on campaign dollars, which makes it ever more difficult for them to be *independent* of the wishes of those who pay the electoral piper. Such dependence, Lessig contends, results in bad governance and a corresponding loss of public trust in government. Similar to Senator Snowe, Lessig asserts that this problem—one he names "dependence corruption"—means that lawmakers have less time to perform their constitutionally ordained duties because they are preoccupied with fundraising. "Between 1974 and 2008," Lessig points out, "the average amount it took to run for reelection to the House went from $56,000 to more than $1.3 million." Worse still, he adds, in "1974 the total spent by *all* candidates for Congress (both House and Senate) was $77 million. By 1982 that number was $343 million—a 450 percent increase in eight years. By 2010 it was $1.8 billion—a 525 percent increase again." In this "fundraising Congress," lawmakers cozy up to the special interests of rich power brokers while distancing themselves from the needs and concerns of their constituents. In other words, the pressure to raise money fundamentally changes Congress and the norms by which it operates. Accordingly, Professor Lessig argues that the idea of corruption must be seen in this light and thus redefined to take into account the problems created by the flood of money into the hallways of Congress and elsewhere.

If the flow of money into politics is a problem, then the media are part of that problem—they are complicit players. That, at least, is the argument advanced by John Nichols and Robert McChesney in their book *Dollarocracy: How the Money-and-Media Complex Is Destroying America* (2013). "The owners of media corporations," they write, "have made their pact with the new order," the economic elites. If indeed there is a crisis of money in politics, then the media help to create that crisis and gain from it. The TV media impact our system of electoral democracy in three basic ways: First, it is in their economic interest that ever more money be pumped into TV political advertising, especially the kind that is slick and acrimonious. Second, sound-bite ads replace the old-fashioned idea of extended discourse and debate. And as Professor Bruce Ackerman has observed, "If your opponents will batter you with hot-button sound bites, it won't do your principle much good if you lose the election. The only good defense is a sound bite offense!" Finally, Nichols and McChesney contend that, in today's TV media environment, the Fourth Estate often does not function as an unbiased fact-checker. Instead, it prefers to cast its own partisan spin on the news or simply to air the kind of sensationalist stories (true or otherwise) likely to appeal to a wide mass of viewers. As discourse comes down, dollars go up. By this measure, the media stand to benefit from the divisiveness spawned by an endless barrage of political attack ads.

Some problems are not new, though the *way* and *degree* to which they become problematic may well be. Times change, circumstances change, people and cultures change, but in the historical mix of things some evils die only to resurrect in different and virulent forms. Thus it is with the issue of money and how it relates to government and the press. Just consider the case of Abraham Lincoln, who was said to be a "man of the people." Our sense of "Honest Abe" is that he was, by and large, beyond reproach. And we all remember the election of 1858, especially the famous Lincoln-Douglas debates. But was it simply his philosophical platform and rhetorical superiority that later put Lincoln over the electoral top? Perhaps. But there may have been other forces at work—say, his secret May 1859 purchase of a German-language newspaper. Just before the general election, Lincoln bought the *Illinois Staats Anzeiger* for $400 and then leased it back to its editor. Why? The condition was that the paper endorse Lincoln's party. Fortuna being what it was, the German vote played a factor in helping candidate Lincoln to secure victory in seven key Northwestern states. To much the same effect in 1900, Isaac Stephenson, a wealthy lumber business tycoon, purchased the *Milwaukee Free Press* to assure positive coverage for Robert LaFollett's bid for governor. So, yes, the way such things manifest themselves may be novel, but the basic problem is hardly new.

Where merit is not the measure, money may be. The formula is quite simple: "Support me and when I get into office I will hire you" (patronage), or, "if you want to keep your government job, you must contribute to my reelection campaign" (assessments). Either way, it's money mixing with politics. And when they do, so the argument goes, the former taints the latter much the same way that a dark dye does when poured into a clear beaker of water. But how does the law relate to money?

Cash & the Constitution

In 1905, the Supreme Court weighed into this debate in a roundabout way. The case involved a baker, Joseph Lochner, and a New York law that prohibited him from working his employees more than ten hours a day or sixty hours a week. He objected. The law, he argued, violated his constitutional liberty of contract. The Court agreed, though by a narrow 5–4 margin. "The general right to make a contract in relation to his business," wrote Justice Rufus Peckham for the majority, "is part of the liberty of the individual protected by the Fourteenth Amendment of the Federal Constitution." It was a big win for business.

The Constitution had been aligned with capitalism. In the process, progressive lawmakers and reformists lost out. Their solace came by way of a forceful dissent issued by a resourceful man who much admired American capitalism—Justice Oliver Wendell Holmes Jr. For Holmes, the liberty protected by the Constitution was "perverted" when tapped to protect mere economic interests. No matter, for the next thirty-three years big business capitalized on this constitutional gift from the Supreme Court. But the world and the Court changed in 1937. Since then, the justices have largely forsaken serious protection of economic liberties in the marketplace and have left those issues to federal and state lawmakers. For progressive reformers this meant that the "moneychangers" had been driven out of the temple of constitutional justice.

Much as Joseph Lochner, the New York baker, took constitutional exception to reformist legislation, so too did James L. Buckley, a New York senator. In 1976 he took constitutional exception to a reformist law, this time the Federal Election Campaign Act. In an unsigned opinion, the justices sustained the Act's limits on individual campaign *contributions*, as well as its disclosure and reporting provisions. However, they struck down limitations on campaign *expenditures*, holding that such restrictions violated the First Amendment.

Three words metaphorically associated with the *Buckley* opinion became the mantra of "special interest" groups bent on influencing elections with their wealth—"*money is speech.*" Since then, the Supreme Court has often reaffirmed that idea and has invoked the Constitution to set aside more and more reform legislation aimed at curbing the influence of money on politics. For progressive reformers this meant that the "moneychangers" had been invited back into the temple of constitutional justice.

The caricature is the same today as it was in 1905 when the Court embraced economic constitutionalism—conservative justices are tapping the Constitution to benefit the power elite, those moneyed few who seek to thwart the popular will by buying the will of lawmakers. In a series of rulings, the justices have invoked the First Amendment to strike down various campaign finance measures. In this sense, the new conservatism aligns with the old conservatism to serve moneyed interests. But is that characterization fair? And what does it mean to say that "money is speech"?

Some vehemently deny the proposition and maintain that the Supreme Court turned in the wrong constitutional direction when it issued its famous (or infamous) declaration. Others, such as Professor Eugene Volokh, think that the Court was pretty close to the conceptual mark: "Well, of course money isn't speech. But so what? The question is not whether the money is speech, but whether the First Amendment *protects your right to speak using your money.*" But even if the proposition or a variation of it is true, should First Amendment protection be extended to corporations? Furthermore, should the Constitution bar reformist attempts to regulate the influence of money on our electoral system? In other words, how far are we prepared to go with the idea that money translates to freedom, a freedom that should be unfettered?

From Brown Bag Bribery to Buying Influence

Nixon provoked the new campaign-financing law of 1974. Its new rules will change the nature of American campaigning.
—Theodore H. White (1975)

Watergate was a watershed event, at least in modern times. It was what put the idea of campaign finance reform back into the American mind. "Watergate revealed all kinds of abuses connected to the campaign finance system," observes Richard Hasen, a leading election law scholar. "Major corporations gave large sums to the Nixon campaign—the usual request was for $100,000—despite the longstanding prohibition on corporate giving to federal candidates. American Airlines," Hasen adds, "was the first corporation to plead guilty to funneling $55,000 in illegal corporate cash, laundered through a Lebanese agent and a Swiss bank, to the 1972 Nixon reelection-effort." Worse still, cash "also arrived to the campaign in paper bags from millionaires. The secret cash allowed for all kinds of out-of-sight dirty tricks, such as breaking into the offices of rivals, planting spies with opposition campaigns, and attempts at outright bribery of officials."

Four-plus decades later, the problem of money in politics continues *despite* the various reform measures enacted into law since the Federal Election Campaign Act of 1971 (FECA) and its 1974 amendments. The picture painted by Richard Briffault of the Columbia Law School is an eye-opening one: "According to the Sunlight Foundation, a little more than 30,000 people—or 1 percent of the 1 percent—provided $1.7 billion, or 28 percent of all disclosed federal contributions in 2011 and 2012. And a small subset of this elite—fewer than 4,000 people—each contributed at least $100,000. This is the group," he stressed, "with demonstrated political interest and financial capacity most likely to contribute more if the court invalidates the aggregate limits."

To cast the data in yet another light, consider the picture painted by Harvard Law Professor Lawrence Lessig: "A tiny number of Americans—.26 percent—give more than $200 to a congressional campaign. .05 percent give the maximum amount to any congressional candidate. .01 percent give more than $10,000 in any election cycle. And .000063 percent—196 Americans—have given more than 80 percent of the individual Super PAC money spent in the presidential elections so far."

To put faces on the figures, Seth Cline writing for *US News Weekly*, identified the top ten biggest donors of the 2012 election:

1. Sheldon and Miriam Adelson: $36.8 million (to Newt Gingrich's and Mitt Romney's Super PACs plus various conservative groups)
2. Bob and Doylene Perry: $21.4 million (to Mitt Romney's Super PACs plus Karl Rove's American Crossroads)
3. Harold and Annette Simmons: $19 million (to Karl Rove's American Crossroads plus other conservative groups)
4. Joe and Marlene Ricketts: $12.9 million (to Super PAC Ending Spending Fund to oppose Obama and promote Romney)
5. Fred Eychaner: $8.1 million (to Obama's Super PAC plus the Super PACs supporting Democrats in the House and Senate)
6. James and Marilyn Simons: $7.7 million (to Senate Democrats' Super PAC, Obama's Super PAC, plus House Democrats' Super PAC)
7. Peter Thiel: $4.8 million (to Super PACs supporting Ron Paul)
8. Robert and Diana Mercer: $3.9 million (to American Crossroads plus Romney Super PAC Restore Our Future)
9. Amy Goldman: $3.8 million (to Super PACs for Obama plus Planned Parenthood)
10. John and Marlene Childs: $3.5 million (to Romney's Super PAC plus to Tea Party group Club for Growth)

In sum, this group alone pumped $121.9 million into the 2012 election.

To talk about the First Amendment and our electoral process is to do so in light of the ever larger amounts of money flowing into campaigns and the politics surrounding them. Ilya Shapiro of the Cato Institute is more than willing to have that conversation: "Restrictions on

campaign donations—particularly 'aggregate' limits on election participation—impede robust political speech and thus rob our democracy of
the vibrancy and dynamism it would otherwise have." Money translates
to a vibrant way of expressing one's political views. And that way is, he
adds, consistent with the American way: "Indeed, restricting the liberty to
engage in election campaigns because such engagement somehow injures
the political system is fundamentally contrary to the constitutional structure of rights and powers. As James Madison said, 'It could not be less
folly to abolish liberty, which is essential to political life, because it nour-
ishes faction, than it would be to wish the annihilation of air, which is
essential to animal life, because it imparts to fire its destructive agency.'"
Given that, Shapiro forcefully contends that "it is impossible to separate
speech from the money that facilitates it." Or so he put it in his Supreme
Court amicus brief in support of Shaun McCutcheon.

Unsavory Lobbyists

While the *McCutcheon* case awaited argument in the Supreme Court, a once
prominent Washington lobbyist linked to the infamous Jack Abramoff and
his unscrupulous lobbying team petitioned the justices to hear his First
Amendment case. Here is how Circuit Judge David Tatel described the
petitioner's behavior: "[Kevin] Ring and the other Abramoff lobbyists
relied heavily on campaign contributions to maintain relationships with
elected officials and promote their clients' political interests. But it was
Ring's other lobbying tactics that got him in trouble." And what were those
tactics? According to Judge Tatel, they "included treating congressional and
executive branch officials to dinners, drinks, travel, concerts, and sporting
events. Ring referred to officials with whom he had the closest ties and
with whom his lobbying efforts were most successful as his 'champions.'
As regular beneficiaries of Ring's largesse, these 'champions' often took
actions that were favorable to Ring's clients." Not surprisingly, the Circuit
Court judges ruled against Ring and he appealed.

In light of the facts, one of the key issues facing the Supreme Court
was whether Ring could be convicted of the offense of "honest-services-
fraud-by-bribery" in the absence of a quid pro quo bribery agreement.

The other key issue was whether the First Amendment permitted jurors to consider evidence of his legal (though suspect) campaign contributions if they were allegedly made to express no more than his appreciation toward public officials and his desire to provide election assistance to them.

On October 7, 2013, the justices refused to hear *Ring v. United States*, and thus let the petitioner's conviction stand. In the process, the implication to be drawn was that certain forms of corruption or the appearance of corruption did not require formal proof of a quid pro quo bribery agreement. As the Center for Competitive Politics and Ronald Rotunda (a noted professor of constitutional law) saw it in their amicus brief, such a result was highly suspect: "The court of appeals' decision amounts to a 'meat-axe' where a scalpel is needed. ... Reasonable, precisely targeted laws regulating gifts to public officials are entirely appropriate and consistent with First Amendment standards." Perhaps, but the Roberts Court was not prepared to engage in such precise tailoring, at least not in a case with such seamy facts. Then again, if quid pro quo bribery was not where the line was to be drawn, then where and how should it be drawn? And if the courts are not the ones to draw the lines, or are not the *best* ones to draw such lines, who is?

The Crisis of the Commission Divided

Created pursuant to the Federal Election Campaign Act, the Federal Election Commission (FEC) is an independent regulatory agency that was founded in 1975; its job is to regulate the campaign finance legislation. The Commission is made up of six members who are appointed by the president. Some argue that its bipartisan structure—by law it can have no more than three members of one political party—produces deadlock and thereby renders it toothless so far as rigorous enforcement goes. For others, however, the FEC is sometimes viewed as too aggressive in how it goes about its regulatory duties in ways insensitive to the First Amendment.

As fate had it, shortly before the *McCutcheon* case was to be argued in the high Court, the United States Senate was considering whether to confirm two of President Obama's nominees to the Commission—Ann

Ravel (a Democrat) and Lee Goodman (a Republican). On the one hand, Ms. Ravel had many of the markings of a progressive, having served as the chairwoman of the California Fair Political Practices Commission. This nominee, Dave Levinthal and Michael Beckel reported, had won much "praise from watchdogs for her aggressive fight to unveil the donors who steered $11 million into ballot measures in the state through a series of nonprofit organizations—transactions her office called the biggest case of 'campaign money laundering in California history.'" On the other hand, Goodman had many of the markings of a limited government man, a private law firm attorney who in 2013 petitioned the Court to hear *Danielczyk v. United States*. In that case he argued for an extension of the *Citizens United* holding. That is, Goodman maintained that the federal ban on campaign contributions to political candidates by corporations violated the First Amendment. (The justices declined to hear the case, which left the federal law intact.)

On Constitution Day (September 17), a Senate Rules Committee approved the nominations of Ravel and Goodman, at which point the existing chairman, Donald F. McGahn, stepped down. McGahn (the former general counsel for the National Republican Congressional Committee) led a bloc of three Republicans who in flashpoint cases interpreted the applicable laws narrowly so as to allow for greater campaign expenditures and contributions. Then again, as McGahn argued in a 2009 op-ed article, the Supreme Court sometimes vindicated his views and those of his conservative colleagues in instances when the Commission was guilty of "overreaching."

The McGahn controversy and the Revel-Goodman nominations symbolized much of the division in law over the question of campaign finance regulation. Both sides seemed firmly entrenched in their views and both sides were determined to change the status quo, either because it was too money-in-politics friendly or too First Amendment hostile. What this meant was that absent some clear and strong signals from the Supreme Court, the FEC would be in an ongoing crisis mode owing to its 3–3 deadlocks in the most controversial but important matters it considered. Or as Trevor Potter, a former FEC commissioner and chairman, put it shortly after *McCutcheon* was argued: "In practice, [certain kinds of violations such as earmarking] are almost impossible to discover and prove because they take place behind closed doors. Moreover, the FEC almost never investigates such issues, and it has been deadlocked and unable to act on most matters for the past five years."

Though Ann Ravel and Lee Goodman were finally confirmed, the question was whether the deadlock in controversial cases would continue. If it does, the crisis of the Commission divided will also continue, thus mirroring the intractable problem of dealing with money in politics. Though it was not a problem likely to go away soon, it was, nonetheless, one that would soon enough become more acute for one political side or another depending on how the justices ruled in the *McCutcheon* case.

2. The Players

Cases in the Supreme Court often serve as vehicles for resolving social problems. In articulating their client's interests, lawyers thus help to shape public policy.
——Kevin T. McGuire, *Supreme Court Bar* (1993)

LAW IS WHAT we make it. Putting the Constitution aside for a moment, the first "we" in the scheme of things are federal, state, and local lawmakers. They are the ones who turn public policy into public norms, both civil and criminal. But what exactly they *mean* when they make those laws is first and foremost the province of lawyers who shape and stretch the law to suit their clients. The next "we," the arbiters of the law, is the judiciary, which considers the laws and the lawyers' arguments and then decides what it all means. In the process, the law evolves, sometimes for the better, sometimes otherwise.

Though the nine justices who ruled upon it determined the final outcome in the *McCutcheon* case, the result was molded in important ways by what the other players in the case did earlier. Those players were several talented lawyers and a noted federal circuit judge. And then there was the petitioner himself: Shaun McCutcheon. There was also one other interested party, a United States senator from Kentucky. In their own ways, they all set the stage for what would become a landmark First Amendment case.

Mr. McCutcheon Comes to Washington

September 30, 2013, Washington, D.C. If you had ventured on that day to 1900 M Street NW, and then up four floors, you would have found him there in a plush, postmodern setting. The striking red decor was stylishly trimmed by sharp slate and subdued white accents. Above the receptionist's desk, the public relations firm boldly proclaimed its name: LEVICK ... and its motto: "Communicating Trust." Just a few feet beyond the opulent art deco leather chairs and across the manicured hall was an elegant display of some twenty crystal trophies lined up in iconic rows. There was the *Business Journal* honor (2012 award for one of the Top Public Relations Agencies) and the 2011 *National Law Journal & Legal Times* award (Best Crisis Management Consultant), et cetera. It all spoke of *power* and *influence*. It impressed Shaun McCutcheon enough to seek out and pay for Levick's services starting in March 2012, and then in late September to come to the nation's capital. He left McCalla, Alabama, for ten days or so to be available up to, and shortly after, the time when his case was to be argued in the Supreme Court.

When asked to describe himself in a single word, the rosy-cheeked McCutcheon was quick to respond: "freedom!" Moments later, he spoke with electric passion when he announced his life mission: "Change the world!" He is a self-described workaholic and single; his work and his politics are his life. "In 'change the world,'" he emphasized, "there are *no* rules." He prided himself on being a sort of wild card: "I'm not conventional," he announced with great glee. That's the way he likes it, whether it be in business or in politics. Though he is not a card-carrying libertarian (he is a *very* proud Republican), there is much in that political creed with which he agrees. And though he is not a formal Tea Party member (again, he is a Republican!), he admires the ethos of the rebellious movement.

His first real interest in government began in the fall of 1985 at Georgia Tech when he enrolled in a politics class there. The course, which included readings on civil liberties and American democracy, changed him and got him thinking more and more about politics while he was busy becoming a businessman.

His least favorite politician?—He did not pause long: Jimmy Carter, the peanut farmer from Georgia who had it all wrong.

His favorite politician?—He answered promptly: Ronald Reagan, the "big picture guy" who had it all right.

The Levick Agency's efforts on McCutcheon's behalf were not confined to inviting journalists and others up to its plush offices to interview its client. There was much more. Their client's fate was not left to chance as was the case with most petitioners who were largely indifferent to the esoteric process that lawyers call appellate advocacy. The world had changed considerably

Shaun McCutcheon

since 1962 when Clarence Earl Gideon went it alone and petitioned the Court by way of a penciled document. The modern norm was not to follow Gideon's example and wait silently and stoically for the justices to hear and decide his case and then to wait another year and a half for a book to come out (*Gideon's Trumpet* by Anthony Lewis). That world was so very *past* tense.

By stark contrast, in the digital age, in the public relations age, everything was offered up in real time and with eye-catching pixels for the wired world to see and hear. And so in the days just before oral arguments in his case, the Levick Agency helped their client place an op-ed in *Politico*, the highly influential political newspaper. Levick also launched a slick website for McCutcheon, replete with high-definition video feed, a downloadable color-coded PDF file, an iconic miniature American flag, and all the relevant tabs:

- About Shaun McCutcheon
- Court Documents (with links to briefs supporting McCutcheon and RNC)
- Speeches & Presentations

- News
- Videos
- Calendar/Announcements
- Contact Us ("for a speaking engagement or press interview")

The site originally offered a one-minute, 41-second, crystal-clear video clip, which began, "I'm Shaun McCutcheon, and I'm a conservative activist from Alabama," stated with perfect calm and confidence. Toward the end of the clip he added: "I'm confident that we have a great argument... and yes, I believe we will overturn the verdict."

The verdict to which McCutcheon referred was that of a three-judge federal court sitting in the District of Columbia. A noted conservative jurist with libertarian leanings authored the opinion of that court, an opinion some found surprising.

The "Wreath of Gratitude"

JANICE ROGERS BROWN—To those who know her, Judge Brown is a kindly, thoughtful, and independent-minded jurist who takes seriously her job as a circuit judge on the United States Court of Appeals for the District of Columbia. The sixty-four-year-old, Alabama-born, African-American jurist has served on that court since 2005, and before that served as an associate justice on the California Supreme Court (1996–2005). At the time of President George W. Bush's nomination of her to the federal court, several leading liberal organizations roundly criticized Judge Brown as being "far outside the mainstream" and "extremely conservative." In the First Amendment community, by contrast, her "libertarian" views were seen in a more favorable light, especially given her forceful dissent in *Kasky v. Nike, Inc.* (California Supreme Court, 2002), wherein she defended the commercial speech rights of the corporate shoemaker.

Judge Brown is part of the *McCutcheon* story because she is the jurist who wrote for a three-judge district court before the matter came to the Supreme Court. Sitting by assignment to the trial level court, she was joined by Circuit Judge Robert L. Wilkins and District Judge James E. Boasberg. At the district level, the case was argued by James Bopp for the plaintiffs (McCutcheon and the RNC) and by Adav Noti for the FEC. The unanimous judgment was rendered on September 28, 2012.

Before the *McCutcheon* case came to her desk, Judge Brown wrote a telling concurring opinion in *Emily's List v. Federal Elections Commission* (2009). The issue there was whether FEC regulations that restricted how nonprofits spend and raise money to advance their preferred policy positions and candidates violated the First Amendment. A group that promoted abortion rights and supported pro-choice, Democratic, female candidates brought the case. The court held that the regulations did indeed abridge the plaintiff's First Amendment rights. In her partial concurrence, Judge Brown stressed that the court need not reach the constitutional question since the regulations at issue were contrary to existing statutory law. "But if we're going to answer an unnecessary constitutional question," she added, "we at least ought to get it right. In light of *McConnell v. FEC* (2003), I have grave doubts about the court's analysis, which bears at most a passing resemblance to the parties' briefs, and which will profoundly affect campaign finance law in this circuit."

Sensitive to her role as an intermediate appellate judge, and duly mindful of precedent, Judge Brown both followed existing law *and* criticized it: "While I have argued courts should not unnecessarily assail legislative acts," she declared, "political speech is the core of what the First Amendment protects." As she understood them, many of the Supreme Court's campaign finance rulings "relied on an ad hoc empiricism ill-suited to the complex interactions of democratic politics. The government has unlimited resources, public and private, for touting its policy agenda. Those on the outside—whether voices of opposition, encouragement, or innovation—must rely on private wealth to make their voices heard."

For her, the Court's "increasingly anomalous campaign finance jurisprudence only impoverishes this essential debate." Worse still, some of its rulings carelessly invoke concepts such as "access and influence (two integral aspects of political participation) as synonyms for corruption. … Such an expansive, self-referential, and amorphous definition of corruption, coupled with lax standards of scrutiny and a willingness to accept as 'evidence' any plausible theory of corruption or claim of circumvention, is likely to doom any argument for protection of core political speech."

She closed on a note of hope and restraint: "Someday the Supreme Court may be persuaded to reconsider this approach. But that cannot be our task."

When the *McCutcheon* case came before her in the federal district court, Judge Brown exemplified a similar kind of judicial moderation. Writing for the court, she began: "The current iteration of the Federal Election Campaign Act imposes contribution limits stratified to track both the identity of the contributor and the identity of the receiver. Individuals, however, cannot necessarily contribute as much as they might wish within these limits; they, and only they, must comply with a second regulatory tier: a set of aggregate contribution limits. Plaintiffs Shaun McCutcheon and the Republican National Committee now challenge these aggregate limits as unconstitutional." And immediately thereafter, she put it plainly: "We reject their challenge."

In the course of her opinion, Judge Brown determined that the aggregate contribution limitations would not be evaluated under strict scrutiny, as the plaintiffs had urged. Relying on the reasoning in the Supreme Court's famous *Buckley* opinion, she explained that contribution limitations are subject to a lower level of review because they implicate a contributor's associational rights more than speech rights: "The transformation of contributions into political debate involves speech by someone other than the contributor." The plaintiffs, however, did not oppose the base contribution limitations regulating the amount that an individual or group can give to a single political candidate or committee. Hence, the court assumed that, in light of *Buckley*, those limitations were constitutional. After all, the government had a sufficiently important interest to prevent actual corruption or the appearance of corruption through contributions given during the election campaign cycle. On that basis, Judge Brown reasoned that the aggregate contribution limitation was also constitutional as a means of preventing evasion of the base limits.

Eliminating the aggregate restriction, Judge Brown maintained, would enable a contributor to give half a million dollars to a joint fundraising committee that included a national party committee and others. Eventually that check could be transferred to a single party committee that coordinated expenditures with a political candidate. "The candidate who knows the coordinated expenditure funding derives from that single large check at the joint fundraising event," she stressed, "will know precisely where to lay the wreath of gratitude." Having justified the aggregate contribution limits, the district court rejected the plaintiffs' subsidiary arguments that they were unconstitutionally low and overbroad. "It is not the judicial role to parse legislative judgment about what limits to impose," Judge Brown concluded.

Her judicial restraint notwithstanding, and reminiscent of what she wrote in the *Emily's List* case, Judge Brown emphasized that "the constitutional line between political speech and political contributions grows increasingly difficult to discern."

It was a disappointing loss. So Shaun McCutcheon and the RNC petitioned the Supreme Court to first hear their case and then reverse Judge Brown's ruling. The question was whether the Court would hold firmly to its precedents and thus deny the petitioners' claims, or whether it would modify those precedents and thus affirm the petitioners' claims. Either way, there was a chance that the justices would borrow a page or two of reasoning from one or both of Judge Janice Rogers Brown's opinions—unless, of course, they elected to perpetuate, in her words, their "increasingly anomalous campaign finance jurisprudence."

Meanwhile, the case was headed to a higher court. "I never believed it when Dan Backer said that this case would go all the way to the Supreme Court," recalled Shaun McCutcheon. But it did.

The Consigliere

DAN BACKER—Sitting to Shaun's right that September day in the Levick conference room was his trusted friend and *consigliere*, Dan Backer (pronounced "Baker"). Though several lawyers represented him, McCutcheon was quick to flag the one he saw as the principal persona in his case: "Dan represents me. I'm very happy with that fact." The two first met in February 2010 at the Sixth Annual CPAC Reaganpalooza event (hosted by the Young Conservatives Coalition) in Washington, D.C. Since then, Backer has played a key role in overseeing the general direction of many of McCutcheon's legal affairs.

Backer was born in Novosibirsk in southwestern Siberia. He came to this country with his parents in 1978 when he was a year old. As a young, naturalized American living in New Jersey, Backer was a high school reb-el-rouser who was once defended by the ACLU in connection with a censorship issue concerning his school student newspaper. He then went off to college, and thereafter to law school at George Mason University. Today, the thirty-six-year old lawyer is the founder and principal attor-ney for DB Capitol Strategies, "a premiere campaign finance and politi-cal law firm boutique" in Alexandria, Virginia. Through his work there, Backer has served as counsel to more than thirty PACs and political orga-nizations along with more than twenty members of the U.S. House and Senate through campaigns, congressional ethics, leadership PACs, and joint fundraising committees. He describes himself as a "staunch defender and advocate at the forefront of free speech and associational rights."

It was precisely that mindset that helped put into motion Shaun McCutcheon's decision to first take his complaint to the FEC, then to fed-eral district court, and ultimately to the Supreme Court. En route to the high court, it was Dan Backer who had McCutcheon's ear; and it was Dan Backer who orchestrated how the case would play out.

The Senator from Kentucky: Hero & Antihero

ADDISON MITCHELL "MITCH" MCCONNELL JR. is a United States sen-ator from Kentucky. He has held that post since 1985. In his own way, he has shown an abiding interest in, and a passionate commitment to, the First Amendment, though many take exception to those views. In 2000, for example, the conservative Republican senator courageously opposed the Flag Desecration Amendment, which would have amended the Constitution to ban a particular form of symbolic political speech. "We must curb this reflexive practice of attempting to cure each and every political and social ill of our nation by tampering with the Constitution," he declared. "The Constitution of this country was not a rough draft. It was not a rough draft and we should not treat it as such."

In 1996 Senator McConnell helped James Bopp establish the James Madison Center for Free Speech. The group "was founded to protect the

First Amendment right of all citizens to free political expression in our democratic Republic. Its purpose is to support litigation and public education activities in order to defend the rights of political expression and association by citizens and citizen groups as guaranteed by the First Amendment of the United States Constitution." So reads the Terre Haute, Indiana, group's mission statement. If you scrolled down to the recent news items section of its website, you would see that the center actively supported challenges to state and federal campaign finance laws. Some of the cases that the center had recently taken to the Supreme Court included *National Organization for Marriage v. McKee* and *Alaska Right to Life Committee v. Miles*, both First Amendment disputes involving election laws.

But what the senator is most known for today in First Amendment circles—what makes him a constitutional hero for many conservatives and a constitutional antihero for many liberals—is his unyielding opposition to (some call it a crusade against) campaign finance reform. His fame in this area is so great that there is even a major First Amendment election law case bearing his name—*McConnell v. Federal Election Commission* (2003). The lawyer representing him in that case was *the* First Amendment lawyer of our times, the noted Floyd Abrams.

Predictably, the Senate minority leader filed an amicus brief in the *McCutcheon* case. Once the Court agreed to hear the matter, Senator McConnell petitioned the justices for leave to have some time set aside for his counsel (Bobby Burchfield) to argue the case. His petition was granted. Shortly afterward, Paul Blumenthal, writing in the *Huffington Post*, observed: "On Oct. 8, Sen. Mitch McConnell (R-Ky.) will argue to the Supreme Court that all campaign contribution limits should be eliminated and that candidates should be able to accept unlimited donations."

Meanwhile, two nonprofit groups (the Public Campaign Action Fund and USAction) took the senator to political task for his involvement in the *McCutcheon* case. In October 2013, they ran thirty-second commercials in his home state charging that his views favored special interest groups and the wealthy. "We want Mitch McConnell to explain to Kentuckians why he thinks unlimited political contributions from bailed-out bankers and big oil CEOs makes our democracy better and America stronger," said David Donnelly, executive director of Public Campaign Action Fund.

Back in Washington, D.C., the question was whether a majority of the justices would heed McConnell's bold First Amendment plea. It was hard to tell. On the one hand, the senator had made similar arguments in the *McConnell* case, which he lost. On the other hand, it was a different Court, one now more sympathetic to his views.

"The Man Behind *Citizens United* Is Just Getting Started"

JAMES BOPP JR. was the lawyer who first argued the *McCutcheon* case before Judge Brown and her colleagues. And he was the lawyer who petitioned the Supreme Court on behalf of Shaun McCutcheon and the RNC. He was a natural choice for any variety of reasons.

Bopp is the general counsel for the James Madison Center for Free Speech. He is also the general counsel for the National Right to Life Committee (NRLC), which is on record as opposing a constitutional amendment to overrule some of the Supreme Court's campaign finance cases. Apart from the other conservative groups he represents (such as Focus on the Family), he is the lead partner of the ten-lawyer, Terre Haute, Indiana–based group known as The Bopp Firm. As proclaimed on its website, the firm "was founded by James Bopp Jr. to provide legal assistance to individuals, elected officials, and Political Action Committees ("PACs") navigating the ever-changing fields of PAC Law, Campaign Finance, Election Law, First Amendment, and Constitutional Law."

In a May 2013 *New York Times* piece, Jeffrey Rosen observed, "As the first general counsel of the National Right to Life Committee, Bopp is perhaps the most prolific anti-abortion litigator of his generation, responsible for encouraging states to pass laws chipping away at *Roe v. Wade* and then defending them in court. And as the longtime leader of the Federalist Society's Free Speech and Election Law Practice Group, Bopp has been credited as being the intellectual architect of the arguments that persuaded the Supreme Court, in *Citizens United*, to equate the free speech of corporations with that of human beings." In other words, in those worlds he was a force to be reckoned with.

"I have been privileged to be associated with Jim Bopp over the past decade on the important issue of the First Amendment," said Senator

McConnell in March 2002. Bopp, McConnell continued, "has probably won and argued more First Amendment campaign finance cases than any lawyer in the country." According to Stephanie Mencimer writing in *Mother Jones* magazine, "The Republican National Committee (RNC) has been a major funder of Bopp's work—paying him at least $1.5 million in fees in cases involving GOP candidates—along with the National Rifle Association and conservative megadonors such as Amway billionaire Betsy DeVos." In April 2013 the RNC named Bopp as its special counsel. "I am very pleased that Jim has agreed to continue his service to the RNC by agreeing to assist our General Counsel, John Ryder, on important issues related to the Rules of the Republican Party. Jim was a conservative leader during his time on the national committee and I appreciate his interest in staying involved going forward," said RNC Chairman Reince Priebus.

When the white-haired lawyer first argued the *Citizens United* case before a three-judge federal court, District Court Judge Royce Lamberth reportedly laughed when Bopp tried to explain why the conservative political documentary *Hillary: The Movie* should be viewed as a form of protected news reporting. "You can't compare this to *60 Minutes*!" exclaimed Lamberth. "Did you read this transcript?" But the result was anything but laughable—Bopp's position ultimately prevailed and in the process altered the course of First Amendment law and added yet more animus to America's culture wars.

Due to an unexpected twist of fate, James

James Bopp Jr.

Bopp did not ultimately represent the appellant, Citizens United, in the Supreme Court. In the eleventh hour, he was pushed out, and the honor went to Theodore Olson of *Bush v. Gore* and same-sex marriage fame. Even so, Bopp's views very much helped shape the law announced in *Citizens United* and in other First Amendment campaign finance cases such as *FEC v. Wisconsin Right to Life* (2006) and *Randall v. Sorrell* (2006), both of which he successfully argued.

In a 2012 interview with NPR's Terry Gross, Bopp was straightforward about how he viewed the campaign finance matters in which he was so deeply entrenched:

> As to limits on contributions, sometimes when I'm cynical, I think, yes, we need to have contribution limits to candidates. Other times I'm more optimistic and see how well Indiana's working without any contribution limits to candidates, as well as, I think, twenty other states, and that there's no real corruption. The corruption is in the heavily regulated and limited states with contribution limits. So then I think, well, maybe not; we don't need them. But one thing's for sure is that contribution limits are way too low. They are $2,500, and you can't even buy a Democrat congressman for $2,500. The anecdotal evidence is that it takes $99,000 in cold hard cash to buy a Democrat congressman. That was the amount Congressman Jefferson of New Orleans had in his freezer.

As for the wealthy and their purported undue impact on our electoral system, here is what Bopp said to Gross: "The wealthy do not have one interest. The wealthy—there are wealthy people on every side of every issue. There are more wealthy people who are liberal than are conservative, and historically the wealthy have given more money to liberal causes than to conservative causes. So there are liberal—there are wealthy people on every side of every issue, so the wealthy people don't control the issues." The wealthy acted no differently in principle than their less well-to-do counterparts, he added: "They are just doing what everybody else is doing, you know, picking sides and helping the side that they support to pursue—try to gain the votes of the American people."

When it came to disclosure laws, Bopp's First Amendment thinking was slightly different. "My own view is," he told a *Boston Globe* reporter in February 2012, "I don't like all the influence of money in politics, but I don't have a solution that's a lot better than saying, let people contribute what they will, then report it, let people know who gave what to whom." On that score, he was of two views. On the one hand, he said, "If I had my way, political actors would disclose their contributions and expenditures. So PACs, candidates, and political parties with respect to their election-related spending would report contributors to them and expenditures made by them." On the other hand, he told Ms. Gross that there have been "efforts to impose disclosure on non-political actors, people doing issue ads, you know, and such as that. And I don't think that is warranted. I don't think any disclosure is warranted because Wisconsin Right to Life wants to urge its senators to vote for or against a particular bill. That's grassroots lobbying."

In an interview with the *New York Times* in January 2010, however, he expressed a less nuanced view: "We had a ten-year plan to take all this down. And if we do it right, I think we can pretty well dismantle the entire regulatory regime that is called campaign finance law. We have been awfully successful, and we are not done yet."

While he is typically aligned with conservative and political groups, some of Bopp's views have, nonetheless, secured a measure of First Amendment support from liberal groups such as the AFL-CIO, the ACLU, and the Reporters Committee for Freedom of the Press. In light of all of this, it was not surprising that James Bopp was picked as counsel for the petitioners (Shaun McCutcheon and the RNC) when the case came before Judge Brown and her colleagues. "At the start," recalled Dan Backer, "he was the RNC's lawyer, and given his enormous experience in our field we all thought, you know, Jim should probably be the point man in this case. So he was the RNC's lawyer, and we were thus happy to go with him."

The day the *McCutcheon* case was to be argued in the Supreme Court, James Bopp was in the Great Hall waiting to enter the courtroom. He was quite affable, chatting with McCutcheon and others. What was unusual was his presence *there* and at that time. Why was he not in the lawyers' lounge organizing his final thoughts before preparing to argue the case?

The answer was simple: once gain, James Bopp had been pushed out in the eleventh hour. Another sudden switch. A week later, when asked about that unexpected turn of events, Bopp voiced great disappointment: "It came out of the clear blue sky; it was very late notice. Yes, I was surprised since they agreed to have me do the argument." As he saw it, others were "trying to get all the credit"—"*unjustified* credit" he stressed. Dan Backer, McCutcheon's friend and general counsel, was the main target of Bopp's barbs.

"When you change battlefields, you change generals." That is how David Bossie, then chairman of the Citizens United group, explained his 2009 decision to replace James Bopp with Ted Olson as the lawyer who would argue *Citizens United* in the Supreme Court.

And so it came to pass that there was a new "general," a most unexpected one.

Reboot the Mission

ERIN E. MURPHY—Internally, this is how things evolved as the time neared to argue *McCutcheon* in the Supreme Court. Bopp was first cut out of the Supreme Court picture when it came to writing the merits brief for Shaun McCutcheon. Dan Backer explained the reason McCutcheon and the RNC had separate briefs was because their interests were not exactly the same. "We thought that Jim was arguing too much of the case in a direction that we didn't think adequately represented Shaun's perspective," Backer said, then added, "We were very lucky to get Michael Morley to come on board and really—in about a week—prepare a fantastic [merits] brief for Mr. McCutcheon. ... It's not a criticism of [Bopp's] intellectual or legal capabilities; it's just that there are two clients with distinct interests and his argument is really much more tailored to his client and less to Mr. McCutcheon."

Mindful of those distinct interests, Backer and his colleagues concluded that the boutique but influential Bancroft firm was best one for them. Though few noticed the significance of it at the time, the August 16, 2013, brief to the Court listed James Bopp Jr. as counsel of record, whereas the McCutcheon brief of August 19 listed Michael T. Morley (with Erin Murphy of Bancroft as co-counsel).

The McCutcheon team then decided to curtail Bopp's involvement even further—he would *not*, as expected, argue their case before the Supreme Court. "Erin Murphy joined our team to help out," said Backer. "She had been giving feedback and support along the way. And it just became clear that … Jim Bopp's arguing the RNC's side of the argument … wouldn't necessarily … take the case in a direction that those of us on Shaun's side of the argument all thought it should go. And so, at the end of the day, I would say that having the Bancroft firm involved was a bit of a compromise."

As for the client's take on it all, McCutcheon was elated: "I am very pleased with the direction in which we are going," he said a week or so before his case was to be argued.

The key points of the hush-hush internal news went external when Tony Mauro, the veteran reporter who had covered the Supreme Court since 1979, broke the story—Erin E. Murphy would argue on behalf of McCutcheon *and* the RNC in the Supreme Court. The two cases of the two clients would no longer be bifurcated; there was now one brief and one set of lawyers representing both McCutcheon and the RNC. (Even so, as late as November 20, 2013, James Bopp insisted that he remained the lead counsel for the RNC.)

The new lawyers were Erin Murphy and Paul Clement. Murphy was a thirty-three-year-old "protégé of former Solicitor General Paul Clement" and a lawyer in Clement's Bancroft firm. Murphy, a Georgetown Law School graduate, was both a surprise pick and a logical one. Apart from her many talents, Erin Murphy was a natural for this case. Why? The answer had to do with the fact that during the 2008–2009 term Murphy had clerked for Chief Justice John Roberts, whose vote in *McCutcheon* would be crucial. And to those few in the know, there was something even more tantalizing: she had served as a Roberts law clerk when the landmark *Citizens United* case was first argued on March 24, 2009. That meant she probably worked on that case, or at least knew much about the Chief's

Erin E. Murphy (left), the advocate; and her co-counsel, Paul D. Clement (right)

internal views of it. "I imagine," said Dan Backer, "that had a lot to do with the fact that the Bancroft firm selected her." (As it turned out, the *Citizens United* case was reargued and decided the term after Murphy left.)

Shaun McCutcheon liked the idea of a fresh face in the game; he relished this rebel approach to litigation in the high court. "I like to do things differently, to shake things up a bit," he said. As for Erin Murphy, he smiled: "She's a very nice lawyer, isn't she?" Indeed, young though she was, Murphy's credentials were impressive, including her considerable experience in federal appellate courts and her briefs on a wide range of civil and criminal issues dealing with First, Second, Fifth, and Seventh Amendments, Due Process Clause, Ex Post Facto Clause, as well as complex securities, tax, and copyright law.

Whatever Supreme Court experience Erin Murphy lacked was more than made up for by her esteemed second chair Paul Clement, with whom she had served as co-counsel in the famed Health Care case of 2012. The two were becoming a celebrity team. As Tony Mauro told it a year earlier, "Clement called Murphy 'a stellar advocate on every level' and praised her 'invaluable' work on the health care cases. 'She worked on every brief we filed in the Supreme Court and on our Eleventh Circuit brief as well,' said Clement. 'Every one of those briefs bears her name and her mark.'" When Mauro asked whether, based on her experience, she wanted to argue before the Supreme Court herself someday, Murphy replied: "I certainly would love to."

And now she had just that chance, and Paul Clement had her back. Few, if any, knew the justices and their quirks and preferences better than Clement, who had his own big class action case to argue (*Willis of Colorado Inc. v. Troice*) the day before *McCutcheon* was to be heard. The bottom line: McCutcheon and the RNC would be well represented by Murphy's insights and considerable talent and Clement's winning experience.

Now that a new firm and a new set of lawyers were on board, a new question arose: who would finance the case? After all, prominent lawyers from a boutique Supreme Court appellate advocacy firm tend to be costly—very costly. When the question was posed to Shaun McCutcheon, the Alabama businessman chuckled: "A little bit by me and a lot by the RNC. We started off on our own, you know, but it got too big. I like to describe it as a corporate takeover. The RNC was watching us, since it is rather hard to sue the FEC without drawing a little attention." (McCutcheon said he never paid Bopp any fees). Dan Backer was a bit more cautious in his answer: "At this point Shaun is financing a portion of the litigation. There's going to be some fee sharing between Shaun and the RNC." But on one thing all agreed: the lion's share of Bancroft's fees was to be paid by the RNC. (In the earlier stages of the case and even afterward, Backer, Jarvin Nayar, and Stephen Hoersting all represented McCutcheon pro bono.)

William Baude, one of Erin Murphy's fellow former clerks at the Court, described her as "immensely talented." It would take just that kind of talent to handle the case she would soon argue before the justices of the Supreme Court.

The Middle Man

BOBBY R. BURCHFIELD—There is a March 21, 2002, C-SPAN video clip of Senator Mitch McConnell introducing the legal team that would challenge the constitutionality of a recent campaign finance law. The senator began by declaring that he was "honored" to be represented by such a distinguished team that included Floyd Abrams, Kenneth Starr, James Bopp Jr., Jan Baran, Kathleen Sullivan, and Bobby Burchfield. McConnell tagged Burchfield, then a partner at Covington and Burling, as a "distinguished election law lawyer" whose advice and counsel the senator said, "I greatly value."

As Burchfield put it during an interview in November 2013: "Political campaigns are the most heavily regulated practice in America." He paused and continued, "I think it is highly ironic that activities at the very core of the First Amendment are so heavily regulated." It was a view that traced back at least to 1992 when Robert Teeter, a Republican strategist for former president George H.W. Bush, contacted Burchfield on behalf of Senator McConnell to work on some campaign finance issues. In the two-plus decades since, that relationship and that interest in election law and the First Amendment have blossomed.

Today, Burchfield is a partner at the Washington, D.C., office of McDermott Will & Emery LLP, where he currently serves as a member of the firm's management committee. Burchfield, a member of the Economic Club of Washington (a group of prominent government and business leaders), often represents the mighty and wealthy; his client roster has included the likes of the RNC, NFL, Exxon, United Airlines, the American Automobile Association, Dow Corning, and BorgWarner. He serves his clients both in and outside of courts and likewise promotes their causes in the legislative arena. Predictably, Burchfield is considered one of the super lawyers" in the nation's capital.

The thick-haired and quick-thinking lawyer has long been very involved in Republican politics. He served as general counsel for George H.W. Bush's 1992 presidential campaign and was outside counsel to Tom DeLay (R-TX) while he was House Majority Leader. Burchfield has advised Republican candidates in every presidential election since 1988. He was part of George W. Bush's recount team in 2000 and served as outside counsel to Rudy Giuliani in 2008. Active in the National Republican Lawyers Association and in the Federalist Society, he is ideally suited to his practice.

In the 1990s, Burchfield appeared before House and Senate Committees to oppose various campaign finance bills, including public financing proposals. He once testified before a Senate Committee chaired by Senator McConnell, this in order to contest the constitutionality of the McCain-Feingold Act (aka the Bipartisan Campaign Reform Act of 2002). In much the same vein, he has served as the outside counsel to the National Republican Senatorial Committee.

Senator McConnell's lawyer: Bobby Burchfield

Burchfield has also championed the Republican cause in several federal appellate courts. For example, he filed amicus briefs for Senator McConnell in two Supreme Court cases: *Nixon v. Shrink* (2000) and in *Arizona Free Enterprise Club PAC v. Bennett* (2011). And he argued on behalf of the petitioners challenging the McCain-Feingold law in *McConnell v. FEC* (2003).

Back in 1997, he was the lawyer for the Bush-Quayle '92 Primary Committee in a legal contest with the Federal Election Commission. The issue involved an FEC decision that required the Bush-Quayle Committee to repay federal matching funds made pursuant to the Presidential Primary Matching Payment Account Act. Burchfield argued that the FEC's repayment determination was inconsistent with the governing statute and regulations and that the Commission had not adequately explained its departure from precedent. In an opinion by D.C. Circuit Judge David B. Sentelle, the court agreed with Burchfield and remanded the case to the FEC to justify or remedy its departure from the relevant law. The year before, he represented a Republican organization in an action in which it had been sued for excluding opponents of then–President George H.W. Bush's reelection at a political rally held on public property. The Republican group, the Strongsville Republican Organization, obtained a permit from the city to use certain municipal property, including the Strongsville Commons, for a political rally to be held on October 28, 1992. In *Sistrunk v. City of Strongsville*, a divided panel of the Sixth Circuit agreed with Burchfield.

Given his credentials, vast appellate experience, and the fact that he had represented the plaintiffs in *McConnell v. FEC* when it was before the Supreme Court, Burchfield was Senator Mitch McConnell's pick to represent him in *McCutcheon*.

"He Isn't Showy"

DONALD B. VERRILLI JR.—He was a law clerk to Justice William Brennan and before that to Judge Skelly Wright on the U.S. Court of Appeals for the District of Columbia. Brennan was one of the architects of *Buckley v. Valeo*, while Wright was one of its severest critics. Now, a man of fifty-seven years, Verrilli was the lawyer charged with defending the provisions of the Bipartisan Campaign Reform Act at issue in the *McCutcheon* case. His official title is solicitor general of the United States, a position he has held since June 9, 2011.

He is tall and unassuming. There is a quiet demeanor about him, combined with a sense of shyness. Still, he is not one to be underestimated. Yale University–educated and Columbia Law School–trained, he earned his stripes as a respected litigator with the Jenner & Block firm, where he co-chaired its Supreme Court practice division. He left the firm to take a job as an associate U.S. deputy attorney general within the U.S. Department of Justice. He also acted as White House deputy counsel to President Obama. Serving in both the private and public sectors, the New York–born lawyer had participated in more than a hundred Supreme Court cases prior to *McCutcheon*. One of those cases, which he argued, was *National Federation of Independent Business v. Sebelius* (2012), the landmark healthcare case.

Lincoln Caplan tagged him as a "lawyer's lawyer." He "isn't showy," Caplan added, "but he is a deeply experienced and a capable advocate who finds ways to make technical legal arguments that persuade a majority of justices. While he's not inspiring, he's often effective." One such example was his presentation in the healthcare case. As CNN's Jeffrey Toobin judged it, Verrilli's performance amounted to "a train wreck for the Obama administration." Similarly, *Mother Jones'* Adam Serwer said Verrilli's performance "may go down as one of the most spectacular flameouts in the history of the court." At the time, after oral arguments had ended and before the Court's landmark ruling came down, few differed with that assessment. One of those few was Thomas Goldstein, the noted Supreme Court litigator and publisher of SCOTUSblog. "Don Verrilli," he observed, "did a fine job." And indeed he did—much to everyone's surprise, he largely prevailed.

Varied as his legal experience was—from telecommunications law to the law of voting rights—Donald Verrilli had a special interest in a body of law germane to his work in the *McCutcheon* case. He taught First Amendment law at Georgetown University Law School from 1992 to 2008. And that professorial experience, together with his expertise as an appellate advocate, would serve him well when the time came to represent the government in the *McCutcheon* case.

The government's lawyer:
Donald Verrilli Jr.

In October 2013, SCOTUSblog posted an on-camera, five-part interview with Donald Verrilli. At the end of that interview, the gentle-mannered advocate looked back on his career in the Solicitor General's office: "I happened to be here during a period of real historical importance," he said. "And it was my responsibility to lead the representation of the United States in these matters of real historical importance. And, therefore, I was able to participate in history, in its making, and have some influence— you know, time will only tell what that was—but have some influence in history going down one path versus another. And…that's an awesome responsibility."

Though it was still too soon to tell, one of those moments of "historical importance" might well be his part in *McCutcheon v. Federal Election Commission.*

3. The Controversy

JAMES CLARK McREYNOLDS was a man of stern conservative convictions. He came to the Supreme Court in 1914 and remained there as an associate justice until 1941. Among other views, the Kentucky-born jurist was a fierce opponent of FDR's New Deal legislation. When it came to laws directed at economic regulation or at social ends, McReynolds had the "single-minded passion of a zealot." He was, Kermit Hall added, a "firm believer in laissez-faire economic theory," which he viewed as constitutionally sacred. Though an appointee of Woodrow Wilson, McReynolds was anything but a progressive once he donned the black robes of a justice. *Time* magazine tagged him "puritanical, intolerably rude, savagely sarcastic, incredibly reactionary, and anti-Semitic." It was that same man who wrote for the Court in *Newberry v. United States*, a 1921 case involving the constitutionality of the Federal Corrupt Practices Act of 1910 (FCPA). *Newberry* was the first such case to come to the Supreme Court. And, as in most of the campaign finance cases that followed in the ensuing decades, the *Newberry* Court was badly divided—the vote in *Newberry* was 5–4 to overturn the 1910 law.

Capitalist Context: Money vs. Money

Before there was a case, before there were legal briefs, and before there was a Supreme Court opinion, there was a controversy. It began in 1918 and involved a contest between two very rich men who wanted to be the next U.S. senator from Michigan. One was Henry Ford, the great auto industrialist. The other was Truman H. Newberry, a member of the privileged elite who served on corporate boards and socialized at posh private clubs.

In 1902 Newberry played a key role in launching the Packard Motor Car Company. A few years later, he served briefly as the secretary of the Navy.

Like his Democratic opponent, Newberry was eager to spend big money in order to secure a seat in the Congress. The problem, however, was the FCPA, which barred profligate spending of the kind well-to-do office-seekers preferred; it placed a $10,000 cap on how much a candidate could spend on his own campaign. The ever-resourceful Newberry cleverly steered around that limit (to the tune of almost $200,000) by way of a campaign committee organized to support his senatorial bid. When Newberry won (albeit narrowly), Ford complained bitterly, demanded a recount, and then asked Congress not to seat Newberry for violating the FCPA. Progressives echoed these sentiments. A grand jury was convened, but nothing came of it. Ford complained again, and with the aid of detectives he proffered enough evidence to indict and convict Newberry along with many involved in his campaign. They were charged with conspiring to violate the FCPA. The verdict: guilty. Newberry's punishment: two years in Leavenworth Penitentiary. His fine: $10,000. He appealed.

As Professor Paula Baker noted, "the Ford-Newberry contest generated the first test of the purpose, meaning, and possible uses of the FCPA, the first national campaign finance legislation that aimed to rein in the amount of money in politics." On the one hand, progressives thought that the Act needed to be read broadly so as to root out not only corruption but also the potential for such. On the other hand, the law's critics argued that the reform movement was a front for partisan politics. Moreover, they added, reformers could rarely prove any real link between contributions and policies. So, the dispute went to the Supreme Court; Justice McReynolds and his eight colleagues would settle the matter.

A well-known and highly talented lawyer represented Newberry in the high court. His name was Charles Evans Hughes—former governor of New York (1907–1910), associate Supreme Court justice (1910–1916), Republican candidate for president (1916), secretary of state (1921–1925), and future chief justice of the United States (1930–1941). The *Newberry* case was argued in the Supreme Court on January 7 and 10, 1921, a mere two months before Hughes took office as secretary of state. On the other side, Solicitor General William Frierson—a relatively undistinguished lawyer whose greatest moment came in defending the National Prohibition Act of 1919—argued the case on behalf of the government. The two advocates quarreled over the proper interpretation of the FCPA—was its text confined to political candidates and thus not applicable to political committees?—and wrangled over whether the law was unconstitutional because it exceeded Congress' Article I, Section 4, powers by regulating primary elections, which were argued to be the domain of the states.

Justice McReynolds agreed with the argument advanced by Hughes, his former associate on the Court. The fifty-nine-year-old jurist spoke for himself and three of his colleagues, which included a surprising vote of approval from Justice Oliver Wendell Holmes. The majority (with a vital fifth vote from Justice Joseph McKenna, who wrote a special concurrence) concluded that Congress had indeed overstepped its proper powers and thus had impermissibly interfered with the sovereignty of the states. McReynolds was emphatic: "Many things are prerequisites to elections or may affect their outcome—voters, education, means of transportation, health, public discussion, immigration, private animosities, even the face and figure of the candidate; but [the] authority to regulate the manner of holding them gives no right to control any of these." As he saw it, history supported his view and Newberry's case: "If the Constitution makers had claimed for this section the latitude we are now asked to sanction, it would never have been ratified." His opinion provoked two powerful dissents, one by Justice Mahlon Pitney (joined by Justices Louis Brandeis and John H. Clarke), and the other by Chief Justice Edward D. White, writing for himself.

And what of the future of campaign finance reform? "If the FCPA applied only to general elections and to the spending of candidates," Professor Baker noted, then "it regulated nothing. In practice, candidates and their committees spent money in primary elections. *Parties* raised and spent funds in general elections, and party activities were not covered by the FCPA." Hence, "Newberryism," as reformers negatively branded it, seemed destined to continue. Outraged by McReynolds' constitutional handiwork, Senators William Borah and Hiram Johnson called for a constitutional amendment, but it never took hold. In 1925 Congress amended the FCPA and excluded primaries from its reach. Sixteen years later, in a case successfully argued by Attorney General Robert H. Jackson and aided by Herbert Wechsler, *Newberry* was effectively overruled in *United States v. Classic* (by a 5–3 vote). As for Justice James McReynolds, he retired from the Court in January 1941, only two months before the case was argued.

And what of Truman Newberry? As it turned out, there was a fly in the ointment of McReynolds' opinion; it allowed Congress, if it so elected, to itself judge the merits of Newberry's campaign maneuvers. Later, the Committee of Privilege and Elections did just that, and the entire Senate thereafter took up the matter. It voted 46–41 to seat Truman Newberry, but only for the remainder of the Sixty-First Congress. Not long after the 1922 election and a change in the Senate's makeup, it seemed likely that Newberry would be unseated if he did not resign. On November 18, 1922, the plump politician did just that.

More than a half century after the *Newberry* ruling, the Court returned to the question of money and its relation to elections. While the justices had considered the matter in 1957 in the case of *United States v. Auto Workers* (6–3 vote), and again in 1972 in *Pipefitters v. United States* (6–3 vote), and yet again the following year in *Broadrick v. Oklahoma* (5–4 vote), it was not until 1976 that the Court took a hard look at the question of how the First Amendment fit into the constitutional calculus of campaign finance laws. The case—and it became the landmark decision in the area—was *Buckley v. Valeo.* The background and ruling of the case? Quite complex.

Enter the Rogues & Reformers

Watergate. The name resonates with gross abuses of executive power associated with President Richard Nixon and the Committee to Re-Elect the President (commonly referred to by its acronym, CREEP) during the 1972 presidential campaign and its aftermath. The June 17 break-in at the Democratic National Committee headquarters in the Washington, D.C., Watergate complex led to journalistic investigations and congressional hearings that uncovered CREEP's extensive corruption. By engaging in blatantly illegal activity and exploiting the absence of effective disclosure laws, CREEP raised a slush fund that financed the break-in and other criminal activities, a cash-on-hand kitty estimated at $5 million of largely illegal donations from corporations (including American Airlines, Gulf Oil, and other companies and their foreign subsidiaries) and rich executives (such as business magnate, aviator, and film producer Howard Hughes and high-stakes investor and financier Robert Vesco, who eventually avoided criminal embezzlement prosecution by fleeing the country). John Gardner, head of the public interest lobby Common Cause, aptly summed it up: Watergate was "a particularly malodorous chapter in the annals of campaign financing," and the public's shock and outcry provided ammunition for congressional reformers to enact new campaign finance measures.

The operative law at the time of Watergate—the Federal Election Campaign Act (FECA) of 1971—imposed stringent reporting requirements (requiring disclosure of all contributors or lenders of $100 or more), restricted campaign spending by a candidate or immediate family members from their personal funds ($50,000 for presidential or vice presidential candidates; $35,000 for senatorial candidates; and $25,000 for House candidates), and placed ceilings on media advertising expenditures established by demographic criteria. Apart from these restraints, however, the 1971 Act regulated no other contributions or expenditures. In that light, the post-Watergate reform measures—the 1974 Amendments to FECA—were amendments in name only, since they far eclipsed the narrow limitations of their predecessor.

Among the most significant revisions to the federal campaign regulatory structure were the following:

- *Contribution limitations*: a $1,000 ceiling for contributions by an individual or group to any candidate in a federal election (primary, runoff, or general); a $5,000 ceiling for contributions by an individual or group to any non-candidate political organization or committee; and a $5,000 ceiling for contributions by a political committee to any federal candidate.
- *Aggregate contribution limitations*: a $25,000 ceiling for all contributions within an election cycle by an individual to federal candidates,

with no aggregate limit on contributions to non-candidate political committees.

- *Individual expenditure limitations*: a $1,000 ceiling on spending by an individual or group "relative to a clearly identified candidate"; the 1971 Act's ceilings on candidate expenditures from personal or family funds were retained.
- *Campaign expenditure limitations*: presidential and vice-presidential candidates were restricted to a total of $10 million in a primary election and $20 million in a general election; ceilings for senatorial candidates were determined by state population, up to a cap of $100,000 in the primary and $150,000 in the general election; candidates for the House of Representatives were limited to $70,000 per election.
- *Public funding for presidential elections*: after raising contribution totals of at least $5,000 in twenty states, a presidential candidate might receive federal subsidies in increasing amounts funded by voluntary taxpayer check-offs.
- *Reporting obligations*: heightened disclosure requirements were imposed on candidate and non-candidate political committees for reports to be filed at designated periods throughout the election cycle with the Federal Election Commission, a new agency created by the 1974 Amendments to FECA.

To campaign reform advocates such as Common Cause, the Center for Public Financing of Elections, and the League of Women Voters, the 1974 FECA Amendments were, no doubt, an occasion for celebration. Finally their hopes for more rigorous cleansing of financial corruption of the federal election process might be realized. Not so for a coalition of conservative and liberal adversaries who viewed the law as trampling core First Amendment rights by circumscribing political speech and authorizing governmental surveillance of political association. No more than two months after passage of the 1974 amendments, a Washington press conference featured James Buckley (a Conservative Party senator from New York and the brother of William F. Buckley), Eugene McCarthy (the former Democratic senator and presidential candidate from Minnesota), and Ira Glasser (the New York Civil Liberties Union executive director), who announced their plans to challenge the FECA revisions in federal court.

En Route to the Supreme Court

The coalition made good on its promise on January 2, 1975, the day after the 1974 amendments became effective, when the challengers filed suit in the U.S. District Court for the District of Columbia. By that point, Buckley and his colleagues had attracted other supporters, including Stewart Mott (the General Motors scion who had been Eugene McCarthy's largest contributor in his 1968 presidential run), the New York Conservative Party, and the American Conservative Union. Representing this phalanx of liberals and conservatives were Yale Law School professor Ralph K. Winter, Brice M. Clagett and John R. Bolton (the former a partner and the latter an associate at the distinguished Washington firm of Covington & Burling), and Joel Gora (counsel for the ACLU).

The defendants named in the case included several federal officials who were to administer the 1974 amendments—Secretary of the Senate Francis R. Valeo, Attorney General Edward Levi, and the FEC, among them. Representing the government were Deputy Solicitor General Daniel L. Friedman, Archibald Cox (former solicitor general under President Kennedy and special prosecutor for the Watergate scandal), and Ralph S. Spritzer (special counsel to the FEC). Concerned that the governmental officials might not avidly defend the law, the FECA's strong supporters—Common Cause, the Center for Public Financing of Elections, and the League of Women Voters—joined by intervention. Lloyd Cutler and others from the respected Washington firm of Wilmer, Cutler & Pickering represented the intervenors, along with Kenneth Guido and Fred Wertheimer as counsel for Common Cause.

The case, *Buckley v. Valeo*, launched a broad-based attack on the FECA Amendments. Based on the premise that money constituted political speech and association in the context of federal election campaigns, the plaintiffs argued that disclosure requirements, contribution restrictions, and spending limitations, whether independent of candidate coordination or tied to public funding provisions, invaded the First Amendment rights of citizens, groups, and candidates. Because FECA explicitly provided for a special and expedited review process of any constitutional challenges, the federal district court did not conduct a full-blown trial; rather, Judge Howard F. Corcoran entered an order adopting extensive findings of fact that had been submitted by the parties, and certified twenty-eight constitutional questions to be determined by the U.S. Court of Appeals for the District of Columbia. Sitting *en banc* (with all of the judges considering the case), the appellate court issued a *per curiam* (or unsigned) opinion that affirmed the constitutionality of all but one provision of the act—requiring disclosure reports from issue advocacy groups.

Thereafter, when the Supreme Court accepted the case for review, it agreed to decide for the very first time in its history the pressing question of whether federal restrictions on campaign contributions and expenditures—considered in the abstract and not in the concrete context of criminal charges for political corruption—violated the U.S. Constitution.

Enter the Justices—Oral Arguments & Internal Deliberations

Monday, November 10, 1975, at 10:04 A.M. "We will hear arguments today in *Buckley* against *Valeo*." With those words, Chief Justice Warren Burger began a full day of oral arguments in Case No. 75-436/437. For a typical case, the parties are given only one hour for arguments, with thirty minutes accorded to each side. But this was no typical case. Seven lawyers presented arguments and fielded questions from the justices for a full two hours in the morning and two more hours in the afternoon.

For much of the first half of the session, the Court's attention strongly focused on the constitutionality of FECA's reporting requirements. The primary question at issue: because of the law's low threshold for disclosure of contributions and expenditures and the wide scope of who would be obliged to report, were the requirements carefully tailored to further the government's legitimate interests in exposing potentially corruptive contributions? An exchange between the chief justice and the ACLU's Joel Gora illustrated this concern:

Burger: I take your argument, Mr. Gora, to be that there is no valid, rational public interest in flushing out and publicizing the names of $100 contributors or $101 contributors, none that can be justified constitutionally; but that there is, indeed, a real public interest in knowing about $10,000 or $100,000 or $500,000 ones.

Gora: Yes, that is our position...

Burger: But you're saying that you can't pick the point where the line should be drawn.

Gora: Well, the point, I think, has to be attempted to be drawn in reference to the purpose of having disclosure. ... There is a presumption that one's politics are one's own business. That's why, when the purpose is in terms of the prevention of corruption, then this Court and the Congress must ask whether the disclosure levels are drawn to meet that purpose.

Surprisingly little argument throughout the day was directed to the constitutionality of the expenditure limitations—particularly the $1,000 ceiling imposed on individuals and groups for spending relative to the election of a particular candidate. Justice William Rehnquist raised the provision himself at the very end of Gora's argument:

Rehnquist: Mr. Gora, unless I missed something, I think that neither you nor Mr. Winter specifically identified Section 608(e) [the independent expenditure restriction] for special attention, did you?

Gora: No, we have not. Section 608(e) is a flat ceiling on the speech of persons completely unconnected to any political candidate or committee. In a statute with a lot of unconstitutionality, we submit that that stands out.

Rehnquist: Well, I should think if there's a problem in requiring someone who spent $100 to disclose it, there would be even more of a problem in flatly prohibiting a person from spending over a thousand dollars.

Gora: That is our submission, Mr. Justice Rehnquist.

Indeed, to the extent that the parties and the justices indicated their concern with expenditure limitations, it was essentially in terms of the potential advantages to incumbents in preventing relatively unknown opponents from gaining electoral headway. On this score, Justice Lewis Powell and the chief justice expressed skepticism over Archibald Cox's defense of FECA:

> *Powell:* Mr. Cox, as I understand you, you expressed the view that a challenger is not disadvantaged by this act. May I put this hypothetical to you: suppose the challenger is in a district from which the member of congress—which the member of congress has served, say, for ten or fifteen years, and therefore is very well known. Assume further that the entire media in that district supports the incumbent. Would you think he would have much of a chance? I realize it would depend on the facts and circumstances, but isn't he disadvantaged?
>
> *Cox:* I will agree with you that you can think of cases where the only way in which a man could win was by having to spend enormous sums of money himself, because everything else was stacked against him.... But if you look at the [candidate expenditure] ceilings, on the basis of the 1974 election, it seems that they give ample chance to challengers to gain recognition; and second, that taking the act as a whole, they hurt incumbents who probably have the greater money-raising capacity, more than challengers....
>
> *Burger:* But the deference that you might give to a congressional judgment as to how much money might be appropriate may not be the same when we're talking about how much incumbents thought challengers might need.... I take it [you] give some weight to the fact that incumbents have a lot of built-in assets that challengers do not have; namely, large office staffs and branch offices out in districts, and that sort of thing?... Plus the newsworthiness to what they do, that the challengers don't always have.
>
> *Cox:* There's no question but that incumbents have advantages; sometimes there are disadvantages, but there are likely,

through name-recognition, to be advantages. My proposition is that this statute does not make the challengers any worse off in that respect than they were before. Now, some have mellifluous voices and others don't. There are all kinds of injustices in the world. I say this statute doesn't make it any worse.

In the flood of arguments dealing with technicalities over the identity of political committees subject to the act, the nature of reporting requirements, the relative advantages of incumbency, the operation of public funding for presidential candidates, and the propriety of the FEC commissioner appointments, what hardly surfaced at all were grander jurisprudential themes. The justices waded in the shallow seaweeds, but rarely plunged into deeper jurisprudential waters. Indeed, little dialogue was heard on a central First Amendment issue at play in *Buckley*: whether in controlling the amount of money contributed or spent in election campaigning (whether to individual candidates or in the aggregate to many candidates), FECA was restricting political speech (lying at the core of the First Amendment) or merely regulating symbolic conduct (lying at the Amendment's periphery). Only Justice Potter Stewart forthrightly raised this point in his exchange with Deputy Solicitor General Friedman:

> *Stewart:* But we are talking about speech; money is speech, and speech is money, whether it be buying television or radio time or newspaper advertising, or even buying pencils and paper and microphones. That's certainly clear, isn't it?
>
> *Friedman:* Money affects speech, but I would not agree that money is the same thing as speech, because not every contribution that is made to a political candidate is used for speech; it may be used for many things. ...We do not question that there is a First Amendment protection to these interests. As we see the issue, it is whether whatever adverse impact the statute has on the exercise of those rights is outweighed by what we deem to be the clearly compelling governmental interest underlying the legislation.

Perhaps it was the inherently complicated nature of the case. Perhaps it was the division of labor among the seven attorneys—three arguing for the appellants (Winter, Gora, and Clagett) and four for the appellees (Friedman, Cox, Cutler, and Spritzer). Perhaps it was the lineup's somewhat artificial truncation of interrelated issues. Whatever the explanation, it is not difficult to conclude—at least with the benefit of hindsight—that the oral arguments appeared relatively insignificant, and at times even entirely collateral, to the matters that eventually emerged as the turning points in the Court's analysis.

As to what truly concerned the black-robed jurists, much more revealing are the individual notes that eight of the justices took before and during their private conference session on the case, held two days after oral arguments. (Interestingly, although Justice William O. Douglas sat in oral arguments on *Buckley*, he was not present at the private conference. On that very day, he retired from the Court, having served for thirty-six years. After having suffered a debilitating stroke in December 1974, Douglas insisted on participating in the Court's business until Justice Abe Fortas persuaded him to leave. Douglas's replacement, Justice John Paul Stevens, took no part in the deliberation or decision of the case.)

The justices' abbreviated jottings on the conference discussions tell much about their preliminary views on the constitutional issues in *Buckley v. Valeo*. All eight indicated their willingness to uphold FECA's disclosure requirements. Characteristic of their views was the commentary by Chief Justice Burger, who penned: "The disclosure provisions are the heart of the whole thing for me. I think that these provisions are constitutional and highly desirable. It is a separate question as to the level at which disclosure is made." Indeed, four of his brethren—Associate Justices William Brennan, Thurgood Marshall, William Rehnquist, and Harry Blackmun—expressed concern over the low levels triggering report obligations, particularly as applied to minor and new parties. Only Justices Potter Stewart, Byron White, and Lewis Powell strongly affirmed the disclosure requirements on their face; as expressed most clearly by Potter Stewart, "It is for Congress to fix these limits and not for us to second-guess them."

Consensus broke down, however, when it came to the contribution limitations. The justices split 4–4 in their preliminary views of the constitutionality of those ceilings. Justices Brennan, White, and Marshall argued in favor of all contribution restrictions, and Rehnquist was willing to vote for all except a candidate's contributions to his or her own campaign. "On contributions, I am as firm as can be to affirm," Byron White asserted. "Giving money is an act, and acts are regulable. Congress has said that the dangers of money to fuel corruption require regulation. Neither content of speech nor censorship are involved here." In contrast, Chief Justice Burger and Justices Stewart, Powell, and Blackmun demonstrated much greater indecision, both as to individual and as to aggregate contribution limitations. Lewis Powell expressed the ambivalent spirit of his colleagues in declaring, "I am not at rest on the contribution limits, but if any part of the act can be sustained [as to regulating monies], I guess this is it."

Certainty reigned, however, when it came to FECA's expenditure limitations. The split was five against (virulently so), and three in favor (more cautiously so). Justices Brennan, White, and Marshall expressed their willingness to affirm the expenditure ceilings as loophole-closing devices in support of the contribution restrictions. "The expenditure limitations are constitutional," Byron White argued, "because otherwise, despite the contribution limitations, you can get and spend all the money you want."

Such logic held no sway with Chief Justice Burger and Justices Stewart, Rehnquist, Powell, and Blackmun, who aggressively expounded on the facial unconstitutionality of the expenditure caps on candidates and their campaign committees, and particularly the independent expenditure limits on individuals and groups. Referring to three of the most influential nationally syndicated columnists in the twentieth century, Burger declaimed: "This [law] has no limitation on the [Jack] Andersons, [James] Restons, [Joseph] Krafts, etc., who are much more influential than those who are precluded by this law from writing or distributing pamphlets. I find this section even more troublesome than the contribution limits. This is pure speech."

In this regard, Justice Powell delivered an even more powerful lambaste: "This statute is a revolutionary change in the system under which we have lived for two hundred years. The entire act, in purpose and effect, perpetrates the grossest infringement upon First Amendment rights." The mild-mannered southern gentleman who became known as a master of compromise pulled no punches on governmental regulation of political expenditures. "Instead of a system that is neutral on its face, where all scramble for all the money they can get, this law rigs the structure for incumbents," he complained. With rhetorical flourish, Powell concluded, "Section 608(e) [the independent expenditure limitation] is the most drastic abridgement of political speech since the Alien and Sedition Acts."

These early views—and those on other dimensions of FECA—were subject to change, of course. There would be more deliberation, more debate, and more development of thought before a final decision was rendered. But that would only take seventy-nine more days.

The Court Ruling—the *Buckley* Opinions

"There was urgency to the matter," election law expert Richard Hasen explained. "The Court felt pressure to decide the case before the 1976 presidential election session." To speed up the process, the justices shared the task of preparing a preliminary draft of the Court's decision—Potter Stewart took up the contribution and expenditure limitations, Lewis Powell the disclosure requirements, William Brennan the presidential public funding scheme, and Byron White and William Rehnquist the issue of the FEC's appointment—and Justice Brennan agreed to meld the segments together.

On Thursday, January 30, 1976, the Court delivered a tome of surprising length and complexity to the legal and political circles that had eagerly awaited its ruling. Coming in at a total of 294 pages in the *United States Reports*, the *Buckley* decision consists of an unsigned opinion of the Court (144 pages), an appendix to the *per curiam* (91 pages), and opinions concurring and dissenting in part from five of the eight justices who participated in the deliberations (59 pages)—all making it one of the longest reported cases in Supreme Court history.

From a bird's-eye view, *Buckley* upheld much of the 1974 FECA Amendments. The Court affirmed the constitutionality of the contribution limitations (i.e., the base and aggregate ceilings), the disclosure requirements, and the presidential campaign public funding system. In contrast, the expenditure limitations (i.e., restrictions on independent spending by individuals and groups, personal candidate spending, and overall campaign spending) were struck, and the appointment scheme for the commissioners of the FEC was held to violate separation of powers. (Four months later, in May 1976, Congress properly reconstituted the FEC.) But unquestionably, the pivotal part of the decision—that which garnered the most attention and criticism from jurists, scholars, lawyers, politicians, and pundits—was the Court's overall characterization of spending money as political speech and the dichotomy made between contributions and expenditures in terms of their differing treatment in First Amendment law.

At the outset, the justices recognized that FECA's contribution and expenditure limitations "operate in an area of the most fundamental First Amendment activities. Discussion of public issues and debate on the qualifications of candidates are integral to the operation of the system of government established by the Constitution." Restricting the amount of money that can be spent on political campaign communication "necessarily reduces the quantity of expression by restricting the number of issues discussed, the depth of the exploration, and the size of the audience reached." This is so, the jurists posited, "because virtually every means of communicating ideas in today's mass society requires the expenditure of money." Simply put, when it comes to political campaigning, money "speaks."

Nonetheless, for First Amendment purposes, the Court reasoned, money "speaks" differently depending on the form of political communication that it takes. As a contribution, money "serves as a general expression of support for the candidate and his views" (i.e., symbolic political expression) and "affiliate[s] a person with a candidate" (i.e., political association); and the amount of money contributed only "provides a rough index of the intensity of the contributor's support for the candidate." Thus, a limitation on the amount of money a person or group can contribute "involves little direct restraint" on political communication, because it "does not in any way infringe the contributor's freedom to discuss candidates and issues." In other words, money really "speaks" when contributions are transformed by candidates into their own speech.

In the form of a political expenditure, however, money "speaks" as an expression of the spender. Independent expenditures explicitly advocate a person's views on the election or defeat of identified candidates (i.e., individual political expression), and group or non-candidate political committee expenditures effectively amplify the voices of their adherents (i.e., associational political expression). Accordingly, the Court explained, limitations imposed on expenditures by persons, groups, candidates, and political parties "represent substantial rather than merely theoretical restraints on the quantity and diversity of political speech."

Given these differences, the *Buckley* decision drew a First Amendment distinction based on the government's stronger justifications for regulating contributions as opposed to expenditures. The Court granted that the prevention of "the actuality and appearance of corruption resulting from large individual financial contributions" was a constitutionally sufficient reason for the contribution limitations. "To the extent that large contributions are given to secure a political quid pro quo from current and potential office holders," the opinion established, "the integrity of our system of representative democracy is undermined." Equally concerning to the Court was the "appearance of corruption stemming from public awareness of the opportunities for abuse inherent in a regime of large individual financial contributions." That was the case for all contributions regulated by the act—the "base limits" of $1,000 on individual and group contributions and $5,000 on political committee contributions to candidates and campaign committees, and the "aggregate limit" of $25,000 on total contributions by an individual or group during any election cycle.

The justices did appreciate that the overall contribution limitation would impose a cap on the number of candidates and committees that a person might otherwise support. Nevertheless, the Court concluded that the aggregate ceiling was a "quite modest restraint upon protected political activity," acting as a loophole-closing measure. It "serves to pre-vent evasion of the $1,000 contribution limitation by a person who might otherwise contribute massive amounts of money to a particular candidate through the use of unearmarked contributions to political committees likely to contribute to that candidate, or huge contributions to the candi-date's political party."

When it came to the expenditure limitations, however, the Court rejected the anti-corruption rationale. Imposing the strictest of constitutional review standards on all of the spending ceilings—for individual and group independent expenditures, for personal candidate expenditures, and for total candidate campaign expenditures—the risk-of-corruption argument collapsed. As long as spending remained truly independent, the Court conjectured, the absence of coordination with candidates and their campaign committees would reduce the risk of actual or apparent corruption, and uncontrolled expenditures might even prove counterproductive to campaigns. And as far as personal candidate and total campaign expenditures were concerned, the anti-corruption rationale simply had no place.

Moreover, to the extent that expenditure limitations were designed by the government to level the playing field for individual political influence, the Court condemned this separate rationale as a per se unconstitutional purpose. Intoning a decidedly non-egalitarian theme, the Court theorized, "[T]he concept that government may restrict the speech of some elements of our society in order to enhance the relative voice of others is wholly foreign to the First Amendment," since it aimed "to secure the widest possible dissemination of information from diverse and antagonistic sources" and "to assure unfettered exchange of ideas for the bringing about of political and social changes desired by the people." This same logic served to invalidate the ceiling on overall candidate campaign expenditures. Reducing "skyrocketing costs of political campaigns" could not justify such restrictions, the opinion concluded, because the "First Amendment denies government the power to determine that spending to promote one's political views is wasteful, excessive, or unwise." With libertarian flourish, the Court concluded, "In the free society ordained by our Constitution it is not the government, but the people…who must retain control over the quantity and range of debate on public issues in a political campaign."

The great divide between contributions and expenditures was the front on which four justices deviated in their separate opinions. Chief Justice Burger would have invalidated contribution limitations for the same infirmities that were heralded for the expenditure limitations. "For me," he wrote, "contributions and expenditures are two sides of the same First Amendment coin." Continuing on this line, the chief emphasized: "The Court's attempt to distinguish the communication inherent in political *contributions* from the speech aspects of political *expenditures* simply 'will not wash.'" To the same effect, Justice Blackmun dissented from the decision to uphold the contribution ceilings, concluding curtly: "I am not persuaded that the Court makes, or indeed is able to make, a principled constitutional distinction between the contribution limitations, on the one hand, and the expenditure limitations, on the other."

Sharing the same-coin view, Justice White argued for the entirely opposite result. First, although recognizing that money facilitates speech, he disagreed heartily with treating campaign expenditures as pure speech. "What the Act regulates is giving and spending money," he observed, conduct that has First Amendment significance merely "because money may be used to defray the expenses of speaking." And in the context of political campaigns, money is not equivalent to speech: "There are, however, many expensive campaign activities that are not themselves communicative or remotely related to speech." As such, White argued for a less stringent standard of review for the expenditure limitations: "[T]his case depends on whether the non-speech interests of the Federal Government in regulating the use of money in political campaigns are sufficiently urgent to justify the incidental effects that the limitations visit upon the First Amendment interests of candidates and their supporters."

Under that standard, given the "mortal danger" that the risks of actual or apparent corruption present to the American system of representative government, the ceilings on contributions and expenditures were constitutionally equivalent. "It would make little sense to me, and apparently made none to Congress," Justice White posited, "to limit the amounts an individual may give to a candidate or spend with his approval but fail to limit the amounts that could be spent on his behalf. Yet the Court permits the former while striking down the latter limitation." Comparatively speaking, it was Congress and not the Court that was more institutionally competent to determine the necessity of expenditure limits. "I would take the word of those who know," White conceded, "that limiting independent expenditures is essential to prevent transparent and widespread evasion of the contribution limits." Furthermore, the overall candidate campaign expenditure limits "have their own potential to prevent the corruption of federal elections themselves." At bottom, White concluded:

"There is nothing objectionable in the attempt to insulate the political expression of federal candidates from the influence inevitably exerted by the endless job of raising increasingly large sums of money. I regret that the Court has returned them all to the treadmill."

Finally, Justice Marshall dissented from the decision to strike the limit on expenditures from a candidate's personal or family funds under his or her control. Criticizing the Court's characterization of this ceiling as an unconstitutional equalization of candidate resources, he redefined the government's purpose. "In my view," Marshall explained, "the interest is more precisely the interest in promoting the reality and appearance of equal access to the political arena." And that purpose is a legitimate one: "In view of [FECA's] limitations on contributions," he reasoned, the personal funds ceiling "emerges not simply as a device to reduce the natural advantage of the wealthy candidate, but as a provision providing some symmetry to a regulatory scheme that otherwise enhances the natural advantage of the wealthy."

Responses to *Buckley*—Pleasing All by Half

Not only the justices themselves, but the parties to the case were dissatisfied with winning only half the battle. Senator James Buckley, who eventually became a D.C. Circuit Court judge, complained that, "by severely limiting the size of individual contributions, today's law has made the search for money a candidate's central preoccupation." And Francis Valeo, the secretary of the Senate, told election law scholar Richard Hasen in an interview, "I knew the minute that they took off the limitations on personal expenditures that you were setting up a Senate of millionaires, or people who could rely on other people's money for their support. ... I was a little hard pressed to see how putting a limitation on how much you could spend was an infringement on your right of free speech."

Major figures in every interested sector of society—political, legal, academic, journalistic, and otherwise—derided the decision as illogical, impracticable, unprincipled, or worse. Politics and media writer Jeffrey Scheuer panned *Buckley's* aftermath: "The Supreme Court has seen fit ... to equate money with speech; hence, our political system is—to put it delicately—an influence auction, awash in hard and soft money." In a similar regard, law professor Cass Sunstein equated *Buckley* with the "discredited" doctrine in *Lochner v. New York* (1905), in which the Supreme Court struck progressive social and economic reform legislation. With more dramatic flair, Joseph A. Califano Jr., the secretary of Health, Education, and Welfare at the time the *Buckley* decision came down, urged the Court to toss its decision "in the same dustbin" with its disastrous 1896 "separate-but-equal doctrine that constitutionally blessed racially segregated schools." And Frank Sorauf, a political science professor and noted campaign finance scholar, put it plainly: "The majority opinion in *Buckley* is one of the Court's less impressive monuments."

True, the ruling has gathered the support of some prominent defenders. For example, law professor Joel Gora, co-counsel for the plaintiffs in the case, asserted that "the academic pundits are dead wrong in rating the *Buckley* decision so poorly." Agreeing with him, First Amendment scholar Eugene Volokh contended: "People either say the Court went too far in allowing restrictions on political contributions and expenditures, or not far enough. I want to do something radical, which is to say that the Court got it pretty much right."

Nonetheless, with its contribution-expenditure dichotomy, the Supreme Court aimed for a delicate Metternichean compromise (the delicate political arrangement in pre–World War I Europe). In the end, however, its First Amendment handiwork in *Buckley v. Valeo* brought no such peace. The battle would only escalate, though it would take time.

Buttressing *Buckley*: The Burger & Rehnquist Courts

However unsatisfying the *Buckley* framework seemed to its critics, it proved to have staying power. Over the next twenty-nine years—the remainder of the Burger Court era and the entirety of the Rehnquist Court era—the justices heard no fewer than fifteen campaign financing cases, thirteen of which involved challenges to federal or state regulations on campaign contributions and expenditures. In those thirteen cases, segments of the Court occasionally voiced opposition either to *Buckley's* affirmation of contribution limitations or to its negation of expenditure limitations. But no majority of five justices ever coalesced around the reversal of either ruling. And despite some significant doctrinal wrinkles written into the First Amendment law of campaign finance regulation— recognizing constitutional distinctions, for example, between ballot measure campaigns and candidate election campaigns, or between nonprofit corporate ideological advocacy and candidate endorsements, or between nonprofit and for-profit spending for ideological advocacy—ultimately the Court reinforced, time and again, the contribution-expenditure dichotomy at the center of *Buckley*.

Adhering to *Buckley's* teachings on 1) the minimal expressive significance and the maximal corruptive potential of contributions and 2) the deference owed to legislative judgments about what to do with them, the Court validated federal and state restrictions on contributions in the following four cases:

- *California Medical Association v. FEC* (1981) upheld FECA's $5,000 limitation on individual and group contributions to a political action committee (PAC). The Court affirmed *Buckley's* reasoning that contributions give rise to meaningful political expression when spent by the PAC.
- *FEC v. National Right to Work Committee* (1982) unanimously upheld FECA's "membership" requirements for a nonprofit corporate PAC. The Court ruled that the PAC could not solicit or accept contributions from individuals who were not sufficiently attached to the corporation (for example, as stockholders, executives, or administrative personnel) to qualify as members.
- *Nixon v. Shrink Missouri Government PAC* (2000) upheld a Missouri law that imposed limits on contributions to candidates for state office in amounts ranging from $250 to $1,000. Relying on "the prevention of corruption and the appearance of corruption" as the basis for its decision, the Court recognized that ceilings lower than those in FECA are permissible as long as they do not substantially hinder a candidate's ability to run for office.
- *FEC v. Beaumont* (2003) upheld a provision of FECA that banned direct corporate treasury contributions to federal election

campaigns, as applied to nonprofit corporations as well as for-profits. Accepting the government's argument that the members of nonprofit advocacy groups would otherwise be able to circumvent their individual contribution limitations, Justice Souter declared for a 7–2 majority of the Court: "Any attack on the federal prohibition of direct corporate political contributions goes against the current of a century of congressional efforts."

Similarly abiding by *Buckley*'s teachings on 1) the substantial expressive significance and reduced corruptive potential of expenditures and 2) the heightened level of judicial review appropriate to legislative regulation of them, the Court invalidated federal and state restrictions on expenditures in the following four cases:

- *Common Cause v. Schmitt* (1982): an evenly divided Court (with Justice O'Connor not participating) let stand a lower-court ruling finding unconstitutional a provision prohibiting certain groups from making independent expenditures of more than $1,000 on behalf of publicly financed presidential candidates. The Court reasoned that the unconstitutionality of expenditure limitations applied equally to individuals and groups.
- *FEC v. National Conservative PAC* (1985) struck the provision of the Presidential Election Campaign Fund Act that prohibited PACs from independently spending more than $1,000 to advocate for the election of a presidential candidate who accepted public funding. Firmly resolving the same issue presented by *Common Cause v. Schmitt*, a six-member majority grounded their decision in *Buckley*'s rationale that government regulation of expenditures violates the First Amendment.
- *Colorado Republican Federal Campaign Committee v. FEC* (1996) (*Colorado I*) struck the "party expenditure" provision of FECA that imposed dollar limits on expenditures of a political party in connection with the general election campaign of a congressional candidate. Rejecting an FEC regulation that presumed coordination between political parties and their candidates, and thus treated

these expenditures as contributions, Justice Breyer's plurality opinion concluded: "We do not see how a Constitution that grants to individuals, candidates, and ordinary political committees the right to make unlimited independent expenditures could deny the same right to political parties."

- *FEC v. Colorado Republic Federal Campaign Committee* (2001) (*Colorado II*) rejected a facial challenge to FECA's ban on coordinated expenditures by political parties on behalf of specific candidates. In reviewing the case once again after remand, the Court held that substantial evidence "shows beyond serious doubt how contribution limits would be eroded if the Court were to strike down the limits on coordinated spending." Although not explicitly equating coordinated expenditures with pure contributions, a five-member majority applied the same standard of review that *Buckley* considered to be appropriate for contribution regulations (i.e., "closely drawn" to a "sufficiently important government interest" in combatting political corruption). Significantly, the four dissenting justices (Rehnquist, Scalia, Kennedy, and Thomas) strongly called for overruling *Buckley* in part so as to apply full strict scrutiny analysis and strike the coordinated expenditure limit, which "sweeps too broadly, interferes with the party-candidate relationship, and has not been proved necessary to combat corruption."

Buckley had not squarely addressed the First Amendment status of corporate spending for political campaign advocacy, and it was in this area that the Supreme Court's analysis took novel and distinct directions. Indeed, the very first case after *Buckley* began the justices' investigation of the constitutional differences between corporate spending in ballot initiative campaigns and candidate election campaigns.

First National Bank of Boston v. Bellotti (1978) struck a Massachusetts law that restricted a corporation from contributing or spending in initiative or referendum campaigns, unless the enacted law would directly impact the corporation's business or property. Justice Lewis Powell's opinion for the Court observed: "If the speakers here were not corporations, no one would suggest that the State could silence their proposed speech." Finding that ballot advocacy is "indispensable to decisionmaking in a democracy," Powell reasoned that "this is no less true because the speech comes from a corporation rather than an individual. The inherent worth of the speech in terms of its capacity for informing the public does not depend upon the identity of its source, whether corporation, association, union, or individual." This declaration was rendered by the former corporate law expert who had served on the board of eleven mega-corporations. And as Professors John Nichols and Robert W. McChesney revealed, no less than two months before Justice Powell joined the Court, he authored a report for the U.S. Chamber of Commerce titled "Attack on American Free Enterprise System"; it urged the group to fortify corporate rights by "assuming a broad and more vigorous role in the political arena."

Bellotti's philosophy of First Amendment value for corporate political campaign advocacy took on added strength in two subsequent cases. Ruling that *Buckley's* contribution-expenditure dichotomy had never contemplated ballot measure campaigns, the Court struck a local ordinance that set a $250 ceiling on personal contributions to PACs established to support or oppose referenda in *Citizens Against Rent Control v. Berkeley* (1981). And in *FEC v. Massachusetts Citizens for Life* (1986) (*MCFL*), the Court granted even more latitude for political campaign advocacy conducted by a narrow class of corporations—those corporations that: 1) are nonprofit and non-shareholder, 2) were organized solely to spend on ideological and express candidate advocacy (and not to contribute to candidates), and 3) accepted no contributions from corporations or labor unions. Justice William Brennan's opinion for a 5–4 majority held that such groups could spend their treasury funds to publicize their views on key political issues, to broadcast the voting records of candidates, and to expressly advocate the election or defeat of any particular candidate.

Broadening *Buckley*: "A Different Kind of Corruption"

Although *MCFL* had hinted that nonprofit and for-profit political campaign spending might stand on different footing, as late as 1990 the Court had yet to drive a First Amendment wedge between the two. That distinction first came in *Austin v. Michigan Chamber of Commerce*, which upheld a state statute barring all corporations (except media corporations) from spending their treasury funds for candidate and issue advocacy of the type that *MCFL* had authorized. Recognizing that the nonprofit *MCFL* refused to solicit contributions from for-profit corporations, the *Austin* Court noted that more than three-fourths of the Chamber's members were business associations, and the nominally nonprofit Chamber received dues and donations from for-profits and largely operated on them. Writing for the majority, Justice Thurgood Marshall explained: "Because the Chamber accepts money from for-profit corporations, it could…serve as a conduit for corporate political spending" in violation of the Michigan campaign finance law.

Importantly, the *Austin* decision did not rely on *Buckley's* quid pro quo corruption rationale to justify the restraint on corporate treasury spending, but rested instead on what Justice Marshall's opinion for the Court called "a different kind of corruption"—namely, "the corrosive and distorting effects of immense aggregations of wealth that are accumulated with the help of the corporate form." Thus, *Austin* significantly moved away from a narrow view of corruption—an exchange of money for political favor—to a broader and more systemic understanding of corruption that focused on the potential of big money to undermine the integrity of the electoral process. Such a capacious definition of corruption effectively granted lawmakers more leeway to regulate campaign finance.

Whatever one's political stripes, electoral corruption is difficult to define. What, for example, is "undue influence"? After all, when we vote for a political candidate, we seek to support the policy positions she staked out during the campaign. We do likewise when we urge fifty of our friends to vote for her, or when we host a fundraising event for her. If we purchase a hundred lawn signs or contribute to a fund to place billboard ads endorsing her, we again do so to show our support. Assume that one of the main reasons we back a candidate is because of her position on minimum wages for workers. What if we belong to a large national union that spends a lot of money derived from our dues (with our approval) for similar political purposes? Finally, what if a for-profit corporation, such as

McDonalds, decides that it wants to respond in kind? At what point do we cross the legal line between proper and undue influence?

Although Justice Marshall's opinion was careful not to invoke the "equality" or "leveling the playing field" rationale rejected in *Buckley*, it found a compelling regulatory interest in the prevention of corruption of the electoral process itself. Accordingly, the Michigan law was "precisely tailored" to further the state's interest in preventing corporate independent expenditures from unfairly influencing elections. In notable part, this was because the corporations could still establish PACs to receive regulated contributions for political campaign expression.

To all of this, Justice Antonin Scalia's dissent rang out with dramatic flourish: "Attention all citizens. To assure the fairness of elections...your Government has decided that the following associations of persons shall be prohibited from speaking or writing in support of any candidate." He boldly announced his opposition: "[T]he Court today endorses the principle that too much speech is an evil that the democratic majority can proscribe. I dissent because that principle is...incompatible with the absolutely central truth of the First Amendment: that government cannot be trusted to assure, through censorship, the 'fairness' of political debate."

While *Austin* was remarkable for its embrace of a broader concept of political corruption, the most sweeping campaign finance decision since *Buckley* was yet to come.

A New Way: The Sins of "Soft Money"

"Soft money." The term—now so disparaged by campaign finance reformers—first came to public consciousness after 1979. That was the year that Congress amended FECA to exempt donations to national or state political parties from contribution and expenditure limitations. The new law intended that such "soft money" (political donations made to avoid FECA restrictions, as distinguished from "hard money" raised and spent subject to FECA restraints) be directed to party-building activities, such as voter registration drives, get-out-the-vote efforts, polling, and the like. But the soft-money phenomenon soon became a funnel for financing federal election campaigns and a loophole for the wealthy who had maxed out on aggregate contribution limitations.

The ploy went like this: national political parties solicited soft money from generous donors (including corporations and unions prohibited from contributing directly to federal candidates or PACs). Thereafter, the indirect process of giving money moved along the following lines:

- Soft money was transferred to state and local parties facing competitive elections.
- Soft money then funded state and local candidate campaigns and party administrative costs.
- And that soft money freed up hard money that was then contributed to federal campaigns under FECA limitations.

As Melvin Urofsky summarized: "Technically, soft money could not go to financing the campaigns of federal candidates, but in fact that is exactly where it went....The transfer allowed state parties to help federal candidates by essentially 'washing' the soft money."

With exploitative fervor, the pursuit of soft money escalated dramatically. As Urofsky reports: "In 1980, the first year that the national committees could raise and spend soft money, it accounted for only 8 percent of their total outlay; by the 2000 election, soft money accounted for 42 percent of the total expenditures of the national committees." Not surprisingly, soft-money gifts typically came from large contributors, "with more than four hundred persons, corporations, or unions each giving $100,000 or more" for the 1988 election alone. And the vast bulk of the soft money landed in federal campaign coffers. In the 1992 election, for example, "barely $2 million of the $80 million in nonfederal funds went to state and local candidates," Urofsky tells us. "The two national parties transferred $15 million to state party committees, nearly all of which they had to use in support of federal candidates. Approximately two-thirds of the soft-money transfers of each party went to ten states considered up for grabs in the presidential election."

Not only the frenzy over soft money, but notorious fundraising improprieties bolstered public calls for reform. Most significant, perhaps, was the 1988 Keating Five Scandal, which involved illegal contributions to five U.S. senators given at the direction of Charles H. Keating Jr., the president of a California savings and loan company under regulatory investigation after the S&L industry's collapse. Keating's and his associates' hard money contributions totaled $324,000, and that sum was far surpassed by soft-money donations to state party committees and others amounting to more than $1,225,000. As told by Herbert Alexander and Monica Bauer, when Keating was asked whether his "financial support in any way influenced political figures to take up [his] cause," Keating responded bluntly: "I want to say in the most forceful way I can. I certainly hope so."

Less momentous perhaps, but certainly not insignificant, were the fundraising shenanigans of the Clinton Administration in the mid-1990s—the allegedly unlawful contributions (totaling over $4 million) channeled by the Chinese government through Chinese-American businessmen to the Democratic Party in order to preserve friendly trade relations, or the tens of millions raised from the well-heeled, who paid for White House "coffee chats" with Bill Clinton or Al Gore and weekend sleepovers in the Lincoln bedroom.

These events and others ensured that salacious reports of campaign finance transgressions and indignities inundated the mass media. According to Rodney A. Smith, "the sleaziness of the Enron debacle and its management's perceived (not proven) attempts to buy government favors with campaign contributions" proved to be the last straw for an American public increasingly outraged by political corruption. In February 2002, Smith informs us, *Gallup Poll Monthly* established that "among people who said they were following the Enron story closely, 80 percent believed new campaign finance laws were necessary." Just as Watergate ushered in the 1974 Amendments to FECA, so the Keating Five and Enron fiascos paved the way for Congress to revise, yet one more time, the federal campaign finance system.

Two Senators, Two Parties, One Solution

Congress's response to campaign finance critics was the Bipartisan Campaign Reform Act of 2002 (BCRA), popularly known as the

"McCain-Feingold" law (for its primary bipartisan senatorial sponsors). BCRA contained a number of discrete provisions tailored for recently detected peccadillos—for example, a restriction on fundraising on federal property (a rejoinder to the Clinton White House indignities), a ban on campaign contributions by minors, a demand that political parties choose between coordinated or independent expenditures after nominating a candidate, and heightened requirements for disclosure and reporting. But the two most significant and controversial provisions in the law addressed 1) the soft-money conundrum and 2) corporate and labor union spending of their treasury funds for electioneering communications.

Title I of BCRA (2 U.S.C. §441[i]) prohibited national party committees or their representatives from soliciting, accepting, or spending any soft money, and proscribed the use of such money by state and local party organizations for activities relating to federal elections. Moreover, federal candidates and officeholders were forbidden to solicit, receive, or spend soft money in connection with any federal election, and they were limited in doing so as to state and local elections. To prevent circumvention of these new regulations, state and local officials and candidates were barred from using soft money for communications promoting or attacking federal candidates. In short, as the Supreme Court later characterized it, Title I aimed to take political parties and candidates "out of the soft-money business."

In addition, BCRA sought to eliminate what some viewed as the "express advocacy" loophole created in *MCFL*. A narrow reading of what constituted express advocacy allowed soft-money expenditures for so-called "issue ads" to escape the law's limitations, prohibitions, and reporting requirements as long as the ads avoided certain "magic words" such as "vote for" or "vote against." To curb this, Title II (2 U.S.C. §434[f]) outlawed corporate and labor union funding of "electioneering communications" with general treasury monies. This new term was defined as any broadcast, cable, or satellite communication that referred to a clearly identified federal candidate if made within thirty days of a primary election or sixty days of a general election. Such political advertising could only be bought by a corporation's or union's PAC using regulated hard money.

Finally, as though compensating for its withdrawal of soft-money donations, BCRA raised some of the original FECA ceilings on hard money contributions:

- Individual contributions to a candidate per election (primary or general) increased from $1,000 to $2,000.
- The aggregate contribution ceiling for individuals raised from $25,000 to $37,500 in an election cycle.
- Within the aggregate, the limit on individual contributions to national political party committees rose from $20,000 to $25,000, and from $5,000 to $10,000 to state party committees.
- Donations from a national party committee to a senatorial campaign were upped from $17,500 to $35,000.
- For the first time, the federal campaign financing law indexed these numbers for inflation, setting them in odd-numbered years for a two-year election cycle.
- FECA's limitations for PAC contributions did not change, and these numbers were not indexed.

The Attack on BCRA Is Launched

Only hours after President George W. Bush signed the bill on March 27, 2002, BCRA was under legal attack. Senator Mitch McConnell issued a press release stating that he had filed suit against the Federal Election Commission that very day "to defend the First Amendment right of all Americans to be able to fully participate in the political process." He hoped to be joined by "a strong group of co-plaintiffs in the very near future." And soon enough he was—by the National Rifle Association, AFL-CIO, U.S. Chamber of Commerce, Republican National Committee, and California Democratic Party, among others. Even the American Civil Liberties Union, which had long supported public financing as a reform measure, came on board. A stellar legal team—the celebrated First Amendment expert Floyd Abrams and former solicitor general and special prosecutor Kenneth Starr—represented McConnell and his colleagues.

Shortly after McConnell's declaration, BCRA's major congressional sponsors—Republican Senator John McCain and Democratic Senator Russ Feingold, along with Republican Representative Christopher Shays and Democratic Representative Patrick Meehan—announced at a press conference that they would intervene in the suit to defend the measure. The Federal Election Commission and the intervenors had their own all-star lineup of counsel: Solicitor General Theodore Olson and Deputy Solicitor General Paul Clement for the FEC; and Seth Waxman, former solicitor general and partner in the distinguished firm of William, Cutler, and Pickering, for the intervenor-defendants.

Although the plaintiffs challenged other parts of BCRA, the two key provisions were assailed for violating free speech liberties, equal protection guarantees, and federalism principles. Title I's regulation of soft-money expenditures, they argued, burdened pure speech and association inherent in the political activities that *Buckley v. Valeo* recognized as protected under the First Amendment. Moreover, by singling out political parties for discriminatory treatment, the soft-money restrictions infringed the equal protection components of both the Fifth and Fourteenth Amendments. And because Congress reached into the realm of soft money—funds raised legitimately under state laws to be used for state and local party election activities such as voter registration, get-out-the-vote drives, administrative expenses, issue advocacy, and the like—Title I also interfered with the structures of federalism at the core of the constitutional scheme. Importantly, the plaintiffs alleged that the legislative record offered scant evidence to support the only justification for such constitutional infringements that the *Buckley* Court had validated: in short, there was no connection between the soft-money bans and the prevention of actual or apparent quid pro quo candidate corruption.

Title II's regulation of corporate and union funding of "electioneering communications" was assailed as directly contravening the First Amendment law doctrines established in *Buckley* and its progeny. Independent expenditures for express advocacy of the election or defeat of particular candidates and for ideological issue advocacy that does not specifically mention candidates cannot be banned—whether or not they influence an election, whether or not they are funded by regulated hard money, whether or not they are made by corporations and unions. These electioneering communications further core political speech values, and that is even more the case in the run-up to election day.

To all appearances, the government lawyers for the defense carried the heavier burden. They had to reconcile BCRA's explicit bans on soft money and electioneering expenditures with a long line of Supreme Court precedents that seemed to nullify such regulations. Even more significantly, they needed to demonstrate that the concept of political corruption that constituted a compelling governmental interest for campaign finance regulation was not the narrow one of quid pro quo candidate influence, but the much broader one recognized in *Austin*.

Now the battle lines were drawn, and the case was submitted to a three-judge federal district court of the District of Columbia. As Melvin Urofsky characterized its ruling, "There is little positive to be said... about the 774-page district court opinion in *McConnell v. Federal Election Commission*. Even recognizing the many complex issues involved in the case, the opinion is so incomprehensible that the three judges had to insert a chart and table of contents to show where each of them stood on particular issues." The end result, Urofsky told us, is that "[a]ll the litigants agreed... that the decision and the resulting orders were so unhelpful and confusing that a stay should be sought so that the orders would not go into effect until the Supreme Court had heard the case." Because of a provision in BCRA itself authorizing expedited review, the case moved on the fast track of direct appeal to the nation's highest court.

The *McConnell* Complex

Ironically, in the eyes of many, the Supreme Court's rulings and rationales in *McConnell* appeared as complex, confusing, or even incomprehensible as those of the district court. When the Court issued its decision on December 10, 2003, "The opinions had the largest U.S. Reports page count (279, excluding the heading and syllabus) and second largest word count (89,684) in Supreme Court history," according to Daniel Lowenstein, Richard Hasen, and Daniel Tokaji. Moreover, the Court presented eight separate opinions, with only five Justices forming a bare majority on the constitutionality of BCRA's major titles. Justices Stevens and O'Connor coauthored the lead opinion on Title I (soft-money ban, contribution limits, and reporting requirements) and Title II (electioneering communications restrictions and disclosure); their opinion was joined fully only by Justices Souter, Ginsburg, and Breyer. The four remaining justices dissented entirely to the holdings on Title I; and whereas Chief Justice Rehnquist and Justice Kennedy objected fully as to Title II, Justices Scalia and Thomas objected only in part.

Surveying the *McConnell* landscape with a bird's-eye view, most of BCRA survived the Court's evaluation, including the hotly contested soft-money and issue-advocacy provisions. The Court generally upheld congressional efforts to "plug the soft-money loophole." As the majority justices recognized, "Both common sense and the ample record in this case confirm Congress' belief that large soft-money contributions to national party committees have a corrupting influence or give rise to the appearance of corruption." Because certain party activities funded by soft money "confer substantial benefits on federal candidates, the funding of such activities creates a significant risk of actual and apparent corruption." *McConnell* also upheld the electioneering communication provision, finding that the "magic-words requirement is functionally meaningless.... The express advocacy line, in short, has not aided the legislative effort to combat real or apparent corruption, and Congress enacted BCRA to correct the flaws it found in the existing system."

Essentially, then, the majority justices: 1) reaffirmed that contribution limitations are not subject to strict scrutiny review; 2) upheld the restrictions on soft money as "closely drawn" to prevent circumvention of the contribution ceilings validated in *Buckley* and to further the important governmental interests of stemming "both the actual corruption threatened by large financial contributions and the eroding of public confidence in the electoral process through the appearance of corruption"; and 3) upheld the regulation of corporate and union electioneering communications funded by treasury monies so as to reinforce the creation of PACs for independent spending on issue advocacy.

Doctrinally speaking, the majority's positions on these three issues could fairly be characterized as unsurprising and predictable. The first proposition—applying a "closely drawn" standard of review, rather than strict scrutiny, to evaluate BCRA's campaign contribution restrictions— was hardly novel. This practice dated from the Court's 1976 decision in *Buckley v. Valeo* and was reinforced thereafter in case after case, the most immediate precedent being *FEC v. Beaumont*, decided only six months before *McConnell*.

The dissenters railed on this score, however, charging the majority with misapplying precedent. "If one is viewing BCRA though *Buckley's* lens," Justice Anthony Kennedy opined for himself and the other three dissenters, "one must conclude [that the act,] unlike contribution limitations, also creates significant burdens on speech itself." Because the act "fundamentally alters, and thereby burdens, protected speech and association throughout our society," Kennedy argued, "[s]trict scrutiny ought apply to review its constitutionality."

But the charge of infidelity to precedent did not stick. Insofar as BCRA limits the sources and the individual amounts of soft-money donations, the Court reasoned, the law only burdens speech to the extent of a hard money contribution limitation. Moreover, "The less rigorous standard of review we have applied to contribution limits," Stevens and O'Connor explained, "shows proper deference to Congress' ability to weigh competing constitutional interests in an area in which it enjoys particular expertise. It also provides Congress with sufficient room to anticipate and respond to concerns about circumvention of regulations designed to protect the integrity of the political process."

Such a deferential posture to congressional expertise was justified, in part, by the majority's holding on the second proposition above—that is, recognition of a "closely drawn" fit between BCRA's soft-money restrictions and Congress's objectives in preventing political corruption and closing loopholes in the campaign finance law. Once again, the Court's disposition was doctrinally foreseeable, following rather logically from the rulings and rationales in *Nixon v. Shrink Missouri Government PAC* and *Colorado II*. Indeed, the majority relied explicitly on both cases in upholding Title I's soft-money bans. Quoting *Shrink Missouri Government*, Justices Stevens and O'Connor asserted, "Take away Congress' authority to regulate the appearance of undue influence, and 'the cynical assumption that large donors call the tune could jeopardize the willingness of voters to take part in democratic governance.'" In addition, the coauthors deployed *Colorado II* to great effect: "[B]ecause the First Amendment does not require Congress to ignore the fact that 'candidates, donors, and parties test the limits of the current law,' these interests have been sufficient to justify not only contribution limits themselves, but laws preventing the circumvention of such limits ('[A]ll Members of the Court agree that circumvention is a valid theory of corruption.')."

What vexed the dissenters here was their perception that the Court had underhandedly stretched the accepted boundaries of political corruption that Congress can proscribe. As per Justice Kennedy, *Buckley* established that campaign finance regulation withstands constitutional challenge only if it targets contributions that entail "demonstrable quid pro quo danger." But now the *McConnell* majority had expanded the anti-corruption rationale to permit regulation of "any conduct that wins goodwill from or influences a Member of Congress." And this objective, the dissenters emphasized, is per se unconstitutional. "There is no basis, in law or in fact, to say favoritism or influence in general is the same as corrupt favoritism or influence in particular," Kennedy declared. "By equating vague and generic claims of favoritism or influence with actual or apparent corruption, the Court adopts a definition of corruption that dismantles basic First Amendment rules, permits Congress to suppress speech in the absence of a quid pro quo threat, and moves beyond the rationale that is *Buckley*'s very foundation."

Nevertheless, the majority would not be constrained by such a "crabbed view of corruption, and particularly of the appearance of corruption." The Stevens–O'Connor joint opinion stressed what they saw as obvious: "Under this system, corporate, union, and wealthy individual donors have been free to contribute substantial sums of soft money to the national parties, which the parties can spend for the specific purpose of influencing a particular candidate's federal election. It is not only plausible, but likely, that donors would seek to exploit that gratitude." For the five justices, drawing the permissible boundaries of campaign finance law tightly around quid pro quo corruption "ignores precedent, common sense, and the realities of political fundraising exposed by the record in this litigation."

Finally, the third proposition above—the constitutionality of Title II's ban on corporate and union electioneering communications funded by treasury monies—was described by the *McConnell* majority as a doctrinal clarification of sorts. Neither the First Amendment nor *Buckley* prohibited BCRA's regulation of "electioneering communications," Justices Stevens and O'Connor maintained, because there is not a hard-and-fast constitutional line between express candidate advocacy and ideological issue advocacy. "[T]he presence or absence of magic words [such as "vote for" or "vote against"] cannot meaningfully distinguish electioneering speech from a true issue ad," the Court remarked. Rather, issue ads publicized within thirty- and sixty-day periods prior to elections are the "functional equivalent" of express advocacy. "[A]lthough the resulting advertisements do not urge the viewer to vote for or against a candidate in so many words," the joint opinion contended, "they are no less clearly intended to influence the election." Relying on *Beaumont v. FEC* and *Austin v. Michigan Chamber of Commerce*, the majority extended the constitutional prohibition on corporate and union treasury funding of express candidate advocacy to BCRA's restriction on such funding of electioneering communications. And the *McConnell* decision invoked those precedents to defend BCRA's constrained impact on issue advocacy: "Because corporations can still fund electioneering communications with PAC money, it is 'simply wrong' to view the provision as a 'complete ban' on expression rather than a regulation."

A full measure of the dissenters' ire was vented against this Title II ruling. Disparaging the majority's anxiety over a flood of political dollars flowing from colossal corporate coffers, Justice Scalia declaimed, "The premise of the First Amendment is that the American people are neither sheep nor fools, and hence fully capable of considering both the substance of the speech presented to them and its proximate and ultimate source. If that premise is wrong, our democracy has a much greater problem to overcome than merely the influence of amassed wealth."

Furthermore, despite Title II's exemption of media corporations, Justice Clarence Thomas rode the slippery slope to indict the Court for the "chilling endpoint" of its reasoning: "outright regulation of the press." Naturally, "media corporations often wish to influence elections," and "[w]hat is to stop a future Congress from determining that the press is 'too influential,' and that the 'appearance of corruption' is significant when media organizations endorse candidates or run 'slanted' or 'biased' news stories in favor of candidates or parties?"

As a spokesman for all the dissenters, Justice Kennedy lambasted the Court's "new and serious intrusion" on the First Amendment. "The majority compounds the error made in *Austin*," he bemoaned, "and silences political speech central to the civic discourse that sustains and informs our democratic processes." Failing to follow the implications of Justice Powell's majority opinion in *National Bank of Boston v. Bellotti* as to corporate participation in the electoral process, "the majority's ready willingness to equate corruption with all organizations adopting the corporate form is a grave insult to nonprofit and for-profit corporations alike, entities that have long enriched our civic dialogue." Since "[c]ontinued adherence to *Austin* cannot be justified by the corporate identity of the speaker," Justice Kennedy concluded, "*Austin*'s errors stand exposed, and it is our duty to say so."

A Reconfigured Tribunal: Enter the Roberts Court

All told, although *McConnell* may not have dramatically altered the First Amendment doctrine of campaign finance regulation, it did reinforce *Austin*'s expanded vision of political corruption and its restricted vision of corporate political speech rights. Given *McConnell*'s narrow five-member majority, however, would its highly contested rulings long endure—especially with changes in the membership of the Court?

Two full years did not pass after the *McConnell* decision before the Supreme Court was reconfigured. John Roberts became the seventeenth and current chief justice of the United States on September 29, 2005, after being nominated by President George W. Bush upon the death of William Rehnquist (whom Roberts served as a law clerk from 1980 to 1981, when Rehnquist was still an associate justice). Recognized generally as having a conservative constitutional philosophy like his former boss, Roberts's particular views on federal election campaign reform were publicly unknown.

That was surely the case on Wednesday, September 14, 2005—the afternoon of the third day of his confirmation hearings—when Senator Samuel Brownback quizzed Roberts on his sense of *McConnell's* validation of BCRA's restrictions on corporate and union campaign electioneering. "I did not think there was any way the Court would hold that this is constitutional," Brownback asserted, "because you're limiting political free speech, and right when people are making their decision." Careful not to reveal his hand, Roberts replied ambiguously: "That was a case where the Court's decision was driven in large part by the record that had been compiled by Congress.... [I]t's no great insight—that the extensive record carried a lot of weight with the justices." No great insight, indeed—either into the case or into John Roberts's leanings as to campaign finance jurisprudence.

Even more significant for the future of *Buckley v. Valeo* and its legacy was Justice Sandra Day O'Connor's resignation from the Court on January 31, 2006. A centrist on the Court in campaign finance cases, she had not been a steady ally in either the regulatory or deregulatory camps. O'Connor "changed her mind on the constitutionality of corporate spending limits in candidate elections three times," Richard Hasen explains. "In *MCLF*, she seemed to agree that for-profit corporate spending could be limited to PAC spending. In *Austin*, she sided with the dissenters in holding such limits unconstitutional. In *McConnell*, without explanation, she sided with the majority in reaffirming *Austin*." Vacillation aside, the justice was a key swing vote in more recent decisions such as *Colorado II* and *McConnell*, where she cast the crucial fifth vote for the 5–4 rulings that accepted Congress's expansive definition of corruption of the political system and that staved off the dissenters' call for overruling *Buckley v. Valeo* altogether. Indeed, in *McConnell*, O'Connor joined Justice Stevens in coauthoring the lead opinion.

Samuel Alito—a former Princeton University/Yale Law School-educated judge from the U.S. Court of Appeals for the Third Circuit—became O'Connor's replacement on January 31, 2006. President Bush's second selection to the Supreme Court had a prior appellate record revealing a "substantial libertarian dimension to his jurisprudence as well as a conservative one," as legal scholar Ilya Somin characterized it. Although

Alito had not ruled in a campaign finance case, his libertarian streak emerged in appellate court opinions he authored on other free speech issues—including the invalidation of a public school anti-harassment code (*Saxe v. State College Area School District* [2001]) and the striking of a ban on paid alcohol advertisements in student newspapers (*Pitt News v. Pappert* [2004]). And even though his senatorial confirmation hearings in January 2006 did not expose his perspectives on federal regulation of elections, there was reason to anticipate that Alito's ascension to the high court would move its campaign finance law in a more deregulatory direction.

After *Austin* and *McConnell*, many questions remained as to governmental regulation of election campaign spending—particularly corporate spending for election-related speech. For example, what would be the real upshot of *Bellotti* and its progeny? Is corporate political speech valued only for the public's enlightenment, and therefore subject to regulation for the greater public interest; or is corporate political speech per se valuable because corporations, like other persons, enjoy First Amendment rights against governmental infringement? For another example, what would be the real upshot of *Austin*? In terms of political corruption, why isn't there a constitutional equivalency between independent expenditures flowing from a thriving corporation's treasury and such spending from a multimillionaire's enormous bank accounts? For yet another example, of course, what would be the eventual upshot of *McConnell*? Would its fragile rulings on soft-money restrictions, prohibitions on corporate and union electioneering using treasury funds, and a systemic concept of political corruption survive? Or the ultimate upshot of *Buckley*? Would its First Amendment framework distinguishing candidate contributions and independent expenditures have staying power?

The answers to these questions—and more—awaited consideration by Chief Justice John Roberts's Court on a later day. And those days were not long in coming.

4. The Court

Stare decisis is, after all, the bedrock principle of the rule of law. Not only does it promote stability and encourage judges to decide cases based on principle rather than on a preference for one or another of the parties before them, but it also serves importantly to reduce the politicization of the Court.

—Geoffrey Stone (2007)

Overwhelmingly, Supreme Court justices are not influenced by landmark precedents with which they disagree.

—Jeffrey Segal & Harold Spaeth (1996)

STARE DECISIS. The words derive from the Latin maxim: *stare decisis et non quieta movere*. Translated it means "to stand by decisions and not disturb the undisturbed." Put plainly, the idea is to stand by things decided. In law, this is reflected in the doctrine of honoring precedent. Judges invoke *stare decisis* when an issue has been previously brought to them and a ruling issued. In such circumstances, judges adhere to the earlier ruling—though this is not always the case.

The doctrine of *stare decisis* was certainly an important issue in the lead-up to the *McCutcheon* ruling. That is, would the justices of the Roberts Court hold to precedent and reaffirm *Buckley v. Valeo* as they had many times earlier? Or would they instead take their constitutional cue from Justice Clarence Thomas, who boldly declared in 1996, "I would reject the framework established by *Buckley v. Valeo*." Concurring in part and dissenting in part in his *Colorado I* opinion, Justice Thomas wrote about the infirmity of *Buckley*'s contribution-expenditure dichotomy, the very issue now before the *McCutcheon* Court: "In my view, the distinction lacks constitutional significance, and I would not adhere to it."

How firmly would the Roberts Court abide by *stare decisis*? To what notion of that doctrine would a majority adhere? For example, would five justices adopt the view espoused by the Cato Institute in its *McCutcheon* amicus brief that "abandoning the *Buckley* distinction would be consistent with *stare decisis*"? Or would they instead be more influenced by what the government argued in its merits brief in *McCutcheon*?—"In the nearly four decades since *Buckley*, this Court has consistently reaffirmed the foundational distinction between expenditure limits... and contribution limits."

The question of *stare decisis* is one that comes up time and again in judicial confirmation hearings—and it certainly did so in those of then–circuit court judges John Roberts and Samuel Alito. During his 2005 hearings, Judge Roberts told Senator Arlen Spector, "[S]ettled expectations in the application of *stare decisis* is a very important consideration." He likewise assured the members of the Senate Judiciary Committee that judges, including Supreme Court justices, needed to "be bound down by rules and precedents." To that end, he invoked Alexander Hamilton and James Madison. "The founders," he explained, "appreciated the role of precedent in promoting evenhandedness, predictability, stability... [and] integrity in the judicial process." That said, he nonetheless conceded that other factors could well prompt the justices "to revisit a precedent under the principles of *stare decisis*." Then again, "if an overruling of a prior precedent is a jolt to the legal system," he added, "it is inconsistent with principles of stability." Even so, "the principles of *stare decisis* recognize that there are situations when that's a price that has to be paid."

Judge Alito expressed his views on the subject at his 2006 confirmation hearings in a similarly two-minded fashion: "Well, I think that when a precedent is reaffirmed, each time it's reaffirmed that is a factor that should be taken into account in making the judgment about *stare decisis,* and when a precedent is reaffirmed on the ground that *stare decisis* precludes or counsels against reexamination of the merits of the precedent, then I agree that that is a precedent on precedent." But the matter was not that simple, not that black and white. "Now," he cautioned, "I don't want to leave the impression that *stare decisis* is an inexorable command, because the Supreme Court has said that it is not; but it is a judgment that has to [take] into account all of the factors that are relevant and that are set out in the Supreme Court's cases."

There was, to be sure, much wiggle-room in the statements of both jurists. But in the eight years preceding *McCutcheon*, both Roberts and Alito provided signs of how they viewed *stare decisis* in the nine campaign finance cases decided by the Court between 2005 and 2012. How much they and their colleagues honored precedent—including that of *Buckley v. Valeo* and other cases—was important to the lawyers arguing *McCutcheon* and to the press corps that had to explain it all to the public.

The votes of Chief Justice Roberts and Justice Alito would prove crucial to the outcome in *McCutcheon*. The question was whether their past votes and statements were meaningful indicators of how they might rule. Would they join ranks with Justices Anthony Kennedy, Antonin Scalia, and Clarence Thomas (all foes of *Buckley* and most campaign finance laws), or would they join Justices Stephen Breyer, Ruth Bader Ginsburg, Sonia Sotomayor, and Elena Kagan (all ardent defenders of many such laws)?

For some, the answer was clear—deregulation was the mantra of the Roberts Court. For others, it was less so—the 2012 National Health Care Case proved that nothing is certain while the vote of John Roberts hangs in the balance.

Three Cases, Three Years, Three Losses

Shortly after Roberts and Alito joined the Court, it took on a steady diet of campaign finance reform issues—in three controversial cases over three consecutive years. The challenged measures were declared unconstitutional in all three decisions (two by narrow 5–4 rulings). Significantly, Alito and Roberts voted with the majority in every case. And although *Buckley* continued its authoritative role as governing law, each decision negated, again and again, any potential for expansive readings of the precedent that might validate the government's regulatory efforts. Indeed, every decision suggested that the tide might be turning in favor of subverting *Buckley*—if not a quick death by a single fatal body blow, then a slow death by incremental cuts.

The first case in the line-up was *Randall v. Sorrell* (2006), which invalidated Vermont's statutory limitations on 1) campaign expenditures made by candidates for state office and 2) contributions to those candidates made by individuals, organizations, and political parties. While unable to reach a consensus, six justices agreed that the First Amendment's speech and association guarantees were violated by both sets of constraints.

Announcing the decision of the Court and authoring an opinion joined only by Roberts and Alito, Justice Stephen Breyer explained that 1) the expenditure restraints clearly failed on the strength of *Buckley*, and 2) the contribution limits were unconstitutional because, given their very low maximum levels (between $200 and $400 per candidate in a two-year election cycle), they imposed "disproportionately severe" burdens on First Amendment interests that were not "carefully tailored" to the government's primary interest in preventing candidate corruption.

In support of its law, the State of Vermont argued that *Buckley*'s ruling on the unconstitutionality of expenditure limitations should either be overruled or distinguished. Justice Breyer's plurality opinion, however, would have none of it. "Departure from precedent is exceptional, and requires 'special justification,'" Breyer wrote. "And we do not perceive the strong justification that would be necessary to warrant overruling so well established a precedent." Nor was the Court persuaded by Vermont Attorney General Sorrell's argument that a secondary governmental purpose—reducing a candidate's time and effort in raising money—was a sufficient basis for distinguishing *Buckley*. Breyer noted that the *Buckley* Court acknowledged that "Congress was trying to 'free candidates from the rigors of fundraising'"; thus, it was "highly unlikely that fuller consideration of [the] time protection rationale would have changed *Buckley*'s result." In this light, the *Randall* judgment was preordained: Vermont's expenditure limits were not substantially different from those imposed by the 1974 FECA Amendments and successfully overturned by *Buckley*, Breyer concluded, and they similarly failed strict scrutiny review.

Three concurring justices, all of whom disparaged *Buckley*'s continuing precedential force, joined in the judgment. "Viewed within the legal universe we have ratified and helped create, the result the plurality reaches is correct," Justice Kennedy reasoned; but given his "skepticism regarding that system and its operation," he would vote only on the judgment. Much more voluble were the views of Justices Thomas and Scalia. "Far from making the case for *Buckley* as a rule of law," Thomas wrote in his concurrence (joined by Scalia), the plurality "demonstrates that *Buckley*'s limited scrutiny of contribution limits is 'insusceptible of principled application,' and accordingly is not entitled to *stare decisis* effect." Since "statements of general support are as deserving of constitutional protection as those that communicate specific reasons for that support," Thomas declared, "I would overrule *Buckley* and subject both the contribution and expenditure restrictions" of Vermont's law "to strict scrutiny, which they would fail."

Particularly intriguing was Justice Alito's decision to file a brief concurring opinion on the issue of *Buckley*'s authoritative force, although he had joined sections of Justice Breyer's plurality opinion that were based on that precedent. "Only as a backup argument, an afterthought almost, do respondents make a naked plea for us to 'revisit *Buckley*,'" Alito observed. But Vermont had failed to substantiate its invitation to reexamine precedent. "Whether or not a case can be made for reexamining *Buckley* in whole or in part," Alito determined, "what matters is that respondents do not do so here, and so I think it unnecessary to reach the issue." One was left to wonder at the larger implications of this statement: Was the justice suggesting that such a reexamination should occur in a future case? Was he hinting that, if a more complete presentation on the issue were given, he would be amenable to joining forces with Kennedy, Thomas, and Scalia in opposition to *Buckley*'s contribution-expenditure distinctions? If a solid phalanx of four existed for that, then could the new chief justice be persuaded to ally himself to the cause? And if Roberts agreed to join the four, would it be to an outright reversal of *Buckley*'s dichotomy? Or would it be something more surreptitious, such as a series of decisions that diluted *Buckley*'s framework by creating exclusions, exceptions, and mitigations—"stealth overruling," as it were?

Answers to these questions were only dimly perceived in the next campaign finance controversy before the Court. *FEC v. Wisconsin Right to Life* (2007) (*WRTL*) involved a corporation that planned to spend treasury funds for issue advocacy during the blackout period created by the "electioneering communications" provision in Title II of BCRA. Wisconsin Right to Life (WRTL) challenged that provision, which prohibited corporate and union treasury funding of political advertising within thirty days of a primary election and sixty days of a general election, as a potential barrier to WRTL's broadcast campaign. Its advertising aimed to encourage viewers to contact specific senators and urge them not to filibuster the Senate's consideration of federal judicial nominations.

By a narrow 5–4 vote, the Court held that the Title II ban, which had been declared constitutional *on its face* four years earlier in *McConnell*, could not be upheld *as applied* in the context of the case. Chief Justice Roberts authored a plurality opinion, joined by Justice Alito, that did not expressly overrule *McConnell*, but severely diluted its precedential force by imposing a broad exemption to Title II's applicability. WRTL's ads, the chief justice described, "may reasonably be interpreted as something other than an appeal to vote for or against a specific candidate," and as such "are not the functional equivalent of express advocacy." Therefore, the corporation's advertisements—and all other issue advocacy like them—"fall outside the scope of *McConnell's* holding" and cannot be constitutionally regulated. The plurality opinion conceded that campaign advocacy and issue advocacy are sometimes difficult to distinguish, because candidates "are intimately tied to public issues involving legislative proposals and governmental actions." Whatever the difficulty, however, the Court's jurisprudence in the area required such line-drawing. "In drawing that line," the Chief added, "the First Amendment requires us to err on the side of protecting political speech rather than suppressing it."

Unsurprisingly, Justices Kennedy, Scalia, and Thomas concurred in the judgment of the Court, but argued for the unconstitutionality of Title II in its entirety. They rearticulated their First Amendment views in opposition to the electioneering communications regulation—essentially, the rationales that they had first voiced in their *McConnell* dissents. To contend that *McConnell* should be overruled, of course, they were obliged to face the issue of *stare decisis*. Justice Scalia addressed it head-on: "*Stare decisis* is not an inexorable command" or "a mechanical formula of adherence to the latest decision," he maintained. "This Court has not hesitated to overrule decisions offensive to the First Amendment...and to do so promptly where fundamental error was apparent."

To the concurrers, "*any* test providing relief to WRTL"—including the standard adopted in the chief justice's plurality opinion—"is incompatible with *McConnell*'s facial holding, because WRTL's ads are in the 'heartland' of what Congress meant to prohibit." In other words, the vast majority of corporate and union pre-election ads regulated by Title II would have to be deemed First Amendment–protected issue advocacy under the plurality's test, and therefore the regulation itself was unconstitutionally overbroad. "In light of the longstanding acceptance of the clarity of *Buckley*'s express-advocacy line," Justice Scalia posited, "it was adventurous for *McConnell* to extend *Austin* beyond corporate speech constituting express advocacy." Moreover, he resolved: "Today's cases make it apparent that the adventure is a flop, and that *McConnell*'s holding concerning [Title II] was wrong."

The dissenters—Justice David Souter writing for himself and Justices John Paul Stevens, Ruth Bader Ginsberg, and Stephen Breyer—agreed with their concurring brethren on only one basic point: that the plurality's "as applied" analysis essentially overruled *McConnell* without saying so. At the outset of his opinion, Souter summed up "the significance and effect" of the *WRTL* judgment as turning on three things. First, "the demand for campaign money in huge amounts from large contributors, whose power has produced a cynical electorate." Second, a tradition of "congressional recognition of the ensuing threat to democratic integrity" and its efforts "in a century of legislation" to restrict "the electoral leverage of concentrations of money in corporate and union treasuries." Finally, and perhaps most importantly, the *McConnell* decision, "declaring the facial validity of the most recent Act of Congress in that tradition [is] effectively, and unjustifiably, overruled today."

Here, then, were the dissenters calling out the Court for an unprincipled exercise of stealth overruling. As they understood it, the plurality opinion "simply inverts what we said in *McConnell*." The *McConnell* majority recognized that only a "genuine" or "pure" issue ad "without campaign advocacy" might escape regulation. "But the principal opinion inexplicably wrings the opposite conclusion from those words," Souter complained. "[I]f an ad is susceptible to any reasonable interpretation other than as an appeal to vote for or against a specific candidate, then it must be a 'pure' or 'genuine' issue ad." This reading of the precedent "stands *McConnell* on its head."

Apart from featuring a stark exercise in stealth overruling, the *WRTL* decision was notable for two understated propositions that lay like potential landmines in the field of campaign finance jurisprudence. At the end of his plurality opinion, Chief Justice Roberts quoted the text of the First Amendment's free speech clause; then he urged his readers to consider that "when it comes to drawing difficult lines in the area of pure political speech between what is protected and what the Government may ban, it is worth recalling the language we are applying." To that effect, he casually added: "*McConnell* held that express advocacy of a candidate or his opponent by a corporation shortly before an election may be prohibited.... We have no occasion to revisit that determination today."

And similar to his posture in *Randall v. Sorrell*, Justice Alito insisted on filing a brief concurrence in *WRTL*, even though he joined the most significant sections of the chief justice's lead opinion. Recognizing that the Court's "as applied" ruling avoided the need for going any further, Alito warned, "If it turns out that the implementation of the as-applied standard set out in the principal opinion impermissibly chills political speech...we will presumably be asked in a future case to reconsider the holding in *McConnell v. Federal Election Commission*" that facially upheld BCRA's Title II.

Once again, what were the inferences to be drawn from these evocative statements? Were they omens of things to come? Were Roberts and Alito signaling their willingness to join Justices Kennedy, Scalia, and Thomas in overruling *McConnell*—either in its entirety or at least as to its ruling on Title II's ban on corporate and union electioneering communications? If they were, how far would this trend go? Would it stop only with *McConnell*, or would it proceed to threaten the First Amendment framework originally set out in *Buckley v. Valeo*? At this point in the process of stealth overruling, the answers to the questions were anyone's guess.

Davis v. FEC (2008), the third in the trio of campaign finance reform cases considered by the early Roberts Court, marched along a different analytical path than those developed in *Randall* and *WRTL*; nonetheless, the decision reinforced the image of the Court as hostile to electoral speech regulations. Acting with newfound consensus, a narrow majority of five justices invalidated a BCRA provision, colloquially known as the "Millionaire's Amendment," that enabled a House and Senate candidate to raise money more easily when faced with a so-called "millionaire" opponent who used a substantial amount of personal wealth to finance his or her campaign. Generally put, after a "millionaire" committed enough personal funds to the race to reach a threshold amount set by the statute, that spending threshold triggered a number of FECA exceptions advantageous to his or her opponents. Among them, an opposing candidate was then entitled to accept contributions three times larger than those that FECA ordinarily permitted; FECA's aggregate contribution limitation was lifted for an individual's donations made to eligible candidates; and political parties were authorized to make unlimited expenditures coordinated with a candidate opposing a "millionaire." Not surprisingly, these exceptions ended when the "millionaire's" war chest and the opponent's campaign fund reached financial parity.

Justice Alito authored the opinion for the Court, which was joined by Chief Justice Roberts and Justices Kennedy, Scalia, and Thomas. Their decision turned on two key determinations. First, the majority held that, while the Millionaire's Amendment "does not impose a cap on a candidate's expenditure of personal funds, it imposes an unprecedented penalty on any candidate who robustly exercises that First Amendment right." In other words, "millionaire" candidates who choose to make large personal expenditures "to engage in unfettered political speech" will "shoulder a specially and potentially significant burden if they make that choice"— being subject "to discriminatory fundraising limitations."

Justice Stevens criticized this logic in a dissenting opinion joined in pertinent part by Justices Souter, Ginsburg, and Breyer. "The Millionaire's Amendment quiets no speech at all," he asserted. "On the contrary, it does no more than assist the opponent of a self-funding candidate in his attempts to make his voice heard." In theory and in practice, "[e]nhancing the speech of the millionaire's opponent, far from contravening the First Amendment, actually advances its core principles." But this line of reasoning did not prevail over the more formalistic arguments of the majority justices, who were taken aback by the amendment's facially discriminatory treatment of electoral opponents. "We have never upheld the constitutionality of a law that imposes different contribution limits for candidates who are competing against each other," Alito avowed.

The second turning point for the decision was the Court's treatment of the government's justifications for the Millionaire's Amendment. The law was enacted and defended as a necessary means to open up the electoral playing field to less prosperous candidates by leveling the campaign spending advantages of more affluent candidates. These purposes, as the dissenters viewed them, were sufficient to validate the discriminatory burden imposed on a "millionaire's" political speech rights. "[R]educing the importance of wealth as a criterion for public office and countering the perception that seats in the United States Congress are available for purchase by the wealthiest bidder," Justice Stevens asserted, "are important Government interests." But the majority railed at the very suggestion that the First Amendment could ever endorse equalization of electoral opportunities as a campaign finance goal.

To this end, Justice Alito's opinion nailed down three jurisprudential propositions that, over the course of the Court's campaign finance decisions, appeared to be somewhat in flux:

1. Although a narrow five-member majority in *McConnell* had applied a "closely drawn" standard of review to analyze the constitutionality of BCRA's other major provisions, the five-member majority in *Davis* (including the *McConnell* dissenters) determined that "strict scrutiny"—requiring a compelling governmental interest, instead of merely an important one—must be applied whenever a

law, like BCRA's Millionaire's Amendment, "imposes a substantial burden on the exercise of the First Amendment right to use personal funds for campaign speech."

2. Although the *Austin* and *McConnell* Courts had refused to tie *Buckley v. Valeo* to "a crabbed view of corruption" (the quid pro quo corruption rationale), the *Davis* Court did precisely that. Citing Justice Thomas's dissenting opinion in *Nixon* for support, the *Davis* majority endorsed his proposition that "preventing corruption or the appearance of corruption are the only legitimate and compelling governmental interests thus far identified for restricting campaign finances."

3. Again, although the *MCFL*, *Austin*, and *McConnell* precedents had accorded First Amendment legitimacy to governmental designs to combat "the corrosive and distorting effects of immense aggregations of [corporate] wealth" on the political process, the *Davis* decision dismissed the goal as entirely illegitimate. In stark and uncompromising language, Justice Alito described the governmental objective of equalizing the political playing field as perilous state paternalism. "The argument that a candidate's speech may be restricted in order to 'level electoral opportunities' has ominous implications," he stressed, "because it would permit Congress to arrogate the voters' authority to evaluate the strengths of candidates competing for office.... [I]t is a dangerous business for Congress to use the election laws to influence the voters' choices."

In all of this, the majority justices, time and again, cited *Buckley* as mandating the results of *Davis*. But the Court—whether in *Buckley* or elsewhere—had never before rejected equalization as illegitimate per se for any form of governmental regulation. As Richard Briffault astutely observed, *Buckley* "had held that the First Amendment's protection of campaign expenditures precluded advancing equality by leveling down the spending of the more affluent, but no Court decision, including *Buckley*, had barred a regulation intended to promote equality by leveling the resources of the less wealthy up."

Much as the *Davis* Court constrained *Buckley* by a narrow interpretation of its doctrine, Justice Alito and his colleagues did not trouble its central framework. The Millionaire's Amendment was not a major component of FECA, and its invalidation did not touch the contribution-expenditure dichotomy at the heart of *Buckley*'s First Amendment handiwork.

What was ominous in *Davis*, rather, were the implications of its holding for the future of public campaign funding systems for state elections. At the time of *Davis*, nearly two dozen states and localities had adopted laws that either relaxed contribution and expenditure limitations or provided supplementary public funds for candidates faced with high-spending, privately financed opponents. "Such measures—sometimes known as 'trigger' or 'fair fight' laws—have been seen as crucial to persuading candidates to accept public funding and the spending limit that always accompanies public subsidies," Professor Briffault explained. "Without the option of raising and spending above the public funding spending limit when running against a high-spending candidate, few serious candidates would accept public funding." Previously, these laws generally prevailed in federal district and circuit court challenges, but after *Davis* the "trigger" or "fair fight" laws were clearly vulnerable to First Amendment attack—particularly because they typically served "equalization-of-electoral-opportunities" objectives.

The dark and menacing clouds hovering over public campaign funding structures were yet to burst, however. In the meantime, a much greater threat to campaign finance law loomed on the horizon—in a case that, strangely enough, involved a movie.

Hillary

David Bossie, the president of a Washington-based conservative advocacy group called Citizens United, has long been involved in scrutinizing alleged electoral improprieties committed by Democrats; among other things, he worked for Senator Fred Thompson in investigating the Whitewater scandal. When Michael Moore's award-winning documentary film, *Farenheit 9/11*, captured public attention, it gave him an idea. He was stirred by the movie's economic successes (as of 2014, it was the highest-grossing documentary of all time, coming in at over $222 million worldwide). And though he disagreed with the movie's political positions, he was also taken by its impact as a searing cannonade against George W. Bush's 2004 reelection.

The prospect of responding in kind by producing documentary diatribes to further Republican causes intrigued Bossie. So he converted his organization into a movie studio, and looked for suitable liberal targets. One of the most irresistible was a politician whom Citizens United had attacked ever since she was America's First Lady—Hillary Rodham Clinton. Once Senator Clinton launched her campaign for the 2008 presidential election, Bossie determined to make her the incorrigible punching bag of his next film.

Hillary: The Movie featured ninety minutes of news clips, foreboding music, and slashing critique by a marquee list of conservative commentators—all to highlight the Clintons' political scandals (including the Whitewater and White House FBI files controversies, among others), to savage Hillary's character, and to slice into her electoral chances. Typical of the film's hardcore harangues was that of Dick Morris, a disaffected advisor to the Clinton Administration: "She's deceitful, she'll make up any story, lie about anything, as long as it serves her purposes of the moment." Agreeing that Hillary was a liar, the right-wing firebrand Ann Coulter delivered the movie's only compliment: Hillary "looks good in a pantsuit." Amidst all of this bashing, there was one declaration that *Hillary* carefully avoided: at no point did the film expressly advocate for the candidate's electoral defeat.

David Bossie intended that the documentary run as an on-demand cable movie, free to viewers at Citizen United's expense, during the entire 2008 primary election period. The only catch? As a nonprofit corporate PAC funded in part by donations from for-profit corporate treasuries, Citizens United could not finance the cablecast (or television advertisements for it) during the pre-election black-out periods—that is, as long as *Hillary* was classified as an "electioneering communication" within the meaning of federal campaign finance law. To prevent such entanglements, the organization sought a Federal Election Commission ruling that the movie was not subject to the strictures of 2 U.S.C. §441(b), the provision which codified the ban on corporate-funded electioneering communications in Title II of BCRA.

James Bopp Jr.—the counsel for Citizens United—was the man who prevailed on the FEC for its approval. A graduate of Indiana University (where he led a chapter of the conservative Young Americans for Freedom) and of the University of Florida Law School, Bopp had previously represented the anti-abortion group Wisconsin Right to Life in its victorious suit against the FEC. Now, once again, the commission looked unfavorably on another of Bopp's clients: it found that *Hillary's* denunciations of Clinton amounted to an electioneering communication. "The marketplace for my movie was completely and totally shut down by the Federal Election Commission," Bossie told Philip Rucker, a *Washington Post* reporter. Although the film passed quickly through movie theaters and was available on DVD, *Hillary* never became a cablecast blockbuster.

Bopp immediately filed suit in a federal district court alleging that §441(b) was unconstitutional as applied to issue advocacy pieces such as *Hillary* and its advertisements. (In addition, Citizens United challenged BCRA's disclaimer and disclosure requirements on an "as applied" basis.) Based on its reading of *McConnell*, the three-judge court recognized §441(b) as facially constitutional, and ruled unanimously that the statute was constitutional as applied to *Hillary*, as well. As the judges perceived it, the movie was "susceptible of no other interpretation than to inform the electorate that Senator Clinton is unfit for office, that the United States would be a dangerous place in a President Hillary Clinton world, and that viewers should vote against her." In other words, it was tantamount to impermissible candidate advocacy. As for Citizens United's disclaimer and disclosure claims, the jurists observed that "the Supreme Court has written approvingly of disclosure provisions triggered by political speech even though the speech itself was constitutionally protected under the First Amendment." Given this analysis, the FEC's characterization of the film was determined to be an "electioneering communication." Hence, the defendant's summary judgment motion was granted.

Oral Arguments in the Supreme Court—
Judging by the Book

Bossie insisted on appealing to the nation's high court, but he decided to do so with another attorney, one with an even more impressive record of Supreme Court adjudication who could command respect from the justices. That man was Theodore Olson—the lawyer from the distinguished D.C. firm of Gibson, Dunn, & Crutcher who had argued and won *Bush v. Gore* (2000) and who thereafter served as solicitor general under President Bush. Notably, as the government's lawyer, Olson had successfully defended BCRA's restrictions on corporate electioneering communications in *McConnell v. FEC* six years before, but now he was positioned to attack that law in the service of a corporation's political advocacy. Interesting, as well, was Olson's personal link to *Hillary: The Movie*. The documentary was dedicated to his deceased wife, Barbara Olson, who had died as a passenger on American Airlines Flight 77 when it crashed into the Pentagon on September 11, 2001. An inveterate critic of Hillary Clinton, Barbara had worked with Bossie to investigate the Clinton Administration scandals in the 1990s and had authored the book *Hell to Pay: The Unfolding Story of Hillary Rodham Clinton*. In this light, as Philip Rucker reported it, Bossie claimed that Ted Olson "had an emotional connection" to fighting for Citizens United.

An eminent legal tactician who understood the jurisprudential inclinations of the justices, Olson decided to play his hand more conservatively in order to appeal to the stealth-overruling preferences of Justices Roberts and Alito as revealed in their 2006–2007 campaign finance rulings. Accordingly, when oral arguments in *Citizens United v. FEC* were heard in March 2009, Olson asked the Court to construe §441(b) narrowly to apply only to electioneering commercials, and not to an issue advocacy documentary such as *Hillary*, produced by a small nonprofit corporation and broadcast as video-on-demand.

But when Malcolm Stewart, the deputy solicitor general defending the FEC, offered his rebuttal, it became apparent that a majority of the Court was inclined not to mince the greater First Amendment issues. The question that sent Stewart tumbling down the proverbial rabbit hole was asked by Justice Alito. "Do you think the Constitution required Congress to draw the line where it did, limiting this to broadcast and cable and so forth?" he inquired. What about "providing the same thing in a book? Would the Constitution permit the restriction of all those as well?"

To all appearances, the Princeton University/Yale Law School graduate, who clerked for Justice Harry Blackmun in 1989 and had been given the highest rank for a career lawyer in the solicitor general's office shortly before the *Citizens United* oral argument, either did not detect the slippery slope ahead of him in this line of reasoning or did not fathom how to stop the fall. Rather than stressing that §441(b)'s restriction on electioneering communications did not facially apply to full-length books, or that the FEC's interpretation of §441(b)'s independent expenditure limitation to include such books could give rise to a strong case of "as applied" unconstitutionality, the deputy solicitor general conceded the point. "Those [prohibitions] could have been applied to additional media as well," Stewart curtly answered.

"That's pretty incredible!" Alito exclaimed. "You think that if a book was published, a campaign biography that was the functional equivalent of express advocacy, that could be banned?" Stewart strove to recover ground. "I'm not saying it could be banned," he rejoined. "I'm saying that Congress could prohibit the use of corporate treasury funds and could require a corporation to publish it using its—"

"Well," Justice Kennedy interrupted, "suppose it were an advocacy organization that had a book." The Justice, sensing the weakness in Stewart's argument, decided to pile on, and continued, "Your position is that, under the Constitution, the advertising for this book or the sale for the book itself could be prohibited within the sixty- and thirty-day periods?" Unenthusiastically, Stewart agreed.

Now the chief justice came in for the kill. "If it has one name, one use of the candidate's name, it would be covered, correct?" Roberts probed. "If it's a five-hundred-page book, and at the end it says, 'And so vote for X,' the government could ban that?" Struggling to cover his hindquarters, Stewart continued to expose the ungainliness of his position. "Well," he explained, "if it says 'vote for X,' it would be express advocacy and it would be covered by the preexisting Federal Election Campaign provisions."

Assessing the overall impact of the oral arguments, Jeffrey Toobin incisively observed, "Through artful questioning, Alito, Kennedy, and Roberts had turned a fairly obscure case about campaign finance reform into a battle over government censorship. The trio made Stewart—and thus the government—take an absurd position: that the government might have the right to criminalize the publication of a five-hundred-page book because of one line at the end."

As fortune would have it, that absurdity enabled the conservative justices to rally to a much more expansive understanding of the *Citizens United* case. Originally, the chief justice purportedly wrote a draft opinion for the Court that gave a victory to the appellant along the narrow lines proposed by Theodore Olson. But the draft of a concurring opinion authored by Justice Kennedy—representing the typical deregulatory posture of Justices Scalia, Thomas, and himself—argued that BCRA's restrictions on electioneering communications were facially unconstitutional, that contrary precedents must be overturned, and that §441(b)'s prohibition on corporate independent expenditures expressly advocating the election or defeat of federal candidates (a restriction first put in place by the Taft-Hartley Act of 1947) must be gutted. This dramatic and extensive critique ultimately won favor with both Roberts and Alito, and the chief then assigned to Kennedy the task of writing the opinion for a five-member majority of the Court.

As Toobin characterized it, Roberts "came up with a strategically ingenious maneuver." Unwilling to threaten the integrity of the Court by "violating [its] own procedures to engineer the result he wanted," the chief justice secured the approval of his colleagues to withdraw Kennedy's opinion and set the case for reargument in the fall. "On June 29, 2009, the last day of the term," Toobin described, "the Court shocked the litigants—and the political world—by announcing, 'The case is restored to the calendar for reargument.'" And the new questions presented "told the parties that the justices were considering overruling two major decisions in modern campaign finance law," namely *Austin* and *McConnell.* "As every sophisticated observer of the Court knew," Toobin explained, "the Court did not ask whether cases should be overruled unless a majority of the justices were already prepared to do so."

Corporations Are Persons, Aren't They?

In 1886—the same year in which the Statue of Liberty was dedicated in New York Harbor—American liberty was given a new face. The liberty that was once accorded only to individuals was handed over to corporations, as well. In *Santa Clara County v. Southern Pacific Railroad*, a unanimous Supreme Court declared that corporations were "persons" under the Fourteenth Amendment and were entitled to the blessings of liberty. Thus, the Court converted an amendment primarily designed to protect the rights of African-Americans into an amendment whose major effect, for the next seventy years, was to protect the rights of corporations. Remarkably, as historian Howard Zinn reported, "Of the Fourteenth Amendment cases brought before the Supreme Court between 1890 and 1920, nineteen dealt with the Negro, 288 dealt with corporations." Once personhood had thus been transformed, it was entirely predictable that corporations would eventually seize First Amendment liberties for their own expression, as well. And they did so in celebrated First Amendment cases protecting corporate press freedoms, as in *New York Times, Inc. v. Sullivan* (1964), corporate associational freedoms, as in *NAACP, Inc. v. Alabama* (1964), and corporate political speech freedoms, as in *First National Bank of Boston v. Bellotti* (1978), among others.

These famous First Amendment decisions were much in the air during the second set of oral arguments in *Citizens United* on the morning of Wednesday, September 9, 2009. Once again, Theodore Olson was the spokesman for the appellant. The veteran First Amendment attorney, Floyd Abrams, appeared on behalf of Senator Mitch McConnell, as *amicus curiae* in support of Citizens United. Facing off against them on behalf of the Federal Election Commission was Solicitor General Elena Kagan, who had been confirmed as President Obama's nominee earlier in 2009, only a few days before the first oral arguments in the case. Prior to her appointment, the renowned dean of the Harvard Law School had never argued an appellate case. Thus, not only was *Citizens United* her debut performance before the Supreme Court, but it was her first appellant oral argument. Accompanying her was Seth Waxman, a distinguished Supreme Court litigator from the D.C. firm of WilmerHale and the former solicitor general during the Clinton Administration, who represented Senator John McCain and others as *amici curiae* in support of the FEC.

Shortly after Citizen United's counsel took the podium, Justice Ruth Bader Ginsburg seized upon the First Amendment implications of corporate personhood. "Mr. Olson, are you taking the position that there is no difference in the First Amendment rights of an individual?" she asked. "A corporation, after all, is not endowed by its creator with inalienable rights. So is there any distinction that Congress could draw between corporations and natural human beings for purposes of campaign finance?" Olson invoked the force of precedent in his sweeping response. "What the Court has said in the First Amendment context, *New York Times v. Sullivan*," he argued, "and over and over again, is that corporations are persons entitled to protection under the First Amendment."

Lighting upon a distinction that had politically portentous overtones, Justice Ginsburg pressed her point: "Would that include today's mega-corporations, where many of the investors may be foreign individuals or entities?" In essence, she aimed to provide a compelling government purpose for regulating corporate behemoths to prevent foreign influence in the nation's elections. "Nowadays," the justice continued, "there are foreign interests, even foreign governments, that own not one share but a goodly number of shares." But Olson was prepared for this query: "I submit that the Court's decisions in connection with the First Amendment and corporations have in the past made no such distinction. … I'm saying that the First Amendment applies. Then the next step is to determine whether Congress and the government has established a compelling governmental interest and a narrowly tailored remedy to that interest." Putting a fine point on the matter, Olson concluded, "Certainly, the government has not advanced it in its briefs: that there is some compelling government interest because of foreign investment in corporations."

Justice Alito offered a helping hand in this debate by asking, point-blank, "Mr. Olson, do you think that media corporations that are owned or principally owned by foreign shareholders have less First Amendment rights than other media corporations in the United States?" To this, Olson predictably responded, "I don't think so, Justice Alito, and certainly there is no record to suggest that there is any kind of problem based upon that....We are talking about a prohibition that covers every corporation in the United States, including nonprofit corporations, limited liability corporations, subchapter S corporations, and every union in the United States."

Not willing to let the former solicitor general off her hook, Justice Ginsburg pounced again: "You have used the word 'prohibition,' Mr. Olson. One answer to that is that no entity is being prohibited; it is a question not of whether corporations can contribute, but how." She then clarified her general point: "The corporation can give, but it has to use a PAC."

"I respectfully disagree," Olson countered. "The corporation may not expend money. It might find people, stockholders or officers, who want to contribute to a separate fund, who could then speak." But that option, he concluded, "is more like surrogate speech."

Shortly before Olson's time was up, Justice Sonia Sotomayor asked her first question of the day—in fact, her first question in her first Supreme Court hearing. Sotomayor, the Court's third female and first Latina justice, was a Princeton University/Yale Law School graduate, like her colleague Samuel Alito. She had served as a New York federal district court judge for six years and as a Second Circuit appellate court judge for eleven years before being nominated by President Obama as the replacement for retiring justice David Souter. Her confirmation hearings and the Senate's ratifying vote were held in August 2009, one month before the second set of oral arguments in *Citizens United*. Because the chief justice scheduled the hearing for September 9, a month before the typical opening of the Court's term on the first Monday in October, *Citizens United* was the first case on which Justice Sotomayor sat.

The most junior justice chose to focus on the narrower challenge to BCRA that the appellant had launched only five months before. Sotomayor questioned Citizen United's counsel as to his client's current position on that legal posture. "Mr. Olson," she asked, "are you giving up on your earlier arguments that there are statutory interpretations that would avoid the constitutional question?"

"No, Justice Sotomayor," Olson replied, "there are all kinds of lines that the Court could draw which would provide a victory to my client.

There are so many reasons why the federal government did not have the right to criminalize this ninety-minute documentary that had to do with elections."

Floyd Abrams, the First Amendment maven, began his oral argument by reflecting on an important lesson from *New York Times v. Sullivan* that ought be applied to *Citizens United*. That lesson? Where vital First Amendment interests are severely burdened, it may be wiser for the Court boldly to resolve the constitutional issue rather than cautiously walking the narrow path of statutory interpretation.

This suggestion sparked a sharp reaction from Justice Ginsburg: "Mr. Abrams, *New York Times v. Sullivan* did not involve overruling precedents of this Court that had been followed by this Court and others. So I think the situation is quite different." Abrams was willing to concede the point, but only technically. "That's true, Your Honor," he responded. "But it did involve overruling 150 years of American jurisprudence. I mean, there was no law at that point that said that actual malice—"

Ginsburg would not be deterred from driving her point home, and interrupted Abrams in mid-sentence: "We do tend to adhere to our precedents. ... The question that was posed here is, is it a proper way to resolve this case, to overrule one precedent in full and another in part?"

Despite the justice's apparent disfavor for a constitutional vindication of corporate political speech rights, Abrams stuck to his guns. "And what I'm urging on you, Your Honor, is that [where] there is an ongoing threat to freedom of expression ... it is worth our moving away in this case from looking for the narrowest way out, and determining [the constitutional issue] now."

When the questioning turned to Solicitor General Kagan, Justice Antonin Scalia hit a note of political pragmatism. "Congress has a self-interest," he asserted. "[W]e are suspicious of congressional action in the First Amendment area because ... I doubt that one can expect a body of incumbents to draw election restrictions that do not favor incumbents. Now is that excessively cynical of me? I don't think so."

"I think, Justice Scalia, it's wrong," Kagan responded pragmatically. "In fact, corporate and union money go overwhelmingly to incumbents. This may be the single most self-denying thing that Congress has ever done."

Calling on statistics for corporate PAC spending over the last two election cycles, she argued, "[W]hen corporations play in the political process, they want winners … and the way to get those winners is to invest in incumbents … in double digits times more than they invest in challengers."

Justice Anthony Kennedy would have none of it. For him, the problem was, purely and simply, censorship of corporate critics of governmental officials. "Corporations have lots of knowledge about environment, transportation issues," he asserted, "and you are silencing them during the election." For Kagan, however, there was a crucial difference between corporate lobbying of governmental officials and corporate buying-up of electoral candidates: "[C]orporations can lobby members of Congress in the same way that they could before this legislation. What this legislation is designed to do, because of its anticorruption interest, is to make sure that that lobbying is just persuasion and it's not coercion."

As Kagan's argument proceeded, Justice John Paul Stevens offered her a helping hand, inviting her to recommend a basis narrower than the facial unconstitutionality of §441(b) to resolve the case. For example, couldn't the justices create an exception for nonprofit ideological corporations like Citizens United, or for "ads that are financed exclusively by individuals even though they are sponsored by a corporation"? Seizing the opportunity handed her, Kagan responded immediately, "Yes, that's exactly right.… [N]onprofit organizations of the kind here [could] fund these ads out of separate bank accounts—not PACS, just separate bank accounts—which include only individual expenditures." Then leading her to his desired conclusion, Stevens inquired, "Then why is that not the wisest narrow solution of the problem before us?" Kagan had finally arrived where Stevens wished her to go: "Well, it is—it is certainly a narrower and I think better solution than a facial invalidation of the whole statute."

In her waning time before the justices, Kagan was forced to address the fateful flaw in the government's first oral argument in March. Thankfully, the question came from an unequivocal ally. "May I ask you one question that was highlighted in the prior argument," Justice Ginsburg queried, "and that was if Congress could say no TV and radio ads, could it also say no newspaper ads, no campaign biographies? Last time the answer was yes, Congress could.… Is that still the government's answer?"

Ripples of laughter filled the chamber when Kagan forthrightly declared: "The government's answer has changed, Justice Ginsburg." After silence resumed, the government's counsel explained the modification: "It is still true," she said, that BCRA's electioneering communication restriction, "which is the only statute involved in this case, does not apply to books or anything other than broadcasts; §441(b) does, on its face, apply to other media." Given that distinction, Kagan needed to mitigate the potential for First Amendment dangers: "I should say that the FEC has never applied §441(b) in that context. So for sixty years a book has never been at issue.... I don't think that it would be substantially overbroad ... if I tell you that the FEC has never applied this statute to a book."

"But we don't put our First Amendment rights in the hands of FEC bureaucrats," Chief Justice John Roberts protested.

Realizing that she needed to address the issue of the statute's theoretical extension, Kagan put a different spin on the matter: "What we're saying is that there has never been an enforcement action for books. Nobody in Congress, nobody in the administrative apparatus has ever suggested that books pose any kind of corruption problem, so I think that there would be a good as-applied challenge with respect to that."

When it was all said and done, the justices knew that the second round of oral arguments were for naught. That morning, all nine had entered the courtroom fully aware of the impending resolution of the case. A majority of five already had the votes for the opinion they wanted—an expansive ruling that went far beyond any more moderate "as applied" interpretation of the governing statute. Notwithstanding the arguments of Solicitor General Elena Kagan, the five conservative justices were determined to deep-six the campaign finance prohibitions on corporate speech.

Wrangling Over First Amendment Reasoning

On the morning of Thursday, January 21, 2010, Justice Anthony Kennedy announced the decision of a narrowly divided Court in *Citizens United v. FEC*. His tempered description of the ruling and reasoning of the five majority justices was followed by some twenty minutes of an impassioned dissenting statement by Justice John Paul Stevens. Although eight of the nine jurists had upheld BCRA's disclosure, disclaimer, and reporting requirements (with Justice Thomas writing strongly against Congress's abridgement of anonymous political expression), the Court's facial invalidation of §441(b)'s restrictions on corporate independent expenditures and electioneering communications—and its overruling of *Austin v. FEC* and the part of *McConnell* that had validated those restrictions— were the targets of a vitriolic debate among the justices.

Running fifty-four reported pages, Justice Kennedy's opinion (joined in pertinent part by Chief Justice Roberts and Justices Scalia, Thomas, and Alito) fervently embraced lofty and abstract First Amendment principles that tolerated no distinctions disfavoring corporate speakers. Striving to fend off the dissenters' searing counterarguments, Kennedy (assisted by Roberts's and Scalia's concurring opinions) endeavored to justify the Court's broad-based decision as fully consistent with the dictates of *stare decisis* and of judicial preference for narrower "as applied" rulings. More notable still were the scalding—and oftentimes scornful—attacks launched by Stevens' dissent (joined by Justices Ginsburg, Breyer, and Sotomayor). Almost twice as long as the majority opinion, the ninety-page rejoinder—the lengthiest authored by Stevens during the entirety of his judicial career—appeared to be his full-throated swan song, delivered only five months before he retired from the Court. Trenchantly and methodically, he addressed the majority's rationales, point by point, to undermine them and to embarrass their proponents. Whether in substance or tone, the *Citizens United* decision was the exposed site of a pitched jurisprudential battle over the First Amendment's meaning and the future of campaign finance reform.

The structure of the majority's analysis rested on four conceptual columns:

1. The case could not be resolved on narrower grounds than a full-fledged reconsideration of *Austin* and *McConnell*. The exception to §441(b) recognized in *Wisconsin Right to Life* for pure issue advocacy could not apply, Justice Kennedy argued, because *Hillary: The Movie* constituted express advocacy of her electoral defeat. After all, the movie called Senator Clinton

"Machiavellian" and questioned whether she was "the most qualified to hit the ground running if elected president," and such commentaries were no more than veiled attacks on her candidacy. "It is not judicial restraint to accept an unsound, narrower argument just so the Court can avoid another argument with broader implications," Kennedy concluded.

This invocation of judicial duty galled Justice Stevens and the dissenters, who viewed the Court's decision to reexamine the facial constitutionality of §441(b) as judicial overreaching, pure and simple.

2. §441(b) was a "ban" on core political expression based on the corporate identity of the speaker. Such an identity-discriminatory ban is presumptively invalid under the First Amendment, since free speech protections have long been extended to corporations even though they are not natural persons. Thus, the principle that the government cannot "distinguish among different speakers, allowing speech by some but not others" applies to corporate speakers, as well.

Both the Court's depiction of corporate speech as "banned" and its characterization of the First Amendment as tolerating no corporate identity–based distinctions severely rankled the dissenters. "Neither Citizens United's nor any other corporation's speech has been 'banned,'" Justice Stevens stressed. "The real issue in this case concerns how, not if, the appellant may finance its electioneering." Taking on the basic premise underlying the Court's ruling—that is, the First Amendment's bar on identity-based distinctions—Justice Stevens caustically declared, "While that glittering generality has rhetorical appeal, it is not a correct statement of the law. … The conceit that corporations must be treated identically to natural persons in the political sphere is not only inaccurate but also inadequate to justify the Court's disposition of this case."

3. §441(b)'s independent expenditure limitations on corporations must fail strict scrutiny review for the very same reason that similar independent expenditure restrictions on individuals and groups

failed in *Buckley*. They could not be justified as necessary to serve the only governmental interest for campaign finance regulation that *Buckley* and its progeny recognized as truly compelling—namely, prevention of the actuality and appearance of quid pro quo candidate corruption. To bypass *Buckley* and *Bellotti*, "the *Austin* Court identified a new governmental interest in limiting political speech: an antidistortion interest." Such an interest is illegitimate per se. "When Government seeks to use its full power, including the criminal law, to command where a person may get his or her information or what distrusted source he or she may not hear," Justice Kennedy concluded, "it uses censorship to control thought. This is unlawful."

That the Court portrayed *Austin*—and by its force, *McConnell*—as "radical outliers" or "aberrations" in First Amendment tradition clearly offended the dissenters. "The Court has it exactly backwards," Justice Stevens charged. "It is today's holding that is the radical departure from what had been settled First Amendment law." By denying the validity of *Austin* and *McConnell's* holdings, Stevens chided, the Court was turning its back on one hundred years of legislative and judicial history. "The majority's understanding of corruption would leave lawmakers impotent to address all but the most discrete abuses."

4. The Court was justified in overriding *stare decisis* and overruling *Austin* and the part of *McConnell* that rested on *Austin's* authority. "This Court has not hesitated to overrule decisions offensive to the First Amendment," Justice Kennedy maintained.

The dissenters' response as to *stare decisis* was more voluminous in length and voluble in tone. "[T]he majority blazes through our precedents," Justice Stevens instructed, "overruling or disavowing a body of case law." His last words scorched the Court's decision as "backwards in many senses." He listed them, one by one: "It elevates the majority's agenda over the litigants' submissions, facial attacks over as-applied claims, broad constitutional theories over narrow statutory grounds, individual dissenting opinions over precedential holdings, assertion over tradition, absolutism over empiricism, rhetoric over reality." For Stevens, the Court's reversal of *Austin* and *McConnell* came down "to nothing more than its disagreement with their results." The justice stated the obvious: "The only relevant thing that has changed since *Austin* and *McConnell* is the composition of this Court." Thus, the *Citizens United* ruling "strikes at the vitals of *stare decisis*, the means by which we ensure that the law… will develop in a principled and intelligent fashion," ensuring society "that bedrock principles are founded in the law rather than in the proclivities of individuals."

Undoubtedly, it was the dissenters' searing accusations of judicial imperialism and non-judicious activism that moved Chief Justice John Roberts to write a concurring opinion (joined by Justice Alito) to address principles of judicial restraint and *stare decisis* implicated in *Citizens United*. "It should go without saying," Roberts asserted, "that we cannot embrace a narrow ground of decision simply because it is narrow; it must also be right. … There is a difference between judicial restraint and judicial abdication." Moreover, in balancing between respecting precedent and rectifying constitutional law, "we must keep in mind that *stare decisis* is not an end in itself. … Its greatest purpose is to serve a constitutional ideal— the rule of law." It followed, then, that *Austin* ought not be retained if it "does more damage to this constitutional ideal" than overruling it would damage the value of fidelity to precedent. And because *Austin* "departed from the robust protections we had granted political speech in our earlier cases," the Court "must be willing to depart from that precedent."

The high court battle in *Citizens United* was pitched, and the intellectual and emotional heat was intense. One academic commentator, Georgetown University law professor Mark Tushnet, held a more measured view of the decision. "Restrictions on political spending—and on contributions to organizations that spend money on campaigns—have always hung by a thread from the First Amendment," he wrote. "*Citizens United* cut the thread." However tempered his perspective, it was overwhelmed by the firestorm of penetrating and passionate reactions released by the Supreme Court's ruling in America's political precincts.

Feuding over the Future of Campaign Finance and the First Amendment

Within hours after the Court announced its landmark ruling, *Citizens United* was tossed about like a football in a championship tournament skirmish. Politicians seized the bully pulpits in turn to declare their approval or dismay. Senate Minority Leader Mitch McConnell, who had challenged BCRA on First Amendment grounds in 2003, was overjoyed: "For too long, some in this country have been deprived of full participation in the political process. With today's monumental decision, the Supreme Court took an important step in the direction of restoring the First Amendment rights of these groups by ruling that the Constitution protects their right to express themselves about political candidates and issues up until Election Day. By previously denying this right, the government was picking winners and losers. Our democracy depends upon free speech, not just for some but for all."

Senator Patrick Leahy (D-VT), chair of the Senate Judiciary Committee, was less thrilled, to say the least: "The Supreme Court's divided opinion is likely to change the course of our democracy and could threaten the public's confidence in the Court's impartiality.... There is clear reason for ordinary citizens to be concerned that this divisive ruling will, in reality, allow powerful corporations to drown out the voices of everyday Americans in future campaigns. This ruling is, no doubt, yet another victory for Wall Street, at the expense of Main Street America. Our founding document begins 'We the People,' and...enshrines the power of our government in the people, not in corporations and powerful special interests."

Finally, President Barack Obama left no mistake as to where his administration and the Democratic Party stood on the decision: "With its ruling today, the Supreme Court has given a green light to a new stampede of special interest money in our politics. It is a major victory for big oil, Wall Street banks, health insurance companies, and the other powerful interests that marshal their power every day in Washington to drown out the voices of everyday Americans. This ruling gives the special interests and their lobbyists even more power in Washington, while undermining the influence of average Americans who make small contributions to support their preferred candidates. That's why I am instructing my Administration to get to work immediately with Congress on this issue. We are going to talk with bipartisan Congressional leaders to develop a forceful response to this decision. The public interest requires nothing less."

Corporate-interest lobbyists vied against public-interest advocates in timely press reports on the decision. Robin Conrad, the executive vice president of the U.S. Chamber of Commerce's litigation center, reflected the views of the nation's largest business association, which had spent $136 million on political lobbying in 2009 alone. "Today's ruling protects the First Amendment rights of organizations across the political spectrum," Conrad gushed, "and is a positive for the political process and free enterprise." His ideological opponent, Common Cause President Bob Edgar, saw the death of democracy without future public funding for federal elections. "The Roberts Court today made a bad situation worse," he argued. "The path from here is clear: Congress must free itself from Wall Street's grip so Main Street can finally get a fair shake."

But what really caught the country's attention was the additional rebuke that President Obama reserved for his State of the Union address on Wednesday night, January 27, 2010, just six days after *Citizens United* came down. Speaking generally to the nation and specifically to six of the Supreme Court justices sitting directly in front of him, Obama aimed his rhetorical fire at their ruling. "With all due deference to separation of powers," the former University of Chicago constitutional law professor declared, "last week the Supreme Court reversed a century of law that I believe will open the floodgates for special interests, including foreign corporations, to spend without limit in our elections."

This rare reprimand—a reproach delivered in the justices' faces and over national television—drew a rare response. Justice Samuel Alito, one of the five-member majority in the case, shook his head in disagreement at Obama's description of their decision, and appeared to utter the words "not true." This sharp and stark exchange electrified the press, which avidly reported the continuing tussle between the major players. After Chief Justice John Roberts complained several months later to a group of University of Alabama law students that the annual address had "degenerated to a political pep rally"—a breach of decorum that he found "very troubling"—the president issued a press statement smacking him back. "What is troubling," Obama replied, is that this decision "drown[s] out the voices of average Americans" in the election process.

The Interlude between *Citizens United* and *McCutcheon*

The Roberts Court's path from *Citizens United* to *McCutcheon* was short, but very telling. The "gang of five" that coalesced in 2010 to vindicate corporate and union political speech rights continued to speak with one voice. This newfound unity—exhibited, once again, in three cases decided over three years—served two purposes: to solidify recent First Amendment victories over election campaign regulations and to point to future extensions of this deregulatory trend.

In *Republican National Committee v. Federal Election Commission* (2010), the Court declined to note probable jurisdiction and summarily affirmed a decision of the U.S. District Court for the District of Columbia. The case involved a challenge to the soft-money fundraising bans for national political parties—those Title I provisions of BCRA that the Supreme Court upheld in *McConnell* and left undisturbed in *Citizens United*. Importantly, the RNC alleged only as-applied violations of its First Amendment rights, so the federal trial court's ruling did not present an opportunity for the justices to reconsider Title I's facial constitutionality. Of course, *Citizens United* upended the broader and systemic view of political corruption that *McConnell* had relied upon, and recognized only the narrower concept of quid pro quo corruption as a justification for any campaign finance regulation. It is not difficult to imagine, then, that Justice Kennedy's clan of five will eventually seize the day once again to strike down these soft-money limitations in a lawsuit that squarely attacks them as unnecessary to prevent candidate corruption.

Whereas the Supreme Court temporarily stayed its hand in 2010, it slapped it down with thunderous force in its 2011 decision in *Arizona Free Enterprise Club's Freedom Club PAC v. Bennett*. Ever since the Court's 2008 ruling in *Davis v. FEC* (the Millionaire's Amendment case), ominous clouds hovered over public funding systems for state election campaigns;

now they burst in a torrential downpour. Chief Justice Roberts, writing for the expected five-member majority, confirmed and extended *Davis's* logic in holding that the matching funds provision of the Arizona Citizens Clean Elections Act violated the First Amendment. Similar to the federal law invalidated in *Davis*, the Arizona statute provided additional public funds to certain state office candidates who were severely outspent by privately funded opponents. On the strength of *Davis's* reasoning, the Court found once again that such discriminatory fundraising advantages imposed an unacceptable penalty on the exercise of First Amendment rights to use personal funds for campaign speech. "If the law at issue in *Davis* imposed a burden on candidate speech," Roberts asserted, "the Arizona law unquestionably does so as well."

Moreover, as in *Davis*, the First Amendment penalty inflicted by the Arizona public funding reform could not be justified for equalizing campaign fortunes. "'Leveling the playing field' can sound like a good thing," the chief conceded. "But in a democracy, campaigning for office is not a game. It is a critically important form of speech." And the First Amendment established that, "when it comes to such speech, the guiding principle is freedom—the 'unfettered exchange of ideas'—not whatever the State may view as fair."

In the most important dissenting opinion in her first year on the Court, Justice Elena Kagan took up the lance for the dissenters. Arizona's public funding system, she explained, "does not discriminate against any candidate or point of view, and it does not restrict any person's ability to speak." To the contrary, by providing more public funds to many candidates, "the program creates more speech and thereby broadens public debate." In essence, Kagan concluded, Arizona's law "promotes the values underlying both the First Amendment and our entire Constitution by enhancing the opportunity for free political discussion to the end that government may be responsive to the will of the people."

Powerfully reasoned, perhaps, and eloquently argued—but unpersuasive, nonetheless. The foursome in the dissent could not move the fivesome in the majority away from the greater implications of *Davis* and *Citizens United*. No state or locality that enacted a "trigger" or "fair fight" law, which provided greater subsidies to encourage skittish candidates to accept public funding, could expect to survive a First Amendment challenge. As a result, the Roberts Court effectively shattered the prospects for public financing reforms serving "equalization-of-electoral-opportunities" objectives.

Less dramatic, but no less significant was the Supreme Court's third campaign finance case in the three years following *Citizens United*. The aim of the 2012 decision in *American Tradition Partnership v. Bullock* was to cement the five-member majority's ruling in *Citizens United* and to extend its force against any state or local restrictions on corporate-funded independent expenditures. An uncharacteristically short *per curiam* opinion (of 150-some words) heralded the Court's judgment that a Montana law forbidding a corporation to fund any candidate-related speech fell by the same First Amendment sword as the federal law in *Citizens United*. "The question presented in this case," the opinion stated, "is whether the holding of *Citizens United* applies to the Montana state law. There can be no serious doubt that it does."

The trio of *RNC–Arizona Free Enterprise Club–American Tradition Partnership* was important for more than its precedential value. It revealed that *Citizens United* was, indeed, the moment of a tectonic shift in the Roberts Court's campaign finance jurisprudence. No longer tentatively moving First Amendment law by stealth overruling, the majority of five boldly rewrote First Amendment law by overt overruling. No longer pretending, in Geoffrey Stone's words, "to respect a precedent while in fact interpreting it into oblivion," the newfound majority of five rejected *stare decisis* to reformulate First Amendment law. No longer uncritically protecting the precincts of *Buckley*, the majority of five critically questioned the logic of its First Amendment framework.

In short, at the threshold of *McCutcheon v. FEC*, the Roberts Court is not exactly what it once was. It is, in the words of Jeffrey Toobin, "engaging in a long-term project to deregulate campaigns. A blessing on unlimited aggregate contributions is the next logical step for them to take—and they have five votes."

5. The Briefs

Our democracy would be energized if freed from contribution limits. More political speech leads to better informed voters, and the kind of speech fostered by campaign contributions—political ads—tends to educate voters who are less inclined to search out information on their own.

—Cato Institute, amicus brief in *McCutcheon*

One of the most important steps to beat back government by faction has been the adoption of campaign contribution limits, of which aggregate contribution limits are an essential component. In the absence of aggregate contribution limits, donors of substantial means could give effectively unlimited sums directly to candidates and parties, marginalizing the role of the People as a whole and ensuring the dominance of powerful factions after elections conclude.

—Brennan Center for Justice, amicus brief in *McCutcheon*

FIRST AND FOREMOST, appellate lawyers communicate with the Court through their briefs. This is especially true of lawyers who litigate before the Supreme Court. As with the briefs in which a party petitions the Court to hear a case (known as a petition for a writ of certiorari), the main briefs of the central parties ("merits briefs") must comply with Rule 33 of the Supreme Court's rules. That is, the briefs must be presented in booklet form, using a standard typesetting process with a "typographic" appearance, produced on "paper that is opaque, unglazed, $6^1/_8$ by $9^1/_4$

inches in size, and not less than 60 pounds in weight, and shall have margins of at least three-fourths of an inch on all sides." The merits briefs must be 15,000 or fewer words in length. The respective briefs of the appellants (Shaun McCutcheon and the RNC) had to be presented in a "light blue" booklet whereas that of the respondent (FEC) had to be in a "light red" booklet. There were also the "reply briefs" which had their own word limitations and color codes.

Though the Court is very much about form, it is even more concerned with substance. While lawyers must be highly attentive to the record of the case and the applicable law governing it (particularly the Court's own precedents), the better appellate advocates must also be able to provide the justices with some "big picture" and policy arguments as to why their client should prevail. By the same token, they must be able to demonstrate how the law would be undermined if their opponent's claims were to prevail. This "build and destroy" approach must, of course, be executed with great craft, nuance, and dignity.

In *McCutcheon v. Federal Election Commission*, some of the most renowned appellate lawyers—for the parties and for those submitting "Friend of the Court" or amicus briefs—tendered an array of sophisticated arguments about the intricacies of election law and how it related to the First Amendment issues at hand. But not all of them were known entities, which is the way Shaun McCutcheon liked it—that "outsider" flair appealed to him.

The Case for the Appellants

James Bopp is the point man for opponents of campaign finance law. Among other things, he "had first advised the winning plaintiff, the conservative group Citizens United, about using its campaign-season film *Hillary: The Movie* as a deliberate test of the limits on corporate political spending." And, as David Kirkpatrick noted in the *New York Times*, it was Bopp who "shepherded the case through appeals to the Supreme Court as part of a long-term legal strategy that he says he has just begun." That strategy led in time to his involvement in the *McCutcheon* case, which he argued in the Court of Appeals for the District of Columbia. Thereafter, he wrote the petition urging the Court to review the case. And thanks to Bopp's efforts, the justices agreed to hear the matter.

So, the next step was to prepare and submit the merits brief on behalf of Shaun McCutcheon. But that did not happen; someone else was chosen to do that. Even before the decision was made to replace him as the attorney to argue the case, he was shoved out of the picture and replaced by a young unknown. That galled him.

Michael T. Morley was the new man, the one who replaced James Bopp. Morley is a Climenko fellow, lecturer on law, and legal research and writing instructor at Harvard Law School. Though few really noticed it at the time, he was the counsel of record on the merits brief for Shaun McCutcheon.

In the decade after graduating from Yale Law School, he clerked on the U.S. Court of Appeals for the Eleventh Circuit, then worked for over three years as a litigation associate at Williams & Connolly, where, among other things, he helped prepare the prevailing merits briefs in a U.S. Supreme Court case. He then accepted a Schedule C appointment in the George W. Bush Administration as special assistant to the general counsel of the Army in the Pentagon. Morley was awarded the Army Meritorious Civilian Service Award and the Army Staff Lapen Pin for his service. He was also a member of the Republican National Lawyers Association.

Impressive as his credentials were, Michael Morley had little on his résumé evidencing any special First Amendment expertise. Given that, he seemed an unusual candidate to author such an important brief in a case with landmark potential. Then again, one of the courses he was teaching at Harvard was a class titled "Election Litigation." And while he had prepared an amicus brief submitted to the Court on behalf of some military and veterans groups in a free speech case decided the year before (*United States v. Alvarez*), this was his first merits brief in a First Amendment case.

As the former senior editor of the student-edited *Yale Law Journal*, Morley was skilled at crafting legal arguments and presenting them cogently, at least in an academic way. He began his brief for McCutcheon by explaining the applicable campaign finance law and how it developed in response to the "scandalous corruption" that first invited it. And he conceded, as he must, that the *Buckley* Court had upheld FECA's aggregate ceiling on campaign contributions, this on the ground that such a limitation was needed as a "corollary" to the limitations on individual contributions, which the Court had also upheld. In other words, if limits were needed to prevent the corruptive influence of individual contributions, then by the same logic they were needed to prevent that same effect if produced by aggregate contributions. Absent such an aggregate limitation, a person could legally "contribute massive amounts of money to a particular candidate through the use of unearmarked contributions to political committees likely to contribute to that candidate," said the *Buckley* Court. Though conceding that, Morley added, "[T]he Court emphasized that the issue had 'not been separately addressed at length by the parties'" in *Buckley*. Translated: the justices needed to consider this issue anew, albeit by way of thorough briefs and robust arguments.

Morley tendered three basic arguments in his brief for *McCutcheon*:

1. Contribution limits substantially burden fundamental First Amendment rights and are therefore subject to rigorous review.
2. The aggregate contribution limits do not further any constitutionally permissible government interest. Whether a person contributes the legally permissible amount to one candidate or twenty candidates makes no constitutional difference, as the risk of corruption or the appearance of corruption remains the same as to each candidate: non-cognizable.
3. And even assuming that the aggregate limits furthered a legitimate governmental interest, they were not sufficiently tailored to satisfy First Amendment requirements.

Among other things, what was significant about the Morley brief was its modesty about what lawyers refer to as the "strict scrutiny test," which when applied is almost impossible for the government to satisfy. It is the test that Professor Gerald Gunther once referred to as "fatal in fact." And it was the legal test James Bopp urged the Court to employ when he first petitioned the Court on behalf of Shaun McCutcheon.

Here is how Mr. Morley dealt with this issue: "whether this Court chooses to characterize its standard of review as 'strict,' 'exacting,' 'close,' or 'rigorous,' the key point in this case is that aggregate contribution limits effectively impose a 'substantial burden' and 'penalty' on an individual who wishes to 'robustly exercise First Amendment rights' by supporting too many candidates or political committees." Moreover, Michael Morley did not have to hammer the "strict scrutiny" point home; there were others who would do that for him.

James Bopp was one of those other players. Incredibly, he was still in the game, though not as counsel for McCutcheon on his merits brief. Instead, Bopp was the author of the merits brief submitted to the Court on behalf of the RNC. In that brief, he proudly flew the "strict scrutiny" banner, and with constitutional vigor. Consistent with that bold spirit, Bopp also argued that "the contribution/expenditure scrutiny dichotomy in *Buckley* should be overruled, modified, or held inapplicable to aggregate limits." A similar point was made by Morley, but in a subtler way—in a footnote. What was also important in the Bopp brief for the RNC was the argument that "the government must specifically prove a 'large'-conduit-contribution risk and may not meet its burden with broad-brush theories of corruption instead." It was just those broad-brush theories that the defenders of the aggregate limits law hoped the justices would endorse and apply.

One of the briefs to which Morley directed the Court in his brief was the one prepared by Bobby Burchfield on behalf of Senator McConnell. In that amicus brief, Burchfield argued that "strict scrutiny *must* apply" and that the Court should reject any test that "relaxed First Amendment review of contribution limits." When it came to the Court's holding in *Buckley v. Valeo*, Burchfield stressed its "analytical shortcomings" concerning the "contribution-expenditure limit dichotomy." This "bifurcated standard of review" had to go, as did the *Buckley* precedent underlying it. Or as he put it: "*Stare decisis* does not compel adherence to the 'halfway house' of *Buckley*.... Accordingly," he added, "amicus Senator Mitch McConnell urges the Court to reconsider the application of less rigorous scrutiny for contribution limits and to accord *full* First Amendment protection to contributions by applying strict scrutiny to *all* contribution limits." Translated: absent some showing of *actual* quid quo pro corruption, no limits on campaign contributions or expenditures should survive constitutional scrutiny.

Joshua Wheeler of the Thomas Jefferson Center for the Protection of Freedom of Expression echoed that position. While his amicus brief (joined by the Media Institute) did not call on the Court to over-rule *Buckley*, it nonetheless argued that there was no proof of any actual harm to the electoral process: "In the absence of a *manifest risk* of quid pro quo corruption, FECA's limit on the number of candidates to whom an individual may contribute at the per-candidate limit cannot survive strict scrutiny review."

The Bopp-Burchfield hard line was fortified by an amicus brief filed by Ilya Shapiro of the Cato Institute, a libertarian group whose views had as of late caught the eyes of certain members of the Roberts Court. Shapiro argued that overruling *Buckley* would improve the integrity and vitality of the electoral process. He quoted political science professor John J. Coleman to stress: "Contrary to what critics charge, 'studies indicate that campaign spending does not diminish trust, efficacy, and involvement.' That's because 'spending increases public knowledge of the candidates, across essentially all groups in the population. Less spending on campaigns is not likely to increase public trust, involvement, or attention.... Getting more money into campaigns should, on the whole, be beneficial to American democracy.' Moreover, 'a deregulated system of campaign finance should be expected to increase electoral competition.' This competition would also reduce the power of incumbency and the corruption that can flow from it."

Other groups also filed briefs in support of Shaun McCutcheon. They included the Center for Competitive Politics, National Republican Senatorial Committee (jointly with the Republican Congressional Committee), American Civil Rights Union, Committee for Justice, Institute for Justice, and Cause of Action. Yet more organizations added their names by way of combined briefs on behalf of the Tea Party Leadership Fund, the National Defense PAC, Combat Veterans for Congress PAC, Conservative Melting Pot PAC, Freedom's Defense Fund, the Libertarian National Committee, the Constitution Party National

Committee, the Free Speech Coalition, the U.S. Justice Foundation, Gun Owners Foundation, English First, Abraham Lincoln Foundation, Institute on the Constitution, Western Center for Journalism, Policy Analysis Center, and the Conservative Legal Defense & Education Fund.

When all the legal dust settled, the sixteen briefs (merit, reply, and amicus) for the appellants made both modest and bold arguments. On the one hand, there was no evidence of any quid pro quo corruption here, so according to the logic of *Buckley* the First Amendment claim should prevail. On the other hand, some of the briefs charged head on against *Buckley* and its contribution-expenditure dichotomy—*Buckley v. Valeo* had to go, it must be overruled.

Shortly before oral arguments in the Court, former Solicitor General Charles Fried, who had filed an amicus brief in support of the government, published an op-ed in the *New York Times*. The seventy-eight-year-old Reagan-era SG and now Harvard Law professor proclaimed his fervent opposition to what Shaun McCutcheon, the RNC, Senator McConnell, and Ilya Shapiro were attempting to do. "If they succeed," he wrote, "individuals will be able, in effect, to direct unlimited amounts of cash to the election campaigns of federal candidates—inviting corruption or the appearance of corruption, which the Supreme Court has consistently held justifies contribution limits."

The Case for the Government

As the government saw it, and as it advised the justices to view it, there was no reason why the Court should even bother to hear the *McCutcheon* case. "The FEC, through its own lawyers and the solicitor general's office," Lyle Denniston observed, "urged the Court to dispose of the case *without* briefing and oral argument, contending that the Court's decision in the *Buckley* case settled the constitutionality of aggregate limits on donations, and arguing that nothing has changed in campaign finance law or the Court's later decisions to alter that." Of course, that did not happen, which meant that the government's lawyers had to address the merits of the case.

The brief prepared by Solicitor General Donald Verrilli and his colleagues was fifty-seven printed pages long (plus appendixes) and consumed some 15,000-plus words. It began with a statement of how substantially the country and our legal system had invested in the status quo. The existing limits on campaign contributions, the brief emphasized, were deeply rooted in our electoral system of governance. Verrilli laid out the history of contribution limits: "For more than seventy years, federal law has generally limited the amounts that individuals may contribute to political candidates, political-party committees and non-party political committees for the purpose of influencing elections for federal office. . . . Both Congress and this [Supreme] Court have recognized that such limits are an important tool in combating corruption and the appearance of corruption in federal politics."

To buttress his case, Verrilli directed the justices' attention to a 1974 congressional report that identified "multiple instances in which contributions to numerous separate entities had been made at the request of a particular candidate." And what better way to do this than by way of an example from the Nixon era. During that period "the dairy industry had avoided then-existing reporting requirements by dividing a $2 million contribution to President Nixon among hundreds of committees in different states, 'which could then hold the money for the president's reelection campaign.'" Worse still, he added, "Shortly thereafter, President Nixon 'circumvented and interfered with' the 'legitimate functions of the Agriculture Department' by reversing a decision unfavorable to the dairy industry." As if that were not enough, "Attorney General John Mitchell [who was also President Nixon's campaign manager] halted a grand jury investigation of the milk producers' association." There were yet other examples, such as the one involving a presidential aide who "promised an ambassadorship to a particular individual in return for 'a $100,000 contribution, which was to be split between 1970 Republican senatorial candidates designated by the White House and [President] Nixon's 1972 campaign.' That arrangement was not unique."

The point: the law was well settled. *Buckley*'s system of regulation had prevented the kinds of abuses that first prompted campaign reform, and numerous courts and state legislatures had relied on the *Buckley* holding to establish precedents and enact laws. In short, the country heavily invested in *Buckley*. Hence, "overruling *Buckley*...would severely disrupt the considerable reliance interests that have accrued over the last four decades." In that regard, Verrilli added, the appellants had failed to provide the Court with the kind of evidence needed to set aside *stare decisis*.

When it came to the First Amendment test the Court should apply to the facts in the *McCutcheon* case, Verrilli greatly distanced the government's position from that urged by the appellants. "The Court in *Buckley*," he emphasized, "declined to apply strict scrutiny to contribution limits, including aggregate contribution limits." Rather, a "lesser" and far more deferential standard should apply. Given the relevant body of First Amendment law, the government was *not* required to prove actual or quid quo pro corruption as a justification. It was enough if the aggregate contribution laws in question sought to prevent "'the appearance of corruption stemming from public awareness of the opportunities for abuse inherent in a regime of large individual financial contributions.'"

There was, of course, more about the nuances of election law, how it evolved, and how it should be interpreted consistent with a wide-ranging body of First Amendment doctrine. But those arguments were for the justices and their law clerks to figure out and later test during oral arguments.

As is customary, reply briefs were filed. James Bopp filed the brief for the RNC and Michael Morley filed the one for Shaun McCutcheon. Though few noticed it at the time, a new name appeared beside that of Mr. Morley—that of Erin C. Murphy of the Bancroft law firm. That name would prove significant as to how the case was handled in the course of oral arguments.

Two Uncommon Liberal Terms: "Deference" & "Originalism"

The name Paul M. Smith is one well known and respected in First Amendment circles, this because of his ardent and insightful defense of free speech principles. Not surprisingly, he filed an amicus brief in *McCutcheon*, one on behalf of eighty-five Democratic members of the House of Representatives. What was surprising, however, was the fact that in this case he weighed in by *opposing* the First Amendment claim. Contrary to his usual First Amendment position, he urged the Court to bow to legislative assessment: "As a matter of relative expertise and democratic accountability, the judiciary should defer to the elected branches' determination that contribution limits are needed." This was the conceptual and constitutional opposite of the kind of strict scrutiny urged in several of the briefs filed on behalf of the appellant. Furthermore, echoing Verrilli, Smith argued that the constitutionality of campaign finance laws did not require proof of actual quid pro quo corruption, but only the appearance of corruption. As for the purported need to overrule *Buckley*, Smith was blunt: "Nothing has changed to justify a departure from *Buckley*. Indeed, this Court has retained the *Buckley* framework over vigorous dissents raising the very same arguments that appellants and their *amici* put forward now."

The amicus brief filed in support of the government by the Brennan Center for Justice made a somewhat unusual argument for a liberal group. It contended that the *original intent* of the framers was to safeguard the integrity of the electoral process against *all* forms of corruption and that this originalist view comported with the founders' understanding of the First Amendment. Originalist arguments, of course, were the constitutional stock-and-trade of Justices Antonin Scalia and Clarence Thomas, two of the most outspoken critics of campaign finance reforms. Drawing on James Madison, James Wilson, Gouverneur Morris, and Alexander Hamilton, among others, the Brennan Center brief (submitted by Daniel F. Kolb) argued, "The historical record leaves no doubt that the founders understood corruption as more than just individual quid pro quo payments for legislation. To them corruption encompassed *any* use of public power for private purposes—not merely theft, but any use of government power and assets to benefit special interests rather than the broader public."

The originalist take on the matter before the Court was buttressed by an amicus brief submitted by Professor Lawrence Lessig. Ever the reformer, the Harvard professor had just published a book on the corrosive impact of money on politics (*Republic, Lost: How Money Corrupts Congress*). Central to Lessig's position was the claim that the arguments tendered by the appellants and the amici supporting them relied "upon a *modern* understanding of the term 'corruption,' in sharp conflict with the term's original meaning." Building on that foundation, Lessig maintained that the "framers had a very specific conception of the term 'corruption'... one at odds with McCutcheon's contemporary understanding of that term." The framers understood corruption, whether of individuals or institutions, as synonymous with "improper dependence." In that regard, his historical research revealed three findings key to an argument in support of the government's position: "1) the framers' dominant concern was the corruption of the institutions of government, not individuals; 2) the framers recognized that democratic institutions could be corrupted through developing conflicting *dependencies*, as they had in England; and 3) corruption of individual officeholders by bribery or other forms of quid pro quo corruption was a real, but secondary, concern."

Taken together, these three amicus briefs were premised on a single basic proposition, the sovereignty of the *people*. As the *amici* in support of the appellee viewed it, that sovereignty demanded that the Court defer to the will of the people as expressed by their representatives in Congress, and that the integrity of the political process be jealously guarded against the evils of any and all forms of corruption.

Other Friends of the Court: Supporting the Appellee

There were more briefs and more arguments. There were also a number of groups that thought it important to their members and their causes that they sign onto a combined brief in support of the government and its defense of limits on campaign contributions, aggregate or otherwise. Those groups, all liberal, included the Campaign Legal Center, AARP, Asian Americans Advancing Justice, Asian American Legal Defense and Education Fund, Common Cause, Citizens for Responsibility and Ethics in Washington, the League of Women Voters, Progressives United, Public Campaign, the Communications Workers of America, Greenpeace, NAACP, Sierra Club, American Federation of Teachers, Main Street Alliance, Ourtime.org, People for the American Way, Rock the Vote, U.S. PIRG, Working Families Organization, and Demos.

Enter & Exit the American Civil Liberties Union

When it comes to money and the Constitution, the current position of the nation's oldest civil liberties organization is this:

> The ACLU does not support campaign finance regulation premised on the notion that the answer to money in politics is *to ban political speech.* ... In our view, the answer to that problem is to expand, not limit, the resources available for political advocacy. Thus, the ACLU supports a comprehensive and meaningful system of *public financing* that would help create a level playing field for every qualified candidate. We support carefully drawn *disclosure* rules. We support *reasonable limits on campaign contributions* and we support stricter enforcement of existing bans on coordination between candidates and Super PACs.

Though the language quoted above would strike some as a reaffirmation of the ACLU's longstanding opposition to many campaign finance laws, a closer examination of the italicized language makes it obvious that the matter is not really that clear—nuance is important. That is, the ACLU supports: 1) *certain kinds* of public financing of elections along with 2) *carefully crafted* disclosure requirements, and 3) *"reasonable limits"* on contributions. Note the absence of any reference to *campaign expenditures* along with any reference to limits on *aggregate campaign contributions.* The first omission might fairly be understood as opposition to such laws, or to many of them. The second omission, however, might fairly be construed as the ACLU having no position on aggregate limits. Then again, it may support such limits provided they are "reasonable." But what, in the group's judgment, is reasonable?

Were the limits as applied in the *McCutcheon* case "reasonable" in the minds of the members of the ACLU's board? No one knows since no answer was ever provided to that question. This was so even though the ACLU had played a major role in campaign finance cases dating back to 1972, and then in 1976 when the group contested the laws at issue in *Buckley v. Valeo*. Between 1976 and 2010, when it filed a brief contesting the campaign finance laws in *Citizens United v. FEC*, the national ACLU had filed fourteen briefs in the Supreme Court, all of them challenging various aspects of campaign reform laws. In that almost forty-year period, the ACLU participated in almost every important Supreme Court campaign finance case and took what some viewed as an absolutist First Amendment position by arguing against limitations on contributions, expenditures, or both. But after *Citizens United*, the national ACLU pled the proverbial Fifth and went silent. It expressed no position in such cases either pending in or before the Supreme Court. Why?

The answer: there was division in the ranks. Some of the new ACLU guard broke away from the traditional party line. Some of them were no longer the tried and true defenders of the First Amendment when it came to campaign finance cases (and picketing near abortion clinics). Or as they saw it, money was ruining the American electoral system so badly that the First Amendment should not be invoked to defend its all-too-harmful impacts on that system.

For Burt Neuborne—the former ACLU legal director and a New York University Law professor—the ACLU's longstanding position on this First Amendment issue had become problematic, to put it diplomatically. "I've marched proudly behind the ACLU's First Amendment flag for almost fifty years," he likes to say. "On campaign finance reform," he is quick to add, "I believe the ACLU's adamant opposition to limits on massive campaign spending by the super rich gets the constitutional issues wrong." Where Neuborne was once supportive of challenges to campaign finance laws, he now publicly applauds many such laws notwithstanding his colleagues' First Amendment challenges to them. And he makes his views known in his capacity as the founding legal director of the Brennan Center for Justice, which has *defended* many campaign finance laws including the one in the *McCutcheon* case. "I confess to having supported the ACLU position in *Buckley*. As the corrosive effects on democracy of uncontrolled campaign spending became increasingly clear, however, I joined several former ACLU leaders—Norman Dorsen, Aryeh Neier, John Shattuck, and Mort Halperin—in opposing the organization's campaign finance position." From where he now stands, First Amendment liberty cuts the other way: "Limiting the power of a few individuals and corporations that exercise disproportionate political influence solely because of their enormous wealth has nothing to do with censoring a speaker's message; it is desperately needed to preserve the integrity of the egalitarian democracy the First Amendment was designed to protect."

Not so fast, counsels Nadine Strossen, the ACLU's distinguished past president and a law professor at New York Law School. "The benefits of added free speech, and added voices, and added opinions," she stressed in 2010, "will go across the political spectrum. So I completely disagree with the many pundits who have been saying, 'Oh, this is going to benefit Republicans, or benefit conservatives, or benefit big business.' Not at all!" To think otherwise, she argues, is to put groups like the ACLU in a perilous place when it comes to taking positions on controversial campaign issues. As she sees it, what the *Citizens United* decision did was to "unshackle *all* corporations, including nonprofit corporations, such as the ACLU, which itself was mentioned expressly in the Supreme Court's decision, along with the Sierra Club, and the National Rifle Association, as well as unions. [Hence,] all of us will be able to speak more and all of us will be able to receive more information."

Not surprisingly, Strossen opposes some of the very campaign reform measures that Neuborne and his followers endorse. For her, such laws are a kind of "Incumbents Protection Act; they make it much harder for a non-incumbent challenger to mount a campaign unless it is a wealthy individual. But if you're talking about middle-class people trying to pool their resources to finance a campaign of a non-wealthy individual, or to advocate an issue that merely mentions the name of a candidate, that itself was a crime." Thus, for Strossen the principle of egalitarian democracy cuts precisely the other way: "The rhetoric makes it seem as if, oh, it is going to empower the little folks. In fact it does exactly the opposite."

So, there is robust division in the group; some strongly favor certain campaign finance laws while others strongly oppose them as violative of the First Amendment. When it comes to this hot-button issue, there is yet another ACLU side—the silent ones. Of the twenty amicus briefs filed in the *McCutcheon* case, one was conspicuously absent—that of the ACLU.

For whatever reasons, the group most known for defending civil liberties, especially those involving First Amendment rights, opted to remain silent.

In 2013 it was silent, but it was not always so. The ACLU had long been at the forefront of this controversial issue, filing merits and amicus briefs in support of the First Amendment claims in such landmark campaign finance cases as *Buckley v. Valeo* (Joel Gora, counsel of record) and *Citizens United v. FEC* (Steven R. Shapiro, counsel of record). Its story in this fight goes back forty-plus years to a time when Richard Nixon's Justice Department used the Federal Election Campaign Act of 1971 (FECA) to silence and punish its critics. At first, the ACLU role was that of providing free legal counsel to those critics; the district court case was titled *United States v. National Committee for Impeachment.* Soon enough, the ever-outspoken ACLU was itself a named plaintiff in a case contesting certain provisions of FECA. That case: *American Civil Liberties Union, Inc. v. Jennings.* Here is the short story of both cases, drawn largely from an account by Joel Gora, a Brooklyn Law School professor, who has worked with the ACLU on campaign finance issues for almost forty years and who was one of the main litigators in the *Buckley* case.

"Three old-time dissenters came to the ACLU offices in New York with an incredible story. In September of [1972] the group had run a two-page advertisement in the *New York Times* advocating the impeachment of President Richard Nixon for the bombing of Cambodia and praising those few hardy—and clearly identified—members of Congress who had sponsored an Impeachment Resolution." As Gora tells it, the "advertisement was turgid, wordy, legalistic, and not very slick, but it embodied the essence of what the First Amendment stands for: the right of citizens to express their opinion about the conduct of their government, free from fear of sanctions or reprisals from that government. Nonetheless, before the ink on the advertisement was barely dry, the federal government had hauled the group into federal court." All of this occurred despite the fact that such speech would otherwise seem to be protected by the Court's landmark First Amendment rulings in *New York Times, Inc. v. Sullivan* (1964) and *Brandenburg v. Ohio* (1969), both of which offered considerable protection for those who criticized government officials.

Those rulings notwithstanding, Richard Nixon's Justice Department tapped the FECA to wage war on the Administration's liberal critics.

"The government," Gora noted, "claimed that the expenditure of funds on the advertisement was for the purpose of influencing the outcome of the elections, thus rendering these individuals a political committee. The government threatened them with injunctions against further speech unless they complied with the law, filed reports with the government and disclosed their contributors and supporters. All of this was for simply sponsoring an advertisement publicly criticizing the president of the United States on a crucial issue of the day."

While all of this was going on, the ACLU took the matter into its own organizational hands. In order to test the use of FECA to censor political speech, in September 1972 the group submitted to the *New York Times* a proposed political ad expressing its stern disapproval of the Nixon Administration's opposition to court-ordered busing. Fearful of criminal prosecution under FECA, the *Times* declined to run the ad, whereupon the ACLU went to the federal district court in the District of Columbia seeking declaratory and injunctive relief. The court granted the motion for a preliminary injunction, which allowed the *Times* to publish the ad. That case was *American Civil Liberties Union, Inc. v. Jennings.*

The other case, *United States v. National Committee for Impeachment,* involved a political ad that ran in the *Times* in May 1972. That piece was titled: "A Resolution to Impeach Richard M. Nixon as President of the United States." It was worded as an impeachment resolution similar to the one brought against President Andrew Johnson. Nearly half of the ad charged that Nixon unconstitutionally "arrogated to himself the power to declare war and the power 'to make Rules for the Government and Regulation of the land and naval forces,' which are committed by article I, section 8, clauses 11 and 14 of the Constitution solely to the Congress." Among other things, the ad also contained two contributions coupons, which appeared at the bottom of the page. Nixon's Justice Department claimed the ad violated FECA's certification requirements. Those requirements barred the solicitation and acceptance of contributions unless and until certain detailed and complicated filings had been submitted to the government.

The ACLU and the Committee ultimately prevailed in their respective cases, though on different legal grounds. The spirit of those victories is captured in the following statement from the opinion in the *Jennings* case: "Groups concerned with the open discourse of views on prominent national issues may...comfortably continue to exercise these rights and feel secure that by so doing their associational rights will not be encroached upon."

At that point in time, several years before the Court's seminal ruling in *Buckley v. Valeo*, liberals opposed the government's use of federal campaign laws while conservatives applauded it. Back then, and for many years afterward, the ACLU was at the vanguard of defending what it saw as revered First Amendment principles against the evils of certain campaign reform laws. Time, however, changed that.

Fast-forward nearly three decades: The news broke in the *Washington Post* on June 19, 1998. Here is how it began: "There's been a major breakthrough in the battle to reform the campaign money system," wrote E.J. Dionne. "As the House of Representatives joined a bitter debate this week over a measure to fight some of the more egregious campaign abuses," he added, "a group of luminaries from the American Civil Liberties Union has broken with the organization's opposition to the principles underlying the bill." There was division in the ranks and it had become public. "In a statement that will be formally released in the next few days," the article continued, "the nine leaders—among them, former ACLU president Norman Dorsen, former executive director Aryeh Neier, former legal director Burt Neuborne and former legislative director Morton Halperin—dispute the ACLU's view that placing 'reasonable limits on campaign spending' violates the First Amendment."

The controversy continued. By 2010, after the ACLU filed its amicus brief in *Citizens United* and the Supreme Court's decision in the case invalidated a section of the Bipartisan Campaign Reform Act, the group's official policy concerning campaign finance issues modified. An April 19, 2010, press release announced that the group had voted to "revise its policy." The vote was a close one: 36–30. There were two revisions: 1) "The policy accepts spending limits as a condition of voluntary public financing plans," and 2) "The policy permits reasonable limits on campaign contributions to candidates. This contrasts with prior policy, which opposed all such limits."

As indicated in its press release, "since 1970 [the ACLU had] taken up the issue on its agenda at least twenty-two times." Though the ACLU had "resolved" the matter, peace reigned for only eleven days. The headline in the *Wall Street Journal* proclaimed the end of that diplomatic truce: "The ACLU Approves Limits on Speech."

Floyd Abrams (a noted First Amendment lawyer), Ira Glasser (the former executive director of the ACLU), and Joel Gora (an ACLU lawyer and Brooklyn Law School professor) took aim at the April 19 policy: "Over the objections of some key senior staff and by a very narrow vote, the ACLU National Board of Directors rejected core aspects of... [its] longstanding policy" of vigorously contesting campaign finance restrictions as incompatible with the First Amendment. More specifically, they charged that the "organization will now accept 'reasonable' government limitations on contributions to candidates. The ACLU doesn't say what 'reasonable' means, so the government will doubtless supply the definition." Speaking bluntly, the trio added: "Nonetheless, we've come to this: the premier First Amendment organization in America now favors limitations on the First Amendment in the area in which all agree it must have its most powerful application—political speech during election campaigns. ... This is a self-inflicted wound from which the ACLU will not soon recover."

Shortly afterward, Susan N. Herman, president of the ACLU, weighed into the controversy with a letter to the *Wall Street Journal*. "The board has been debating campaign finance regulation for nearly forty years," she wrote. "It convened a special committee in 2007 to revisit the organization's policy on the issue and heard from a number of First Amendment experts including Messrs. Abrams and Gora. The decision to revise the policy in order to permit reasonable limits on contributions to candidates is an acknowledgment that very large contributions may lead to undue influence or corruption that can undermine the integrity of the electoral process." That said, she nonetheless conceded: "Reasonable minds can certainly hold legitimate but divergent views on an issue as important and complicated as this." What could not, however, "be disputed is the ACLU's unwavering commitment to protecting the First Amendment."

Would the controversy linger? Or had there finally been a meeting of the minds? Fast-forward again to 2013: nearly two weeks before the *McCutcheon* case was argued, Steven R. Shapiro, the ACLU's current legal director, spoke to a small audience at the group's national office in Washington, D.C. While the ACLU had taken no formal position on *McCutcheon*, and former ACLU officials had done likewise, Shapiro nonetheless openly volunteered his take on the case: "I would be shocked if the Supreme Court upheld the law." Stressing the perceived outcome, Shapiro (the same man who was the ACLU's lead counsel in *Citizens United*) was nonetheless careful not to state the group's own position. As for the division within the ACLU, he preferred to keep such matters off the record.

However constitutionally problematic the aggregate contribution law was, it did not convince the ACLU to revisit its 2010 policy and thereafter take a public stand in *McCutcheon*. For some, that fact was shocking. For others, it was a welcome relief.

6. The Arguments

POLITICAL THEATER was their purpose and the Supreme Court was their backdrop. On the morning of oral arguments in the *McCutcheon* case, demonstrators held black and yellow signs that read MCCUTCHEON IS CORRUPTION while others displayed small black and white signs that read PROTECT OUR DEMOCRACY and DEMOCRACY IS NOT FOR $ALE. Both before and after the arguments, several protesters paraded around near the steps of the Court dressed up as $100 bills. Beside them was a white-haired man waving a pole with a fake American flag bearing VISA and Chevron icons for stars and large bills for stripes.

A small square platform, with lectern atop and replete with sound system, had been set up in preparation for fifteen or so featured speakers scheduled to address the crowd and TV cameras. They included Congressman John Sarbanes (D-MD), Reverend Dr. William Barber II (Moral Monday leader), and representatives from liberal groups such as Greenpeace, Demos, Free Speech for People, U.S. PIRG, and the Main Street Alliance. Similar political rallies occurred that same day

A protester outside the Supreme Court

in seventeen cities across the nation—from Philadelphia to Portland, and from Hartford to Honolulu. Earlier, a huge inflatable "Fat Cat" with the name "McCutcheon" running across its plump belly was displayed near the Capitol building. And a Facebook page ("McCutcheon v. FEC, Money v. People Rally") provided an additional forum for Web protest.

The Communications Workers of America and People for the American Way (PAW), among others, orchestrated much of this exercise in First Amendment freedom. In the days before the oral arguments, PAW provided a digital "*McCutcheon v. FEC* Activist Toolkit." The table of contents for the toolkit had "click-on" headings that read:

- Introduction
- Background of the case
- *McCutcheon v. FEC* talking points
- Protests and actions
- October 7 training and October 8 lobby day
- Submitting a letter-to-the-editor
- Social media tools
- The solution
- Additional resources

And then there was all the construction going on. It seemed metaphoric, the fact that the Supreme Court building was undergoing major renovations to restore the crumbling marble on the façade. Its majestic front side was surrounded by six tiers of scaffolding (the imagistic scrim had been removed earlier). The 1935 structure, first built during the depths of the Great Depression, looked haggard. The rows of wooden planks and lines of supporting steel made it difficult to experience the splendor of this great building designed by the prominent American architect Cass Gilbert, who planned it in the Beaux Arts style to give American meaning to the work of the ancients. But now this once glorious neoclassical temple with its Corinthian columns was in *repair*—things needed to be fixed.

The political and structural spectacle notwithstanding, Erin Murphy and Paul Clement (the lawyers for McCutcheon and the RNC) strolled by the line of people waiting on the marble plaza to enter the Court. Solicitor

General Donald Verrilli and several young lawyers from his office did likewise, as did Bobby Burchfield (counsel for Senator McConnell). Clad in a dark suit, an oxford blue shirt, and a light bronze patterned tie—and flanked by his friend Dan Backer and his publicist Heather Purcell—a confident-looking Shaun McCutcheon marched past the protesters and toward the scaffolding. As he did, cameras clicked to get a photo of him walking into the designated side entrance of the Court.

Once in the building, McCutcheon and the lawyers who had represented him in the early stages (Dan Backer, Jerad Najvar, and Steve Hoersting) chatted as they waited in the Great Hall for the marshal to check them into the Court chamber. Nearby was James Bopp, the lawyer who had first brought the constitutional challenge in the lower court and who, up to a few weeks earlier, was the attorney scheduled to argue the case. (Significant as his role was in *Citizens United*, Bopp was absent from the courtroom the day the landmark case was argued in the high court.) Though Bopp was still said to be part of the *McCutcheon* team, he was not in the plush lawyers' lounge where Erin Murphy and Paul Clement waited before they entered the courtroom.

Above the bench where the justices sat, the floating clock neared ten. As it did, the lawyers took their seats, as did several prominent guests— Senate Minority Leader Mitch McConnell of Kentucky, Democratic Senators Max Baucus of Montana and Tom Udall of New Mexico, and independent senator Bernie Sanders of Vermont. As for James Bopp, he did not sit at the counsel's table, or in the Supreme Court lawyers' section; he sat several rows back in the public section with only his white crop of hair readily visible.

Shortly before the proceedings began, the audience was reminded (yet again) of the rules of the Court—no talking, no eating, no standing up, and no electrical devices such as cell phones, tablets, pagers, and most assuredly no cameras of any sort. What images the public would see of what transpired there would be rendered by the courtroom sketch artist Arthur Lien, whose sketches appeared on SCOTUSblog, among other outlets. Though no cameras are permitted, the Court has long allowed official tape recordings of oral arguments; beginning in 2003, those recordings were digitally made and are available on the Oyez Project website.

Hypothetically Speaking

They all follow the law…but only as they see it. And how they see it depends a little on precedent and a lot on other things, including how well a legal argument does or does not stand up when tested. And so an advocate has to be at his or her best and then some to get the better of the fight during oral arguments. Of course, Fortuna sometimes has its way as in *Citizens United* when Justice Samuel Alito inquired about the applicability of BCRA to books. After that, Citizens United's counsel breathed easier with the knowledge that a mighty blow had been leveled. No such luck, however, favored any of the three attorneys during the fifty-nine minutes of oral argument in *McCutcheon*.

The *McCutcheon* case was one that required, among other things, a *comprehensive* knowledge of First Amendment law combined with a *thorough* understanding of election law (statutory and regulatory), accompanied by a *wide-ranging* grasp of realpolitik as practiced by political parties, political action committees, lobbyists, and millionaires and billionaires who funnel money into politics. This was a complicated area of law with different rules for limits on contributions to candidates, PACs, national parties, and state parties. And then there were differing rules for limits on base contributions and aggregate ones. As it turned out, no one was entirely up to speed in all of those respects. Even so, the exchange went on with each ideological bloc among the justices vying to make its point.

10:00 A.M. Erin Murphy sat next to the man whom many considered to be the finest living Supreme Court advocate in the nation—Paul Clement, the former solicitor general. It was quite unusual that a lawyer so seasoned in the ways of the Court should be second chair to a lawyer so young (thirty-three) and inexperienced. Though she had been a Supreme Court law clerk in 2005, she had never before argued a case in the high court.

10:03 A.M. "We'll hear argument first this morning in Case 12-536, *McCutcheon v. The Federal Election Commission.* Ms. Murphy."

That's how it began when Chief Justice John Roberts invited Murphy, his former law clerk, to begin on behalf of the appellants Shaun McCutcheon and the RNC. In the course of her opening argument, the justices (save Clarence Thomas) interrupted her thirty-eight times to ask questions, make comments, or just interject a little lively humor into the legal discourse. The chief spoke up only twice during her argument.

Barely a minute into her argument, Murphy capsulized her position with rhetorical panache, though not without some confusion: "By prohibiting contributions that are [outside] the modest base limits Congress has already imposed to combat the reality or appearance of corruption, these [aggregate contribution] limits simply seek to prevent individuals from engaging in too much First Amendment activity." That was the point—penalizing people for exercising too much First Amendment freedom—that she had to drive home; that was the argument she used to convince at least five justices who would tip the scales in her clients' favor. But to do that, she would first have to defend her position against the certain onslaught of questions to come from the Court's liberal wing.

Justices Stephen Breyer and Elena Kagan (two of the Court's four liberals) began that onslaught with dialectical force. They peppered the Georgetown University Law Center graduate with hypothetical after hypothetical—all worst-case scenarios, to be sure.

Given that they were both former law professors, this sort of thing was to be expected. Essentially, the two justices conjured up scenarios in which the letter and spirit of existing election laws might be circumvented unless some meaningful limits were placed on aggregate contributions of the kind that Shaun McCutcheon sought to make.

> **Breyer:** Now, we can give each of those forty [supporters] $5,000. They aren't coordinated; they're not established by a single person. Each is independently run. And we know pretty well that that total of $5,000 times forty will go to [candidate] Sam Smith. Okay? What does that violate?

Basically, this is what is known as the *circumvention problem*. That is, the letter of the law is circumvented (and thus not formally violated) while the spirit of the law is functionally violated. In many ways, that has been the history of campaign finance law. Even so, Erin Murphy was not about to yield the point, arguing that existing law already prevented the kinds of evils the justices hypothesized.

Murphy: [N]umerous direct circumvention measures [already exist]. For instance, we have earmarking provisions on earmarking contributions for candidates. We have coordination restrictions on coordinated expenditures with a candidate. There are proliferation restrictions on creating multiple PACs that are all designed [to prevent the kinds of circumvention just mentioned.] ... [And] there are base limits both on what can be given to a PAC ... and on what a PAC can give to a candidate.

Justice Kagan, who as solicitor general unsuccessfully defended the campaign finance law at issue in *Citizens United,* was unconvinced; she thus pursued a similar line of inquiry having to do with the circumvention problem.

Kagan: You have a hundred PACs and each of them says that they're going to support ... the five candidates in the most contested Senate races. There are really only five very contested Senate races, and a hundred PACs say that they're going to support those five candidates. So a donor gives $5,000 to each of those PACs, which support those candidates, the PAC divides up the money, $1,000 goes to each candidate. The total, all those PACs, $100,000 goes to each of the Senate candidates in the five most contested races, twenty times what the individual contribution limits allow.

Justice Kagan and the counsel for the appellants went back and forth as the former revised her hypothetical while the latter attempted to refute each new variation of it.

Kagan: Ms. Murphy, can I give another one? There are 150 House candidates with completely safe seats, all right? ... Anybody can contribute $2,600 to each of these candidates, 150 of them, right? So that makes about $400,000. And then these 150 candidates with completely safe seats just transfer all this money to the one person who doesn't have a safe seat. So that's about $400,000. Double it for a primary and a general election, that's about $800,000 that all goes to one candidate from one donor because of the ability for candidates to transfer money to each other.

Murphy: I think even if you accept this scenario where all of these candidates are independently deciding to give all their money to one candidate, you can't have a law that is designed to prevent this one person from circumvention by prohibiting everybody else from engaging in contributions.

Here, the appellants' counsel took direct aim at Kagan's hypothetical with an "overbreadth" argument. Essentially, Murphy characterized the justice's scenario as suggesting that, in order to remedy this rather unique problem, the law would have to restrict many other persons and PACS from expressing their views by giving money to campaigns. Such an attempt would be unduly overbroad in violation of First Amendment principles. At this point, one of the severest critics of many campaign finance laws intervened with baritone vigor.

Scalia: I can't imagine that if you have a PAC which says we're going to give money to Smith, that's bad, but if you have a PAC that says we're going to give all the money that you contribute to us to Smith and Jones, that's okay. Or Smith, Jones, and three others. It seems to me that that's earmarking.

As the intellectual ping-pong continued, the audience's eyes either stared up at the ceiling or down into their laps, so esoteric had the argument become. After Justices Anthony Kennedy, Ruth Bader Ginsburg, and Sonia Sotomayor weighed in, the chief justice leaned into the microphone to make a point, while bending his index finger as if to draw attention to what he was about to say.

Roberts: Ms. Murphy, we haven't talked yet about the effect of the aggregate limits on the ability of donors to give the maximum amount to as many candidates as they want. The effect of the aggregate limits is to limit someone's contribution of the maximum amount to about nine candidates, right?

Murphy: That's right.

Roberts: Is there a way to eliminate that aspect while retaining some of the aggregate limits? In other words, is that a necessary consequence of any way you have aggregate limits? Or are there alternative ways of enforcing the aggregate limitation that don't have that consequence?

This was the sort of query to which savvy lawyers pay attention, if only because the Roberts vote could decide the outcome of the case. Was the chief justice suggesting it might be possible, without invalidating entirely the aggregate contribution restriction, to rule in favor of the appellants? Was he suggesting it might be possible to do so without overruling any aspect of the Court's seminal decision in *Buckley v. Valeo*? If so, did this mean that he was prepared to break ranks with Justices Kennedy, Thomas, and Scalia (all strong *Buckley* critics) and likewise turn a blind eye to Senator McConnell's brief and that of the Cato Institute? For whatever reason, the fair-haired counsel for the appellants did not really pick up the point and develop it beyond saying much more than "aggregate limits in general are always going to have this effect."

Soon enough her time was nearly at its end: "If I may, I'd like to reserve the remainder of my time," said Murphy as she headed for her chair. Now the moment fell to Senator McConnell's counsel to persuade the justices. Enter Bobby R. Burchfield.

Bold & Broad

Burchfield was no stranger to law and politics. Among other things, in 2003 he was one of the counsel who argued in *McConnell v. FEC*. While he had no extensive First Amendment credentials, he nonetheless was familiar with election law and had appeared in administrative hearings before the FEC. The relationship between the First Amendment and limitations on campaign financing had been something he had been pondering for well over a decade. Writing in the *Weekly Standard* in October 1999, he articulated a view that he still held in the case he was about to argue: "*Buckley* made clear that the only governmental interest in campaign finance sufficient to override … First Amendment concerns is the need to prevent 'corruption,' which the Court defined as the giving of dollars for political favors—essentially bribery." And then with rhetorical verve (and some mixed metaphors) he added, "But free speech is not a loophole, it is the oxygen of democracy." That kind of unwavering argument was about to find its way into his remarks to the Court.

> *Burchfield:* Senator McConnell agrees that this aggregate limit does not pass exacting scrutiny. Senator McConnell believes that all restrictions of this nature should be reviewed under strict scrutiny. To begin with, this is a severe restriction on political speech.

Translated: practically speaking, no aggregate limits should be constitutional. While such a bold and broad argument might well appeal to Justices Kennedy, Scalia, and Thomas, could it convince the chief justice and Justice Alito?

Like Murphy before him, Burchfield went the rounds with Justice Kagan as she spun out yet more worst-case scenario hypotheticals. If the Court were to strike down the aggregate limits, she said, an individual could contribute more than $3.5 million "even before I write checks to independent political action committees. Are you going to say that money isn't going to give me influence?" Burchfield held firm. "No," he insisted. Owing to FEC regulations, he stressed, as soon as money leaves a donor's hands "he loses control over it and the person who receives it makes the direction." Kagan was not persuaded. The money goes to a single party, she stressed. Worse still, "the speaker of the House or the Senate majority leader could solicit $3.6 million … and you're telling me there's just no special influence that goes along with that?" Burchfield returned to a theme he had emphasized in his brief: "Well, we know from the *Citizens United* decision, Your Honor, that gratitude and influence are not considered to be quid pro quo corruption."

But was that all that was involved here, mere gratitude and innocent influence? Or was there more by way of subtle forms of quid pro quo? Such questions, in one form or another, underlay much of what went on in the courtroom that day.

A Case for Judicial Restraint?

Justice Samuel Alito much admired the thought of the late Alexander Bickel. "I discovered the writings of Alexander Bickel advocating judicial restraint," Alito wrote in 1985, "and it was largely for this reason that I decided to go to Yale Law School." Bickel, the great constitutional scholar, was a respected defender of judicial self-control. In his much-heralded book *The Least Dangerous Branch*, Bickel maintained that there are certain kinds of cases involving political questions that turn "ultimately on issues that bring into question the very capacity of judicial judgment." During the course of oral arguments in *McCutcheon*, there were several times when echoes of the ghost of Bickel could be heard.

> *Scalia:* This campaign finance law is so intricate that I
> can't figure it out. It might have been nice to have, you know,
> the lower court tell me what the law is.

He was referring to the fact that, given the procedural posture of the case—the plaintiffs sought a motion for a preliminary injunction and the FEC moved for a motion to dismiss—there was no evidentiary hearing. In other words, there was no opportunity to test the "empirical support," as Justice Alito put it, for the "wild hypotheticals" that Justices Breyer and Kagan had posed. This lack of an evidentiary hearing and a full record also troubled at least two other justices.

> *Sotomayor:* I'm a little confused, okay? I'm confused
> because we're talking in the abstract. This decision was based
> on a motion to dismiss. And there is a huge colloquy about
> what happens and doesn't happen. We don't have a record
> below.

> *Breyer:* Justice Sotomayor is saying: I don't know. And I
> don't, either, because there's been no hearing, there's been no
> evidence presented. There is nothing but dismissal.

What all of this pointed to was the possibility of sending the case back to the trial court for a full evidentiary hearing. When this point first surfaced during her main argument, Murphy countered by pointing out that "the government had an opportunity to make a record and it chose to treat this as a legal case," at which point Justice Scalia interrupted and asked somewhat rhetorically, "Ms. Murphy…do we need a record to figure out issues of law?"

Judging from the exchange between the Court and counsel, the matter was not that simple. "As the argument progressed, it became clear," said the former FEC chairman Trevor Potter, "that the justices really don't know enough about money in politics." In his post-argument op-ed in the *Washington Post*, Potter (who had filed an amicus brief in the case) maintained that the "oral argument revealed that the justices could stand to know much more about the realities of campaign finance law and political fundraising. Part of the problem," he stressed, "is that the Roberts Court has less political experience than any group of justices in Supreme Court history." Even so, he argued, this lack of experience did not seem to be of any great moment: "Despite being out of their depth, the justices seem perfectly comfortable being the ones to decide whether to transform the landscape of campaign finance"—a landscape that had once been tended mostly by the legislative branch of government.

If true, campaign finance cases were highly problematic for the Court. And that problem was compounded where, as here, the counsel arguing the case were (to varying degrees) not seasoned experts familiar with the intricacies of campaign finance law and the realities of politics.

By agreeing to hear the *McCutcheon* case, especially given its procedural posture, had the justices entered into forbidding waters? To draw on a passage from Bickel's *The Supreme Court and the Idea of Progress*, "[E]lections are the tip of the iceberg; the bulk of the political process is below." As the arguments in *McCutcheon* suggested, the deeper the justices dove, the more some of them sensed that there was indeed something gigantic below the iceberg's tip.

The Stealthy Solicitor General

"It's conventional wisdom in some circles," wrote Lincoln Caplan in the *New York Times*, "that [Donald] Verrilli is a fumbling lawyer who can't hold his own at the Supreme Court." For those who doubted that assessment, they needed to look no further than his tax argument in the 2012 Health Care Case in which the chief justice borrowed more than a leaf to fashion his opinion and provide the crucial fifth vote. Could Verrilli repeat that feat?

The justices interrupted Verrilli fifty-one times during the course of his arguments in *McCutcheon*. Unflappable, he marched on with his points, always ready to deflect anything thrown at him. He began by emphasizing what he saw as the extreme nature of the appellants' position.

> **Verrilli:** Now, the appellants in this case have tried to present the case as though the issue were whether there were some corrupting potential in giving a contribution to the nineteenth candidate after someone has already contributed the maximum to the eighteenth. But that is not what this case is about. The appellants are not arguing that the aggregate limit is drawn in the wrong place. They are arguing that there can be no aggregate limit because the base contribution limits do all the work.

The solicitor general was but a minute and twenty seconds into his argument when the chief justice interrupted him to ask a question:

> **Roberts:** The current system, the way the anti-aggregation system works, is he's got to choose. Is he going to express his belief in environmental regulation by donating to more than nine people there? Or is he going to choose the gun control issue?

After some back-and-forth with the chief justice, Verrilli conceded that "the aggregate limit would have the effect of restricting the ability of a contributor to make the maximum contribution to more than a certain number of candidates. That's true. We can't help but acknowledge that. It's math." That said, Verrilli added, Shaun McCutcheon could "spend as much of his considerable fortune as he wants" provided that he did so by way of "independent expenditures advocating the [election of] these candidates."

Eager to weigh in, Justice Scalia took exception: "And that does not … evoke any gratitude on the part of the people? I mean, if gratitude is corruption, you know, don't those independent expenditures evoke gratitude? And is not the evil of big money—$3.2 million, an individual can give that to an independent PAC and spend it, right?"

Later on, other justices pursued the same point, trying to get the solicitor general to flesh out his notion of corruption. What exactly was it? At what exact point did it occur? How exactly is this to be judged? Now the conservatives were spinning the hypotheticals by way of question after question.

> **Kennedy:** You have … two persons. One person gives an amount to a candidate that's limited. The other takes out ads, uncoordinated, just all on his own, costing $500,000. Don't you think that second person has more access to the candidate who's … successful, than the first? I think that was at the root of Justice Scalia's question.

Trying his best, Verrilli resorted to an analogy in order to better explain his point. "If somebody thinks the secretary of defense is doing a great job," he said, "they can take out an ad in the *Washington Post*, spend $500,000 on that ad saying, 'The secretary of defense has done a great job.'" That would be permissible. By contrast, he continued, the same person could not give "the secretary of defense a Maserati," which would certainly not be protected expression. The Maserati example did not serve him well, as Justice Alito both expressed skepticism and inquired further into the question of how *exactly* corruption or undue influence was to be determined.

> **Alito:** Unless the money is transferred to—you have to get it from the person who wants to corrupt to the person who

is going to be corrupted. And unless the money can make it from A to B, I don't see where the quid pro quo argument is.… [J]ust take this example: you have somebody who wants to corrupt a member of the House, and this person's strategy is to make contributions to multiple House candidates with the hope, the expectation, the plan that those candidates are going to transfer the money to the member that this person wants to corrupt. Now, how is that person going to accomplish that given the earmarking regulations, and the limits on how much one member can contribute to another?

Much as he had done in the *Citizens United* case, Samuel Alito raised questions that made it difficult for the government to maintain its position. Still, the solicitor general tried.

> **Verrilli:** [I]n *McConnell* and in *Colorado Republican*, this Court said that earmarking is not the outer limit of the government's authority to regulate here. And the reason the Court said that is because a lot of this can be done with winks and nods and subtly. And so I don't think it's the case that earmarking would work to prohibit that.

Even the liberal justices sensed that the government's position was a hard one to defend in light of the hypotheticals that had just been raised.

> **Breyer:** So what would you think? I was just listening to your dialogue, and you heard—this is pretty tough, we try to construct some hypotheticals, and the counsel says, 'Oh, I've got this part wrong or that part wrong or the other one,' and they may be right. And we can't do this, figuring out all these factual things in an hour, frankly.

Unable to resolve such difficulties, an exasperated Justice Breyer asked, "So what do you think about going into these matters in a district court where the evidentiary aspects of them can be explored at some length?" Meanwhile, Chief Justice Roberts and Justices Scalia and Alito, seemingly averse to Breyer's suggestion, continued to pepper the SG with yet more perplexing challenges.

> *Scalia:* It seems to me fanciful to think that the sense of gratitude that an individual senator or congressman is going to feel because of a substantial contribution to the Republican National Committee or the Democratic National Committee is any greater than the sense of gratitude that a senator or congressman will feel to a PAC which is spending an enormous amount of money in his district or in his state for his election.
>
> *Verrilli:* Well, Justice Scalia, I am not here to debate the question of whether or not the [*Buckley*] Court's jurisprudence is correct with respect to the risk of corruption from independent expenditures.

In light of that, Justice Kennedy made an observation that some may have understood as self-evident and others may have taken as snide—but a remark with notable implications, nonetheless.

> *Kennedy:* I'm coming off the bench with the understanding that your answer is: *Buckley* has settled the issue; no more discussion necessary.

Though it seemed clear, the comment was ambiguous. On the one hand, was Justice Kennedy saying no more than that Verrilli viewed *Buckley*'s contribution-expenditure dichotomy as determinative for the *McCutcheon* case because aggregate limits fall on the contributions side of the constitutional ledger? Accordingly, end of case? On the other hand, did his comment portend much more? Given Scalia's hypothetical scenario, was Kennedy suggesting that *Buckley*'s dichotomy was nonsensical and thus should be scuttled? Unwilling to leave the dialogue there, Justice Kagan weighed in.

> *Kagan:* I suppose that if this Court is having second thoughts about its rulings, that independent expenditures are

not corrupting, we can change that part of the law.

Verrilli: And far be it from me to suggest that you don't, Your Honor.

Beyond the laughter that this exchange provoked, there was another subtle point: the real problem with *Buckley* was that it had not appreciated the functional similarity in corruptive potential for both contributions and independent expenditures. Notably, Justices Kennedy and Kagan posited they be treated the same. But for Kennedy, sound jurisprudence would require that both be deregulated; for Kagan, sound jurisprudence would permit both to be regulated.

Erin Murphy, though eager to respond, was calm in her manner when it came to her rebuttal argument. She arose, approached the lectern, and added her own finishing touches to the Scalia-Kennedy-Kagan-Verrilli exchange.

> **Murphy:** What we're really hearing today is a corruption argument. But as the questioning revealed, once you accept the corruption theory that the Government is putting forward here, there really isn't a way to continue to draw a line between independent expenditures and the $3-point million check to all of these different individuals that is in small-based, limited amounts. Because there's certainly going to be just as much gratitude to the individual who spends $3.6 million directly supporting one candidate through ads on that candidate's behalf.

With that, the matter was submitted at 11:02 A.M.

Portrayals & Predictions

"Obviously, I would have argued the case differently; I am a different person with a different style. I also have considerable experience," James Bopp said a week after the Supreme Court hearing. Three months later, he spoke more pointedly: "The justices got little help from Ms. Murphy.... [They] were extremely aggressive and bullied her, perhaps because she lacked detailed campaign finance experience." Nonetheless, Bopp was willing to speculate that as to the appellants' likely success in the suit: "It appears a majority will strike down all the aggregate limits, but will do so on narrow grounds."

And then there was the press. How the oral arguments came to be seen in the legal community and beyond depended much on how a handful of reporters presented those exchanges to the public. Members of the Supreme Court press corps sat to the left of the bench in rows facing the guest section. From that perch, they took notes. Some ventured predictions about the outcome.

Lyle Denniston, the eighty-one-year-old reporter who has covered the Court for fifty-five years, saw much confusion in the arguments. "At times, it sounded as if it were a debate that one might hear in Congress on potential new campaign finance legislation, rather than a courtroom debate over the limits of the First Amendment as applied to campaign contributions." The SCOTUSblog reporter then posed a question, which he promptly answered: "Will the Court start all over with the issue of limiting campaign contributions, as it did four years ago with independent campaign spending, opening the money floodgates further? Maybe, but there was almost nothing heard in Court on Tuesday that would suggest any such boldness."

Pete Williams of MSNBC echoed Denniston when he predicted with a flair of near certainty that the Court would *not* strike down "all limits" on campaign giving. "That's not going to happen," he stressed. He then elaborated: "It did seem…that [Shaun McCutcheon's] view is going to prevail. At the very least, there seemed to be five votes for the proposition that you ought to be able to give as much money as you like to as many candidates as you want." In that regard, Williams speculated that the chief justice would be the "key vote."

Dahlia Lithwick of *Slate* couched her view in her characteristic, impious way: "Chief Justice John Roberts appears to be the lone justice truly struggling to find some middle position between a constitutional speech right for billionaires seeking to purchase their own Personal Pan Politician and the genuine restriction on speech that follows when you allow someone to contribute to nine separate campaigns but not a tenth."

Adam Liptak, a reporter for the *New York Times* who had once been a First Amendment lawyer at Cahill Gordon & Reindel (Floyd Abrams' firm), noted that the Roberts Court had been "consistently hostile to campaign finance limits in its half-dozen decisions in argued cases on the subject so far. The five more conservative justices have voted together in all of those cases, though Chief Justice Roberts and Justice Alito have taken a more incremental approach than the bolder one called for by Justices Scalia, Kennedy, and Clarence Thomas." In this scenario, the votes to watch were those of the chief justice and Justice Alito.

Whatever the vote, Marcia Coyle of the *National Law Journal* suggested that McCutcheon's critics would be disappointed: "The worst fears of campaign finance reformers played out in real time on Tuesday in the U.S. Supreme Court as a majority of justices appeared inclined to make another major inroad on the regulation of money in elections."

Beyond the armchair predictions and court reporting digestible for lay audiences, there was a technical constitutional point that was of considerable interest to First Amendment lawyers and election officials—did a majority of the justices think that a demanding level of judicial scrutiny should be used in order to decide this case? If the Court were, for example, to use "strict scrutiny" in *McCutcheon*, it would establish a precedent that would make it very difficult, if not practically impossible, to uphold most restrictions on campaign contributions. A few seasoned First Amendment lawyers noticed that the justices were surprisingly silent on this point. Not once during the 13,000-plus words spoken during the arguments did any of the nine justices ever mention the phrase "strict scrutiny." Bobby Burchfield was all too aware of that omission. "The justices' silence on this matter," he said, "left me somewhat less confident that they were likely to adopt our view and use strict scrutiny." Of course, he could still win his case without such exacting review, but a "big win" is every appellate lawyer's dream.

Cartoons & the Specter of Immortality

Sitting where he was in the second row of the public seating section, Shaun McCutcheon had a good view of how his lawyer handled his case, how the government challenged his position, and how the justices responded to it all. "I heard a lot of great ideas," he told Tom Ashbrook of *On Point* radio. "I was very impressed with the Court and the process," he added. Others, however, were not as kind in their assessment of what went on during oral arguments.

As the day wore on, more and more commentary about the case came from more and more quarters. During a press conference that day, President Barack Obama once again took issue with the Court, much as he had done in his 2010 State of the Union Address when he criticized the *Citizens United* ruling. "The latest case would go even further than *Citizens United*," he said. "It would say anything goes: there are no rules in terms of how to finance campaigns." Some thought it was political hyperbole, while others viewed it as a credible prediction.

Tom Toles, the Pulitzer Prize winning political cartoonist for the *Washington Post*, wasn't making any predictions; he was too busy being sardonic. Two days after the *McCutcheon* arguments, the *Post* published a Toles cartoon with a lone Justice standing in front of the Court armed with a gavel. Above the building's majestic columns were inscribed the words, "A Government of the Rich, by the Rich, and for the Rich." Echoing what the round-faced Justice had remarked in oral arguments, a bubble caption read: "It is what it is." And below that, in big bold letters, there was this: "The Scalia Doctrine." By way of a final comic salvo, there was a retort at the bottom right of the cartoon—"It sure isn't what it used to be."

Seemingly indifferent to it all, the justices met in private conference the next day (Wednesday, October 9) to vote on the case, or at least to decide what to do with it. Absent a leak, which was extremely rare, no one will know anything about what went on that day at conference until the justices' papers become public decades later. The public would, however, have a good idea of what went on once the Court handed down its opinion in *McCutcheon*, which was still a while away.

Meanwhile, Shaun McCutcheon was already celebrating. On October 23, 2013, the U.S. Court of Appeals for the Second Circuit struck down a state law limiting the amount of contributions to independent committees to $150,000 per year. The New York Progress and Protection PAC challenged the law. According to a spokesman for the PAC, McCutcheon had

MoveOn.org sent out this cartoon on February 21, 2014, warning of the effects of a Supreme Court ruling in favor of Shaun McCutcheon and the Republican National Committee. Designed by Revolution Messaging for MoveOn.org Civic Action

pledged to contribute at least $200,000 to the group in its effort to back local conservatives including Joseph J. Lhota, the Republican nominee for mayor of New York City (who ultimately lost to Democrat Bill de Blasio). Though he was not a named plaintiff, the ruling in *New York Progress and Protection PAC v. Walsh* was still a victory for the cause McCutcheon was backing. "I am very pleased that another court has decided to rule in favor of free speech," is how he expressed his joy to a *New York Times* reporter.

Though McCutcheon had no sure idea at the time, the New York ruling was an omen of things to come.

7. The Ruling

THE CHILL of a dreadful winter had vanished. Spring had finally come to the nation's capital. Though it was much warmer, a gloomy gray hung over the city, preventing the sun's morning rays from glistening on the Supreme Court's majestic marble. It was Wednesday, April 2, 2014. At about four minutes after 10:00 A.M., Chief Justice John Roberts made an announcement. In a clear and crisp voice, he declared: "I have the judgment of the Court this morning in case 12-536, *McCutcheon versus Federal Election Commission*." Solicitor General Donald Verrilli and his staff sat at the front of the bar section listening with great attention as the chief justice began to speak.

It took the justices 175 days to decide the matter. And now, only a few moments after the announcement, the news was being shared with the world by way of Amy Howe's post on SCOTUSblog, aided by Lyle Denniston, the blog's reporter in the pressroom at the Court. "The Court rules in the chief's opinion that the aggregate limits do not further the permissible government interest in preventing quid pro quo corruption or the appearance of such corruption," she wrote. The vote: 5–4. The majority consisted of the chief justice and Justices Antonin Scalia, Anthony Kennedy, Samuel Alito, and Clarence Thomas, who wrote a separate concurrence. Justice Stephen Breyer dissented and was joined by Justices Ruth Bader Ginsburg, Elena Kagan, and Sonia Sotomayor.

It was the eleventh opinion the chief justice had written explaining the judgment of the Court in a First Amendment free expression case. This one, however, was not a majority opinion, but a plurality. Even so, the *McCutcheon* ruling was another significant decision that bore Roberts's name. Since coming to the Court, John Roberts authored more such majority opinions than any of his colleagues—more than twice as many. Like Justices Oliver Wendell Holmes, Louis Brandeis, Hugo Black, and William Brennan, his name was becoming synonymous with the First Amendment. But unlike the liberal heroes of times past, several of his free expression rulings greatly appeased conservatives while greatly appalling liberals. And that was certainly true of his plurality opinion in *McCutcheon v. FEC*, yet another First Amendment campaign finance case in which the Court divided 5–4.

The Plurality Opinion—the Pillars of Democracy

The chief justice began his forty-page plurality opinion on a high rhetorical note: "There is no right more basic in our democracy than the right to participate in electing our political leaders." From that democratic high ground, he proceeded to build his First Amendment case against the aggregate contribution limits that McCutcheon attacked.

Essentially, Chief Justice Roberts's plurality opinion was constructed on four conceptual pillars—moving steadily from 1) retention of much of the Court's 1976 decision in *Buckley v. Valeo*, to 2) rejection of that precedent for purposes of deciding *McCutcheon*'s specific challenges, to 3) resistance against any broad concept of systemic corruption that can be constitutionally regulated by government, and to 4) reversal of the federal district court's ruling. In the end, Shaun McCutcheon was victorious. FECA's aggregate contribution limitations, which placed a cap on the total amount of money that he could give to candidates and political committees, were declared to be facially unconstitutional. Let us look more closely at those conceptual pillars:

1. **Retaining *Buckley*.** The *McCutcheon* decision did *not* require the Court to revisit several key components of the ruling in *Buckley v. Valeo*. Since McCutcheon challenged only FECA's aggregate contribution ceiling, the Court did not need to reexamine either *Buckley*'s distinction between the First Amendment treatment of contribution and expenditure limitations or the difference in standards of review applied to examine their constitutionality.

Aggregate contribution limits failed under either strict scrutiny or the less rigorous "closely drawn" review test, Roberts explained, so the justices refused to "parse the differences between the two standards in this case." Moreover, the Court declined to reexamine FECA's base contribution limitations restricting the amounts that can be given to a single candidate or political committee within an election cycle. In this respect, the plurality opinion distanced itself from Justice Thomas's bold concurring opinion, which argued for the unconstitutionality of all contribution limitations, whether base or aggregate.

2. **Rejecting *Buckley*.** By contrast, the *McCutcheon* decision *did* require the Court to reevaluate the constitutionality of FECA's aggregate contribution limitations. Although the cap on total contributions given in an election cycle was originally upheld in *Buckley*, the majority did not feel bound by the force of that precedent. The *Buckley* per curiam opinion itself recognized that the constitutionality of the aggregate ceiling "ha[d] not been separately addressed at length by the parties." Moreover, Roberts stressed that the Court had analyzed the validity of the total contribution cap in a cursory manner, in only "one paragraph of its 139-page opinion." Accordingly, the chief justice declared, "[T]his case cannot be resolved merely by pointing to three sentences in *Buckley* that were written without the benefit of full briefing or argument on the issue." Rather, the appellants' "substantial First Amendment challenge to the system of aggregate limits currently in place" merited "plenary consideration."

3. **Narrow notion of corruption.** In assessing the First Amendment interests at stake in *McCutcheon*, the Court emphasized that the proper focus was on "the individual's right to engage in political speech" and association, rather than the dissenting justices' focus on a "collective" or "generalized conception of the public good." As Chief Justice Roberts put it succinctly, the "dissent's 'collective speech' reflected in laws is of course the will of the majority, and plainly can include laws that restrict free speech. The whole point of the First Amendment is to afford individuals protection

against such infringements." Given the correct focus, an "aggregate limit on *how many* candidates and committees an individual may support through contributions is not a 'modest restraint' at all. The Government may no more restrict how many candidates or causes a donor may support than it may tell a newspaper how many candidates it may endorse." Then turning to the constitutionally tolerable justifications for contribution regulations, the plurality strongly reaffirmed the Court's earlier position—the perspective found in *Federal Election Commission v. National Conservative Political Action Committee* (1985), *Davis v. Federal Election Commission* (2008), and *Arizona Free Enterprise Club's Freedom Club PAC v. Bennett* (2011)—that "preventing corruption or the appearance of corruption" was the only legitimate governmental interest to be served. And that concept of corruption must be narrowly understood as "*quid pro quo* corruption," not some broader one of systemic corruption. "No matter how desirable it may seem," Roberts continued, "it is not an acceptable governmental objective to 'level the playing field,' or to 'level electoral opportunities,' or to 'equaliz[e] the financial resources of candidates." Furthermore, "because the Government's interest in preventing the appearance of corruption is equally confined to the appearance of *quid pro quo* corruption," the chief justice concluded, "the Government may not seek to limit the appearance of mere influence or access." By this rationale, the *McCutcheon* Court firmly rejected the dissent's notion of acceptable governmental regulation to prevent pervasive political influence, the kind of influence that an individual might procure by contributing to an unlimited number of candidates and political committees. "The line between *quid pro quo* corruption and general influence may seem vague at times, but the distinction must be respected in order to safeguard basic First Amendment rights," the plurality opinion stressed.

4. **Preventing circumvention**. The *McCutcheon* decision reversed the district court's judgment that, as a "loophole-closing" measure to prevent circumvention of base contribution limitations,

the aggregate contribution ceiling furthered the legitimate objective of stemming quid pro quo corruption and was therefore facially constitutional. "If there is no corruption concern in giving nine candidates up to $5,200 each," Chief Justice Roberts reasoned, "there is no risk that additional candidates will be corrupted by donations of up to $5,200." Even understanding the aggregate limits as aiming only to prevent circumvention of the base limits, he continued, "The problem is that they do not serve that function in any meaningful way." The primary example of circumvention would be a donor "who channels 'massive amounts of money'" to a single political candidate "through a series of contributions to PACs that have stated their intention to support" the candidate. But the plurality opinion considered this example, and others like it, to be "far too speculative." As Roberts explained, "Various earmarking and anti-proliferation rules disarm this example." Among other things, he called on FECA's anti-proliferation rule that prohibits donors from "creating or controlling multiple affiliated political committees," and FEC regulations that further limit "the opportunities for circumvention of the base limits via 'unearmarked contributions to political committees likely to contribute' to a particular candidate." With such "targeted anti-circumvention measures in place today, the indiscriminate aggregate contribution limits...appear particularly heavy-handed."

In effect, the *McCutcheon* Court held that "the aggregate limits violate the First Amendment because they are not 'closely drawn' to avoid unnecessary abridgement" of a political contributor's expressive and associational freedoms. Lastly, the plurality justices pointed to "multiple alternatives available to Congress that would serve the Government's anti-circumvention interest, while avoiding unnecessary abridgement of First Amendment rights"—measures such as "targeted restrictions on transfers among candidates and political committees." After all, if transfers "are the key to the Government's concern about circumvention," then they can be more directly addressed without unduly interfering with First Amendment rights.

Some Rhetorical Flourish

Beyond the central conceptual pillars for its decision, the *McCutcheon* plurality opinion framed its trenchant analysis with rhetorical force. Conceding that the government's goal in reducing the amount of money in politics might be attractive to many, Chief Justice Roberts reminded us: "Money in politics may at times seem repugnant to some, but so too does much of what the First Amendment vigorously protects. If the First Amendment protects flag burning, funeral protests, and Nazi parades—despite the profound offense such spectacles cause—it surely protects political campaign speech despite popular opposition." In conclusion, he tied the right of constituents "to support candidates who share their views and concerns" to the "very concept of self-governance through elected officials." Accordingly, the aggregate contribution limitations "intrude without justification on a citizen's ability to exercise 'the most fundamental First Amendment activities.'"

§ § §

The importance of a Supreme Court victory to Shaun McCutcheon was palpably felt in his own words: "I feel like it is a big win for me," he said upon hearing of the ruling. But the significance of the High Court's decision extended much further, and to legal and political consequences of a far greater measure. Among other ramifications, several loom large:

- **The integrity of the *Buckley* First Amendment framework.** In the thirty-eight years since the Supreme Court's decision in *Buckley v. Valeo*, its basic First Amendment framework for campaign finance regulation—all contribution limitations survive, all expenditure limitations fail—was never seriously threatened. But the win for McCutcheon has put into question the ultimate integrity of that structure. For the first time, the Supreme Court invalidated on its face a FECA provision regulating contributions, one that had been upheld as constitutional in the *Buckley* decision itself (even conceding the brevity of the per curiam analysis). Although Chief

Justice Roberts's plurality opinion was careful not to revisit the constitutionality of FECA's base contribution limitations to political candidates, committees, and parties, the *Buckley* wall between contributions and expenditures, nonetheless, has been breached. One must wonder whether the plurality justices will agree to revisit the constitutionality of the base contribution limitations in a future case, taking up Justice Thomas's invitation to overturn *Buckley*'s First Amendment dichotomy altogether.

- **The illegitimacy of a systemic meaning of political corruption.** The win for Shaun McCutcheon put the last nail in the coffin of any First Amendment–sanctioned concept of systemic political corruption. A solid majority of the Supreme Court justices now has ruled that the *only* legitimate justification for campaign finance regulation is prevention of political corruption narrowly understood—that is, quid pro quo corruption of a candidate virtually akin to bribery. What the current Court will not countenance, then, is any governmental campaign finance regulation directed not solely at the corruption of individual officeholders, but more expansively at the corruption of institutions of government. With such jurisprudential hostility to the prevention of generalized political influence—the kind that is garnered with widespread campaign contributions and expenditures— the future of meaningful and effective campaign finance reform is severely compromised. More immediately, the continuing constitutional viability of BCRA's limitations on "soft money" contributions to political parties is put into serious question. The Supreme Court upheld those restraints in *McConnell v. Federal Election Commission* (2003) on the rationale that a "soft money" donor could buy excessive political influence. By definition, however, such donations cannot be earmarked for a particular candidate, and so will fall outside the purview of quid pro quo corruption. *Citizens United* destroyed one-half of the *McConnell* edifice; it seems only a matter of time before another case demolishes the second half.
- **The rise of "*Citizens United 2*."** *McCutcheon v. FEC* has been popularly billed as "*Citizens United 2*." A majority of the justices lifted the lid on aggregate contributions with respect to Shaun McCutcheon,

the individual. He is now free to donate to as many candidates and political committees as he wishes to support, provided that he observes (at least for the time being) the legal limit imposed for his contributions to each one. The reasoning of the Court's decision will not stop with McCutcheon and other aggressive and generous individual political donors like him. When it comes to political campaign spending, *Citizens United* put corporations and labor unions on the same First Amendment plane as individuals. If there is no total cap on contributions for Shaun McCutcheon and his ilk, there can be no such limitation for corporations or unions either. Eyes will turn to future elections to see whether and how much more money will roll.

Notable as all of this was, it was not enough to please the First Amendment appetite of one the Court's staunchest critics of campaign finance reform.

The Concurring Opinion—"Another Missed Opportunity"

Justice Clarence Thomas is well known for his near-absolutist views of the First Amendment when it comes to matters such as corporate speech, commercial speech, and campaign finance laws. Though he agreed with the result in the case, the justice from Pin Point, Georgia, was critical of the timidity of his fellow conservatives in failing to squarely overrule *Buckley*. "This case represents yet another missed opportunity to right the course of our campaign finance jurisprudence by restoring a standard that is faithful to the First Amendment. Until we undertake that reexamination, we remain in a 'halfway house' of our own design.'"

Briefs like those submitted by James Bopp on behalf of the RNC and the one submitted by Ilya Shapiro on behalf of the Cato Institute had attempted to push the Court in the constitutional direction desired by Justice Thomas. It was a direction that Thomas had long urged and once again reiterated in *McCutcheon*: "The Court's decision in *Buckley v. Valeo* denigrates core First Amendment speech and should be overruled." While it seemed that Justices Kennedy and Scalia (and perhaps Alito) once agreed with that proposition, now he stood alone, much as he had done in the *Citizens United* case.

In the end, Justice Thomas regretted that "the plurality does not acknowledge" that its decision, "although purporting not to over-rule *Buckley*, continues to chip away at its footings." Of course, perhaps that was just the stratagem—chip away at *Buckley* much the same way the conservative Court had chipped away at two of its most famous and controversial rulings, *Miranda v. Arizona* (1966) and *Roe v. Wade* (1973). If that were to occur, what Thomas lost in the short run would be gained in the long run.

The Dissent—Reply to the "Devastating" Attack on Campaign Finance Reform

Writing in his 2005 book, *Active Liberty*, Justice Stephen Breyer emphasized how difficult campaign finance issues are: "The inquiry is complex." And so it was, as evidenced by his forty-three-page dissent in *McCutcheon*. Prior to that case, he had written one majority opinion and two plurality opinions in the First Amendment area of campaign finance law. Notably, in *Randall v. Sorrell* (2006), all five members of the conservative wing of the Court joined him in the judgment, with Justices Stevens, Souter, and Ginsburg dissenting. But now in *McCutcheon*, the liberal wing was with him, albeit in dissent.

Before Justice Breyer summarized his dissent in the courtroom, and just before his opinion had been publicly disseminated, Chief Justice Roberts took a moment in his own delivery to be kind. "There's a thoughtful dissent today," he said, one that compelled the majority to think through its arguments. And as Mark Walsh recounted for SCOTUSblog: "At this moment, Justice Stephen G. Breyer turns to his neighbor on his right, Justice Sonia Sotomayor, and gives a wry smile." But that smile was fleeting.

Justice Breyer's steely dissent hinged on four basic charges:

1. **Abdicating judicial restraint.** Complexity is a matter best left to lawmakers and administrators, not judges. That, at least, was the view that Breyer espoused. What was most problematic about the Court's ruling was that it "substitute[d] judges' understandings

of how the political process works for the understanding of Congress." Because of that, the majority justices "fail[ed] to recognize the difference between influence resting upon public opinion and influence bought by money alone." And because of that they ventured to overturn key precedents, this while creating "huge loopholes in the law." All in all, what they did "undermines, perhaps devastates, what remains of campaign finance reform." Thus understood, *McCutcheon* was a case of brazen judicial activism, rather than a case of judicial modesty, a modesty that is duly deferential to the majority will as expressed in congressional legislation.

2. **Misjudging the facts and their significance.** Justice Breyer is a jurist who favors judicial balancing; some think he favors it too much. On that score, he argued that the majority's view of things was just that, meaning no more than its own isolated understanding of the political process. It was "not a record-based view of the facts." For Breyer, the majority justices, unlike their predecessors, seemed uninterested in the factual record: "In the past, when evaluating the constitutionality of campaign finance restrictions, we have typically relied upon an evidentiary record amassed below to determine whether the law served a compelling governmental objective." That problem was compounded by what the dissenters characterized as "faulty" legal analysis that "misconstrues the nature of the competing constitutional interests at stake. It understates the importance of protecting the political integrity of our governmental institutions. It creates a loophole that will allow a single individual to contribute millions of dollars to a political party or to a candidate's campaign." When placed alongside *Citizens United*, the *McCutcheon* case left lawmakers "incapable of dealing with the grave problems of democratic legitimacy that [campaign finance] laws were intended to resolve."

3. **Corrupting the anti-corruption principle**. While all the justices (or at least eight of them, not counting Justice Thomas) agreed that the anti-corruption principle was an important governmental interest worthy of respect, they disagreed considerably on how that principle should be applied. For Breyer, the plurality

had defined corruption "too narrowly." That legal concept was "a far broader, more important interest than the plurality acknowledges. It is an interest in maintaining the integrity of our public governmental institutions. And it is an interest rooted in the Constitution and in the First Amendment itself." By that measure, it was a principle that had been given short shrift in *McCutcheon*.

4. **Changing the rules in major ways.** "Before today's decision," wrote Breyer, "the total size of Rich Donor's check to the Joint Party Committee was capped at $74,600—the aggregate limit for donations to political parties over a two-year election cycle. After today's decision, Rich Donor can write a single check to the Joint Party Committee in an amount of about $1.2 million." He then asked and answered three rhetorical questions:

- "Will political parties seek these large checks? Why not?"
- "Will party officials and candidates solicit these large contributions from wealthy donors? Absolutely."
- "Will elected officials be particularly grateful to the large donor, feeling obliged to provide him special access and influence, and perhaps even a quid pro quo legislative favor?" Yes ... or at least that is "what we have previously believed."

This last point was aptly captured by Justice Breyer earlier when he made a remark in the course of reading the summary of his dissent in open court: "If the Court in *Citizens United* opened a door, today's decision may well open a floodgate," he declared. Or to draw on what may well become the most quoted line of Breyer's dissent: "Where enough money calls the tune, the general public will not be heard."

Instant Commentary

Reformists and Their Critics

It took less than half an hour before Democracy 21, the liberal group defending campaign finance reforms, posted its reaction to the *McCutcheon* ruling. The group's press release had the following banner:

SUPREME COURT CONTINUED TODAY ON ITS MARCH
TO DESTROY THE NATION'S CAMPAIGN FINANCE LAWS
ENACTED TO PREVENT CORRUPTION

Commenting on behalf of Democracy 21, Fred Wertheimer, its president, spoke in striking terms: "The Supreme Court in the *McCutcheon* decision today overturned forty years of national policy and thirty-eight years of judicial precedent to strike down the overall limits on the total contributions from an individual to federal candidates and to party committees in an election cycle. With its decision today in *McCutcheon*," he added, "the Supreme Court majority continued on its march to destroy the nation's campaign finance laws, which were enacted to prevent corruption and protect the integrity of our democracy." As he saw, the bad had just gotten worse: "With its *Citizens United* and *McCutcheon* decisions, the Supreme Court has turned our representative system of government into a sandbox for America's billionaires and millionaires to play in."

Erwin Chemerinsky, dean of the University of California at Irvine Law School and critic of the Roberts Court's campaign finance rulings, opined that *McCutcheon* was "not surprising, though it was deeply troubling." Thankful that the majority did not go as far as Justice Thomas had recommended, he nonetheless felt that the Court had "widely opened the door to challenges to federal, state, and local campaign finance laws. The Court emphasized the extent to which contributions are a form of speech and stressed the need for proof that any restriction serves to prevent corruption or the appearance of corruption." Such proof, of course, would be difficult to tender. "The result," Chemerinsky pointed out, "is likely to be many more challenges and many more rulings invalidating campaign finance laws of all types."

"Help." That is how New York University law professor Burt Neuborne began an op-ed he authored for a SCOTUSblog symposium on *McCutcheon*. "American democracy," wrote the founding legal director of the Brennan Center for Justice, "is trapped in a sealed box built by the Supreme Court. As the *McCutcheon* decision demonstrates, five justices are slowly but surely pumping the air out of the box."

§ § §

On the other side of the ideological divide, the James Madison Center for Free Speech, a conservative group largely opposed to campaign finance reforms, saw matters quite differently. It happily quoted Reince Priebus, chairman of the Republican National Committee (one of the appellants in *McCutcheon*): "'Today's decision is an important first step toward restoring the voice of candidates and party committees and a vindication for all those who support robust, transparent political discourse. I am pleased that the Court agreed that limits on how many candidates or committees a person may support unconstitutionally burden core First Amendment political activities. When free speech is allowed to flourish, our democracy is stronger.'"

James Bopp, the man who helped found the Center and also represented the RNC in its brief to the Supreme Court, was pleased. Recall that this was the man who first brought the *McCutcheon* case to a federal district court. And he was the one who filed the Supreme Court petition for review in the case. Though the Court had not gone as far as he had wished, it was still another win for Bopp and his cause. "This is a great triumph for the First Amendment," he said in the Center's press release. "This is also a great victory for political parties," he added, "who have been disadvantaged recently by the rise of Super PACs. Political parties serve vital purposes, such as tempering polarization, and this is a step in the right direction to re-empower them."

The libertarian folks at the Cato Institute were likewise happy, although not enthusiastically jubilant, if only because a majority of the justices had not embraced the arguments that the Institute advanced in its amicus brief (though Justice Thomas did so in his concurrence). Ilya Shapiro viewed the holding in the case as both straightforward and predictable. "Despite the 5–4 split among the justices, *McCutcheon* is an easy case if you apply well-settled law." What made it easy for him was the fact that "restrictions on the total amount an individual may donate to candidates and party committees—as opposed to how much he can donate to any one candidate—violate the First Amendment because they do not prevent quid pro quo corruption or the appearance thereof." And it was precisely that corruption-prevention rationale that was the "only government interest that the Supreme Court accepts as a valid one for restricting political-campaign activities." Nonetheless, he preferred Justice Thomas's bolder approach. Or as he summed it all up: "In a truly free society, people should be able to give whatever they want to whomever they choose, including candidates for public office. The Supreme Court today correctly struck down the biennial campaign contribution limits and gave those who contribute money to candidates and parties as much freedom as those who spend independently to promote campaigns and causes. But it should have gone further."

Three First Amendment Litigators

Joel Gora, the Brooklyn Law School professor who had been involved in campaign finance cases on behalf of the ACLU back to the time he argued *Buckley*, took a more analytical look at things: "For my money, the impact of the *McCutcheon* decision may be more modest than its detractors fear or perhaps its supporters hope. The Court left the *Buckley* analytic architecture firmly in place, with the distinction between contributions and expenditures still firmly intact and the validity of base contributions on amounts given to candidates and parties almost completely unquestioned." So what was new? Here he pointed out that "the Court insisted on rigorous justification for the continued *aggregate* limits and found such rationales wanting, and on less drastic alternatives to avoiding circumvention of the base limits available." In addition, although the Court had not overruled that "portion of *Buckley* which had upheld the aggregate limits of forty years ago," it had nonetheless gone to lengths to "carefully explain that intervening enactments by Congress and regulations by the Federal Election Commission had created significant safeguards against circumvention so that the aggregate limitations no longer served the kind of vital purpose the First Amendment demands." By way of a reformist nod, Gora suggested, "The lifting of some statutory restraints on campaign funding may actually stir some serious thinking in Congress about ways to reform the campaign finance system so as to enhance and support the funding of political speech, rather than demonize and demean such activity."

And then there was Floyd Abrams, the nation's leading First Amendment lawyer and the man who had argued in defense of the First Amendment in several major campaign finance cases. As he saw it, the ruling was "sound and solid" and took "full account of the continuing need to protect political expression from the single entity the First Amendment identifies as the most obvious and most dangerous potential source of censorship of that speech: the Congress." Of course, there was a downside, too. "Like other decisions protecting First Amendment interests," he stressed, "it will be condemned by many and misunderstood by more. But a country, as the Court observes, that protects flag-burning, funeral protests, and Nazi parades, can surely provide broad protection to speech urging the election of people to public office."

It did not take long for the public condemnation of which Abrams spoke to become a reality. That reality became manifest at 5:00 P.M. EST as Abrams squared off against Harvard law professor Larry Lessig, the man who called for both a constitutional convention and a constitutional amendment to overrule rulings such as *Buckley, Citizens United,* and now *McCutcheon.* The event was a podcast exchange hosted by the National Constitutional Center in Philadelphia with Jeffrey Rosen, its president and CEO, moderating.

Bobby Burchfield, the victorious RNC lawyer, was feeling quite optimistic when he spoke to some *Wall Street Journal* reporters on April 4: "The political parties are going to take a hard look at some of the more extreme provisions of [the campaign-finance rules] to see if those provisions can withstand review."

Politicians

Always happy to help the press on such occasions, House Speaker John Boehner lauded the ruling. He said it showed that "freedom of speech is being upheld," as reported by Elahe Izadi in the *National Journal.*

In contrast stood Senator John McCain, who wrote in a *Washington Post* online column posted the day *McCutcheon* was decided: "I am concerned that today's ruling may represent the latest step in an effort by a majority of the Court to dismantle entirely the longstanding structure of campaign finance law erected to limit the undue influence of special interests on American politics."

The Press

The press corps was also quick to weigh in, though not in openly partisan ways. The *New York Times'* Adam Liptak labeled the ruling "a major campaign finance decision," one that would "change and most likely increase the already large role money plays in American politics."

In his commentary for SCOTUSblog, Lyle Denniston wrote that the Court had "pressed ahead…with the majority's constitutional view that more money flowing into politics is a good thing—even if much of it comes from rich donors." Notably, Denniston pointed out that *McCutcheon* was "not as sweeping as the Court's ruling four years ago, removing all restrictions on what corporations and labor unions can spend of their own in federal campaigns, which has led to billions of dollars spent on politics through financing that is supposed to be independent of candidates or parties."

The Evening News

As the day wore on, politicians, pundits, and others readied their sound bites for inclusion on the evening TV news. *PBS NewsHour* devoted a long segment to the *McCutcheon* case. In it, Senator Charles Schumer (D-NY) opined that the ruling "turned back the clock on our democracy." Erin Murphy, who successfully argued the case, took exception: "I don't think it is really fair to characterize this [case] as a break from the Court's past precedents." Poised, and peering straight into the camera, she added: "If you look all the way back to *Buckley*…, the Court said…that the only proper way to think about corruption is quid quo pro corruption." It said so, she continued, "because if you go broader than that there is simply no way to draw the limit without infringing on First Amendment rights." The decision, she said, was "a big victory for the First Amendment and for individuals who want to exercise their rights robustly."

Perhaps because of the late-breaking story about a shooting at Fort Hood, Texas, the *ABC Nightly News* with Dianne Sawyer may have opted to bump any *McCutcheon* news. But *NBC Nightly News* with Brian Williams did cover *McCutcheon*. The Court, said Williams, "further opened the floodgates on the role of big money in American politics." Pete Williams, NBC's legal correspondent, echoed that point in his commentary: "The rule undoubtedly means more big money in politics."

Remembrances of Times Past

When all the legal dust finally settled, what happened in the *McCutcheon* case was all too reminiscent of what occurred in a case, *Federal Election Commission v. Wisconsin Right to Life*, that James Bopp successfully argued in 2007. The vote in that case, as in *McCutcheon*, was 5–4. The author of the lead opinion was, as in *McCutcheon*, Chief Justice Roberts. In both cases Justice Thomas called for a broader ruling. And there as here, Roberts did not expressly overrule relevant precedents (*McConnell v. FEC* or *Buckley v. Valeo*). Instead, he wrote in *Wisconsin Right to Life*: "We have no occasion to revisit that determination today." Not today, but perhaps tomorrow. And that tomorrow came seven years later when the Roberts Court, in a majority opinion by Justice Kennedy, expressly overruled *McConnell* in the (famous or infamous, depending on one's view) *Citizens United* case. The chief justice joined in that opinion, though he did issue a concurrence explaining why he "felt justified in setting aside earlier law."

If *Wisconsin Right to Life* was a harbinger of what was to come by way of overruling *McConnell*, is *McCutcheon* a harbinger of what may come by way of overruling *Buckley* in some future case? Perhaps. And maybe even one argued by James Bopp? While it is always risky to peer into a crystal ball and predict a future ruling, it is safe to note that the Roberts Court has yet to see a campaign finance law it liked in the six signed opinions it issued prior to *McCutcheon*. That trend continued; now that number was seven.

As we discussed in chapters 3 and 4, the *Buckley* holding and its First Amendment contribution-expenditure dichotomy had been left undisturbed by the Rehnquist Court. In one of its last campaign finance opinions, that Court (with Chief Justice Rehnquist in the majority) approvingly cited *Buckley* for the proposition that "deference to legislative choice is warranted particularly when Congress regulates campaign contributions, carrying as they do a plain threat to political integrity and a plain warrant to counter the appearance and reality of corruption and the misuse of [collective moneyed] advantages." With the advent of the Roberts Court, that kind of deference became a thing of the past.

Liberals saw such engagement—they preferred to brand it "judicial activism"—as anathema to egalitarian democracy. The First Amendment jurisprudence of the Roberts Court pointed away from rule by the people (democracy) to rule by the rich and powerful few (plutocracy). That, at any rate, is how many progressives portrayed it. Conservatives, by stark contrast, argued that the Roberts Court had finally engaged the First Amendment in a way as to give robust life to its true meaning—to guarantee the right to engage in political speech. For them, the Court's latest ruling marked a near end to a judicial mindset that invoked nebulous fears of corruption to abridge the freedom of men and women like McCutcheon.

Absent some change in the conservative makeup of the Court (the chief and Justices Kennedy, Scalia, Thomas, and Alito), the decisional die has been cast. As legend has it, Julius Caesar spoke the words *alea jacta est* as he crossed the Rubicon. It signaled a point of no return, the very point the Roberts Court may have now reached in *McCutcheon*.

It was a fact: money would remain in politics—much more money. In that regard, former Solicitor General Theodore Olson was prescient when in the course of oral arguments in *McConnell v. FEC* (2003), he told the justices: "Concentrated wealth is nothing if not creative. As this Court has observed, the history of campaign finance reform has been a cycle of legislation followed by the invention and exploitation of loopholes, followed by more legislation to cut off the most egregious evasions."

And so that creativity would continue, but now with yet a little more help from five members of the Court.

Winners and Losers

Beyond the immediate parties in the *McCutcheon* case, who were the big winners and who were the sorry losers? Chris Cillizza, the founder and editor of *The Fix*, a leading blog on state and national politics, answered that question in a *Washington Post* column he wrote shortly after the case came down.

He began his analysis by focusing on *joint fundraising committees.* "These organizations," he wrote, "allow a donor to write a single check that is then split up between a handful of candidates/committees. So, if you wrote a $50,000 check, for example, the first $32,400 would go to the national party committee (that's the current federal donation limit for a single year) and the remaining $17,600 would be parceled out in $2,600 increments to candidates." In other words, before *McCutcheon* "an individual could give only $123,200 in a single election cycle: $48,600 to candidates (which breaks down to eighteen 'max out' candidate donations) and $74,600 to federal party committees." But *McCutcheon* changed the legal and financial equation: "That limit is now gone," which is a win for joint fundraising committees.

What about *party committees*? "The competition among party committees—Democratic Senatorial Campaign Committee vs. the Democratic Congressional Committee vs. the Democratic National Committee, for example—is over," declared Cillizza. "Instead of competing to be the recipient of the $32,400 an individual donor could contribute to a national party committee each year, now the committees are each free to collect $32,400 from a major giver willing to write that sort of check." Are there such donors? Well, yes, but not many: "There were [fewer] than seven hundred people in the 2012 cycle [whom] *McCutcheon* would have affected—that's a financial boon for the party committees." Another winner: the party committees.

Big donors were likewise big winners. After *McCutcheon*, "if such donors wish to spread [their] wealth around to, say, every Republican candidate running for Senate this year, [they] can now do it."

State parties won, too. Before *McCutcheon*, they "had been starved by the aggregate limits," noted Cillizza. "Donors, especially major givers, like to give to the politically sexier causes. And that tends to be federal candidates and national party committees. By the time that giving was done, donors were typically at or close to their $74,600 giving limit to all political action and party committees." But here again, *McCutcheon* changes that: now, "a donor could, theoretically give the federal limit of $10,000 to every single one of the fifty state parties."

Were there losers? The answer to that question was much easier: campaign finance reformers.

Businessman, Litigant, Author

Shaun McCutcheon was elated. After two years of litigation, it was finally over; he had prevailed. The news of his victory came when he was at a steel mill in Harriman, Tennessee. "I am *extremely* pleased," he added joyously. "I can now support a bunch of candidates, and I look forward to doing just that." He then paused, as if to reflect for a moment on what it all meant in the grand scheme of things: "For me, freedom is the theme. It's that simple. More freedom, more freedom, more freedom."

But it was not over, not quite yet. Ever the entrepreneur, McCutcheon rushed to finish his latest adventure. The man at the center of this new finance storm was trying to finish his first book—*Outsider Inside the Supreme Court: A Decisive First Amendment Battle.* "It's mainly about the actual due process from an activist plaintiff's (a D.C. 'outsider') point of view," he said in late March 2014.

True to his adventurous and rebellious spirit, he began his ebook by declaring: "I strongly believe in Freedom of Speech and your right to spend your money on as many candidates and political activities as you choose. Free political speech and assembly are especially important to the future, because we can't change anything in Washington, D.C., if we can't change whom we send to Washington. Supporting those we believe will bring about change—and doing so through transparent contributions— is a good thing." His aim was to provide "a rare inside perspective of the evolution of an important court case from the view of an Alabama businessman." To that end, he hoped that his account would help to "demystify an important part of how our government operates."

And so, after all the exhausting attention he received from the print and electronic media—the countless radio, TV, newspaper, and blog interviews—he had to find some spare time to put his own gloss on the story of his own case. Like George Anastaplo and Elmer Gertz, two men who in 1971 and 1992, respectively, wrote books about their First

Amendment Supreme Court cases, Shaun McCutcheon would record for posterity his take on the events that catapulted him to First Amendment fame.

Try as he might (and aided by Richard E. Cohen, a seasoned correspondent for *Congressional Quarterly*), the ebook was still not available a week after the ruling. But not to worry, the ebook could wait. For now, other things like his April 6, 2014, appearance on *Meet the Press* occupied his time. It pleased him greatly.

Meanwhile life was good: he had money, he could now spend more of that money on his favorite sport, politics, and he was famous—his picture was on the front page of the April 3, 2014, edition of the *Washington Post* (above the fold, no less).

8. *The Reformers*

Every major reform period in American history... has been accom-
panied by numerous amendments to the Constitution, amendments
that were deemed unthinkable until almost the moment they were
passed. If the problems faced at this point in the American journey
are going to be solved, history suggests constitutional amendments
will be a significant part of the process.

—John Nichols & Robert McChesney, *Dollarocracy* (2013)

If there is one thing we absolutely should not be doing, it's tinkering
with our founding document to prevent groups like the ACLU (or
even billionaires like Sheldon Adelson) from speaking freely about
the central issues in our democracy. Doing so will fatally undermine
the First Amendment, diminish the deterrent factor of a durable
Constitution and give comfort to those who would use the amend-
ment process to limit basic civil liberties and rights. It will literally
"break" the Constitution.

—Laura W. Murphy, director,
ACLU Washington Legislative Office (June 2012)

THE EDITORS of the *Nation* have long prided themselves on being staunch
defenders of the First Amendment. This flagship of the Left has been the
editorial home of writers such as George Orwell, Jean-Paul Sartre, I.F.
Stone, H.L. Mencken, and Floyd Abrams, too. Before, during, and after the
McCarthy era, the publication founded in 1865 was an uncompromising

champion of First Amendment causes, though that began to change with the *Buckley v. Valeo* ruling. By January 2011, the *Nation's* editors had become severely antagonistic toward the First Amendment jurisprudence of the day. They editorialized against the "conservative majority of the Supreme Court" for its decision in the *Citizens United* case. They characterized it as a "dramatic assault on American democracy." Outraged by the "role that corporate money plays in politics," the guardians of the progressive publication called for a constitutional amendment. It was amazing: the Left was calling on liberals and others to amend the First Amendment. After the *McCutcheon* ruling came down, that resolve to alter our charter of liberties was even stronger. Significantly, if passed, such an amendment would be the first change to our national Bill of Rights in its nearly 225 years of existence.

There is liberal reform and there is radical reform. Some seek to change statutes while others seek to change constitutions. Both sets of reformers aim to alter our culture and how it reacts to the problem of money in politics. But how best to do that? That is the question. The call for reform is not new. Infuriated by the 1921 Supreme Court ruling in *Newberry v. United States* striking down a section of the Federal Corrupt Practices Act, Senators William Borah and Hiram Johnson unsuccessfully pushed for a constitutional amendment. Since then there have been a variety of legislative reforms and proposed changes to our statutes and Constitution.

What follows are profiles of those who, in a variety of ways, have championed the cause of campaign finance reform in modern times. They include proponents of self-regulation; legislative and administrative reforms, including public financing of elections, tightened disclosure laws, and changes to corporate laws; constitutional amendments; and constitutional conventions.

No PAC Money, Thank You

Jeff Kurzon is a progressive New York attorney. In 2013–2014, he ran for Congress for the Seventh Congressional District in his state. Unlike virtually all other candidates for federal office, he put his ideology on the line and refused to accept any money from PACs or lobbyists.

His platform was simple and straightforward: "We are Democrats. We believe in democracy. We believe in electing officials to serve and advocate for our communities. We believe in hope for a brighter future. We also believe that Lord Acton was correct when he wrote that 'power tends to corrupt, and absolute power corrupts absolutely.'"

At the same time that Shaun McCutcheon was venturing to pump campaign money into New York elections, candidate Kurzon roundly condemned such practices: "I believe that our political system is compromised by money and lifelong politicians who rely on corporate PAC donations and lobbyists to get reelected. These politicians are selfish, lack leadership, and work for these multinational institutions that care most about maximizing profit. These politicians have changed the concept of 'public service' to 'self service.'"

That said, the young progressive did call on his supporters to back him with their wallets: "A generous donation of any size is a vote to change the status quo and get Washington working for the people again." In other words, their financial contributions to his campaign were tantamount to political speech.

Self-rule by the likes of the Jeff Kurzons of the world is a rare thing in American politics. Most progressives of his ilk have a different idea: they prefer *government* to intervene in order to solve the problem of money and politics. Of course, the electoral returns won't be in until November 2014. Should Kurzon lose, will it be because his political opponents outspent him and were aided by PAC money?

A Different Kind of Reform Proposal from an Old-Guard ACLU Lawyer

Joel Gora, now a professor at Brooklyn Law School, has long been a staunch defender of a wide variety of First Amendment causes. Ever since he represented the ACLU in the First Amendment challenge the group brought in *Buckley v. Valeo*, his position has not wavered. Accordingly, he supports the First Amendment challenges brought in *McCutcheon*. Gora delights in quoting Senator Eugene McCarthy, one of the challengers in the *Buckley* case: "The best campaign reform law ever written was the First Amendment."

So what reform, if any, does the seasoned and proud ACLU lawyer think would be desirable and constitutional?

Professor Gora concedes the need to "reduce the disparities that our current campaign finance legal regime has created." Similarly, he believes it is necessary to "expand political opportunity" provided it is not done at the expense of "limiting political speech." Hence, he supports what he labels a "unitary approach" to campaign finance law. Such an approach would contain "no limitations on contributions or expenditures to or by candidates or causes in the public arena." It would require "full disclosure of large contributions as the effective and democratic antidote to improper influence by large contributors over elected officials." Finally, it would call for "meaningful private and public subsidies and funding of candidates and campaigns to facilitate political opportunity and participation." To that end, he has also suggested eight detailed recommendations for reform—from raising individual and committee contribution limits to modest tax credits to mailing privileges and free airtime. As he sees it, "[T]hese are all less drastic remedies than government restriction of political funding and monitoring of political speech and association."

More Light—the Call for Full Disclosure

The acronym is DISCLOSE: Democracy Is Strengthened by Casting Light On Spending in Elections. In political circles it is known as the DISCLOSE Act or H.R. 5175 (S.3628—Senate). Congressman Chris Van Hollen (D-MD) introduced the measure in the House of Representatives on April 29, 2010, and Senator Charles Schumer (D-NY) did likewise on July 21, 2010. The proposed law would amend the Federal Election Campaign Act to prohibit foreign influence in Federal elections, to forbid government contractors from making independent expenditures with respect to such elections, and to establish additional disclosure requirements with respect to spending in such elections, and for other purposes. Though the bill passed the House, it was defeated in the Senate on September 23, 2010.

Ever hopeful, on March 29, 2012, Senator Sheldon Whitehouse (D-RI) introduced the "Democracy Is Strengthened by Casting Light On Spending in Elections Act of 2012" (aka "DISCLOSE Act 2.0"). Among other things, this bill would have required groups disbursing more than $10,000 in campaign-related expenditures to disclose the actual names of their contributors who donated more than $10,000. No longer would generic names like "This ad paid for by Citizens for a Better America" be permitted. The measure died on July 16, 2012, by a 51–44 vote on a procedural motion. Sixty votes were needed to move forward.

"We are determined to prove that transparency is not a radical concept," Senator Tom Udall (D-NM) told the *Washington Post*. "Our bill is as simple and straightforward as it gets—if you are making large donations to influence an election, the voters in that election should know who you are."

According to the *Washington Post*, "Senate Minority Leader Mitch McConnell (R-KY) said the bill was an attempt by Democrats, who have realized they can't 'shut up their critics,' to 'go after the microphone instead, by trying to scare off the funders. As a result of this legislation, advocacy groups ranging from the NAACP to the Sierra Club to the Chamber of Commerce—all of whom already disclose their donors to the IRS—would now be forced to subject their members to public intimidation and harassment.'"

Changing Corporate Laws

In a December 5, 2013, column for the *Daily Beast*, UCLA Law Professor Adam Winkler noted, "In his muckraking classic, *Other People's Money—And How Bankers Use It*, progressive reformer Louis Brandeis famously wrote, 'Sunlight is the best of disinfectants.' In the modern financial system, corporate executives often control funds that don't belong to them." For both Brandeis and Winkler, "transparency and disclosure were effective means of minimizing the risk of executives misusing those funds, either wasting them away negligently or enriching themselves nefariously. Inspired by Brandeis, Congress created the Securities and Exchange Commission to oversee publicly traded companies and to create a more open, reliable, honest marketplace for investors."

In that spirit, the Corporate Reform Coalition was created. It is a group of institutional investors, government reform advocates, and labor unions. Its mission is to pressure the Securities and Exchange Commission to compel disclosure of corporate political spending. To that end, the Coalition helped to gather some 600,000 comments, which were submitted to the SEC as part of a record to influence the agency's rule-making process. The effort, however, came to naught. As Winkler reported, "[T]he Commission closed the shades. In announcing its 2014 'Priorities,' the SEC omitted any mention of corporate political transparency." The commissioners offered no reasons for dropping the proposed disclosure requirement.

"We're incredibly disappointed by this, and we need an explanation for why they removed the most widely supported regulation in their docket," said Lisa Gilbert of Public Citizen's Congress Watch. Winkler agreed: "Due to the SEC's refusal to require transparency, all we can do is guess about disclosure's ultimate effect. In the meantime, corporate executives will continue to funnel other people's money into the electoral process—without those other people ever knowing about it."

"There Is a Special Class"

The *New York Times* named Fred Wertheimer "the dean of campaign finance reformers." E.J. Dionne of the *Washington Post* called him "the eminence grise of the campaign finance reform movement." Sam Pizzigati labeled him "America's elder statesman of campaign finance reform." In 2008 the *Legal Times* tagged him as one of greatest lawyers of the last thirty years. And in 2010 the *Hill* identified him as one of Washington's top lobbyists. He is all of that and more. He is Fred Wertheimer, Brooklyn born and Harvard Law School educated.

There is a 2010 Associated Press photo of Senator John McCain (R-AZ) leaning to his left to hear something Senator Russ Feingold (R-WI) is whispering. Situated in the immediate background between these two giants was a man who could well be their confidential counselor. It was Fred Wertheimer.

At seventy-five, the balding and white-moustached public interest advocate is as outspoken as he was when he first came to Common Cause in May 1971. "There is a special class of citizens in this country today," is how he put it in a 2013 *USA Today* interview. "They are the huge donors to the Democrats and Republicans," he added, having "bought a premium place at the table when it comes to government decisions." And what do we know about them? "They spent $1 billion on presidential and congressional elections. And almost all of that money was in huge contributions, the kinds of contributions that buy influence." Just how big were those contributions? "The amount of money spent in the [2012] presidential campaign was probably between $2.5 billion and $3 billion. The most important development in 2012 is the role played by outside spending groups. They spent

The reformer: Fred Wertheimer

$1 billion on presidential and congressional elections." For Wertheimer, that money defines the privileged class that he criticizes: "That [money] puts those individuals and others in a special category—they have special access [and] special influence with government officials. And that access and influence invariably comes at the expense of ordinary Americans."

It is all vintage Wertheimer. His views have not changed over the years since he coauthored an amicus brief in the 1976 landmark *Buckley v. Valeo* case, wherein he urged the Court to uphold the challenged Federal Election Campaign Act. During his twenty-four-year tenure at Common Cause, he served as legal counsel, legislative director, vice president, and then president. In 1997 he founded Democracy 21, a nonprofit group dedicated to removing the influence of private money from politics. One of its objectives is to provide media and the public with the latest information and analysis on money in politics and campaign finance reform efforts. The man behind it all is the group's president and lead spokesperson, Fred Wertheimer, who gives not a dime of an argument to his foes.

When it comes to the Federal Election Commission, he gives no dime there, either. "The FEC is a huge problem today; [it is] a dysfunctional agency because of the commissioners who sit on it."

What of the Supreme Court? His views are equally critical, but for different reasons. The problem is not that the conservative Court is dysfunctional; the problem is that it is activist. For Wertheimer that is a serious dilemma, especially when it comes to the Roberts Court, which needs to learn a lesson in constitutional restraint. "It is time for this Supreme Court to stop acting like a super-legislature. It is time for this Supreme Court to stop issuing radical decisions that overturn decades of national policy designed to prevent government corruption. A little respect by this Supreme Court for the constitutional right of citizens and Congress to protect the government from corruption is in order." As for the *McCutcheon* case, Wertheimer pulled no punches. "If the Supreme Court strikes down the existing limits on the aggregate amount an individual can give to all federal candidates and all party committees in a two-year election cycle," he wrote in a February 21, 2013, *Huffington Post* blog, "the justices will create a system of legalized bribery in Washington."

What to do? That's where his advocacy group comes in. At each juncture of defeat, it rallies its forces anew with reinvigorated energy and determination, much as it had done in the wake of earlier Roberts Court rulings hostile to its reformist creed. Under Wertheimer's creative and dedicated leadership, the eight-person team at Democracy 21:

- Promotes campaign finance reforms
- Works to develop technologies that allow millions of Americans to make small online contributions
- Files lawsuits and appellate briefs (including an amicus brief in the *McCutcheon* case) to defend the constitutionality of campaign finance laws
- Participates in administrative proceedings to press agencies to administer and enforce federal election laws
- Promotes other government integrity reform measures, including lobbying, ethics and transparency laws and regulations, and
- Serves as a watchdog group to hold federal office holders

accountable for violating campaign finance laws and ethics rules and for misusing public office for personal gain.

And who pays for this reformist crusade? Its mission is made financially possible by funding from the John D. and Catherine T. MacArthur Foundation, the Rockefeller Brothers Fund (created by the sons of John D. Rockefeller Jr.), the Opportunity Fund, and "a number of committed individual donors."

Thus his life work goes on and on. Wertheimer's "Campaign Finance Reform Agenda for 2013" was as robust as any of the past, what with its strong support for measures such as the Empowering Citizens Act (comprehensive legislation to help citizens make small contributions) and the DISCLOSE Act (campaign disclosure legislation). But there was one reformist card the old activist seemed most hesitant to play—amending the federal Constitution. That move was left to a new and bolder breed of reformers.

Reverse the Supreme Court—the Move to Amend the Constitution

U.S. Constitution, Article V—the Amendment Option. Writing in 1833, Justice Joseph Story declared, "A government, which, in its own organization, provides no means of change, but assumes to be fixed and unalterable, must, after a while, become wholly unsuited to the circumstances of the nation; and it will either denigrate into despotism, or by the pressure of its inequalities bring on a revolution." Heed those words; they are gradually becoming the rallying cry of a new generation of reformers.

Consistent with Justice Story's admonition, some 180 years later John Bonifaz and Jeff Clements, cofounders of Free Speech for People, are actively campaigning to amend the United States Constitution and thereby overturn the *Buckley, Citizens United*, and *McCutcheon* precedents, among others. Some of the main groups include:

- Move to Amend
- Free Speech for People

- United for the People
- Public Citizen
- Common Cause
- People for the American Way
- Alliance for Democracy
- Communication Workers of America
- American Sustainable Business Council

Two serious obstacles must be overcome to perform this type of constitutional surgery. First, two-thirds of the members of Congress (sixty-seven senators and 290 U.S. representatives) must approve a proposed constitutional amendment. Second, three-fourths of the states (thirty-eight) must ratify the proposed amendment. It is, to say the least, a most arduous process. Thus it is that, from 1789 to April 2014, approximately 11,539 amendments have been proposed, but only twenty-six have been ratified.

Such difficulties notwithstanding, sixteen states and more than five hundred towns and cities, including Los Angeles and New York, have gone on record in support of a constitutional amendment to undo *Citizens United* and related decisions. And resolutions are pending in the legislatures of twenty-one other states. One of the more popular of these proposed amendments is House Joint Resolution 29, which was introduced on February 14, 2013. Among other things, it provides that "[t]he rights protected by the Constitution of the United States are the rights of natural persons only. Artificial entities established by the laws of any State, the United States, or any foreign state shall have no rights under this Constitution and are subject to regulation by the People, through Federal, State, or local law." That would take care of constitutional protection for corporations, such as Exxon and Pfizer *and* the NAACP and Planned Parenthood, too. HJR 29 also declares that "[t]he judiciary shall not construe the spending of money to influence elections to be speech under the First Amendment." Furthermore, "Federal, State, and local government shall regulate, limit, or prohibit contributions and expenditures ... [and] shall require that any permissible contributions and expenditures be publicly disclosed."

Others like Professor Geoffrey Stone, a critic of *Citizens United*, are far more modest in their proposals. "If I were to propose a constitutional amendment," he wrote in the *Huffington Post*, "here's what I would suggest: 'In order to ensure a fair and well-functioning electoral process, Congress and the States shall have the authority reasonably to regulate political expenditures and contributions.'"

Laura W. Murphy, the director of the ACLU Washington legislative office, takes exception to Geoffrey Stone's idea: "When Professor Stone says federal and state governments 'shall have the power to regulate political expenditures,' he means to give them the ability to place limits on, and control the content of, political speech, even when it is non-partisan and independent of a campaign. This speech," she adds "would include typical 'vote for X' ads, but would also extend to political 'issue' advertisements ('call Senator Reid and tell him to support bill Y'), documentaries by Michael Moore and other political filmmakers, and probably even social media platforms like Twitter or Facebook. The problems with such an approach are many."

Not to be left out of the constitutional picture, Harvard law professor Laurence Tribe has some ideas of his own, what he calls an "ambitious amendment." At one time he urged Congress to work on "meaningful avenues of legislative relief short of a Constitutional amendment." But he has changed his views. Though his "ambitious amendment" says nothing about corporate personhood, here is what it provides: "Nothing in this Constitution shall be construed to forbid Congress or the states from imposing content-neutral limitations on private campaign contributions or independent political campaign expenditures. Nor shall this Constitution prevent Congress or the states from enacting systems of public campaign financing, including those designed to restrict the influence of private wealth by offsetting campaign spending or independent expenditures with increased public funding." On June 18, 2012, Congressman Adam Schiff (D-CA) introduced such an amendment with the drafting help of Professor Tribe.

Difficult as such a constitutional undertaking would be, Tribe is nonetheless optimistic: "Rising to meet this challenge through constitutional amendment will be no easy feat, particularly given the predictable reluctance of Congress to take the necessary action. But it's been done. A groundswell of support for a constitutional convention proved decisive in pressuring a reluctant Congress to propose the Seventeenth Amendment, guaranteeing popular election of U.S. senators."

Another call for a constitutional amendment—perhaps the most surprising—came while the justices busily prepared their respective opinions in McCutcheon. One of their brethren was preparing to release a book urging Americans to reverse some of his former colleagues' constitutional handiwork. The work, which came out on April 22, 2014, was titled Six Amendments: How and Why We Should Change the Constitution. The author was Justice John Paul Stevens.

His short book was offered up against the backdrop of Justice Stevens' coauthored opinion in McConnell v. FEC (2003), his dissents in Colorado Republican Federal Campaign Committee v. FEC(1996), Randall v. Sorrell (2006), Davis v. Federal Election Commission (2008), and Citizens United v. FEC (2010), his critique of Citizens United in his Five Chiefs: A Supreme Court Memoir (2011), and his various criticisms of the Court's campaign finance jurisprudence in public addresses and print and TV interviews. In short, Justice Stevens was a man on a constitutional mission.

Quite apart from Citizens United, Justice Stevens had long harbored serious reservations about vindicating First Amendment claims in most campaign finance cases. Arriving at the Court shortly after Buckley v. Valeo (1976), he witnessed firsthand what Justice William Brennan and his colleagues had wrought in sustaining several of the First Amendment claims brought by Senator James L. Buckley, presidential candidate Eugene McCarthy, and the ACLU. It left him, he recalled in Five Chiefs, with an "extreme distaste" for that precedent. That distaste, he added, "never abated, and I have felt ever since that the Court would have been best served by inserting itself into campaign finance debates with less frequency."

Given that, Justice Stevens thought it was time to resort to Article V for a constitutional remedy. Here, then, is the text of the forty-three words he proposed to amend the First Amendment:

Neither the First Amendment nor any other provision of this Constitution shall be construed to prohibit the Congress or any state from imposing reasonable limits on the amount of money that candidates for public office, or their supporters, may spend in election campaigns.

Northwestern University Law Professor Martin Redish, a noted First Amendment scholar who teaches at Justice Stevens' alma mater, took exception to this amendment draft: "As much as I respect Justice Stevens," he noted, "I believe that his proposed amendment is sorely misguided." He offered three main reasons why he thought the proposal to be ill-advised:

1. Its inescapable impact would be to reduce dramatically the flow of information and opinion to the voters about political campaigns, thereby substantially undermining core goals of the First Amendment and its role as a facilitator of democracy. The simple fact is that speech costs money, and by limiting the amount of money that candidates and supporters can spend, the provision would necessarily limit the flow of often valuable expression that could help the voters perform their governing function in the voting booth.

2. Moreover, Justice Stevens' proposal would have the inescapable effect of locking in non-monetary inequalities—for example, incumbency, political connections, or fame—perversely, in the name of equality. These are inequalities that have traditionally been diluted by opponents' use of money to equalize the voters' awareness of the candidates.

3. Finally, the provision would create an interpretive nightmare. How much money is "reasonable"? Would it differ from state to state? From campaign to campaign? And who gets to decide? Would courts invoke strict scrutiny or rational basis review of the legislature's judgment? To give the authority of determining how much is "reasonable" to a state legislature invites the fox to

watch the hen house: legislators who will stand for reelection will naturally attempt to shape the limits in a way that facilitates their continued victory. Also on an interpretive level, enormous uncertainty would be created by the task of determining who is a "supporter" of a candidate. And even if courts were somehow able to establish coherent interpretive standards for that word, is it appropriate for the Constitution to engage in what amounts to viewpoint-based discrimination by giving preferences to those who are neutral over those who have chosen to support a particular candidate?

"In sum," Redish concluded, "Justice Stevens' proposal would bring about all of these nightmares—political, social, and interpretive. We would be left with a doctrinal morass and a substantial disruption of the flow of information and opinion fundamental to the operation of the democratic process. To be sure, there are problems with our current campaign system, but as Madison suggested in Federalist No. 10, sometimes the cure is worse than the disease."

Cornell Law Professor Steven Shiffrin, another noted First Amendment scholar, took a somewhat different view. "The proposal of Justice Stevens directly speaks to the major evil confronting our elections and our democracy," Shiffrin opined. "Nonetheless, I worry that conservatives on the Court, as they have in the past, will make a distinction between commentary on issues and election commentary allowing the former, but not the latter. They have previously ruled that commentary was about issues rather than candidates even when the purpose and effect of the commentary was to influence the outcome of an election. This loophole could seriously undermine the purpose of the proposed amendment."

Such critiques notwithstanding, Justice Stevens noted in Six Amendments that he was "confident that the soundness" of his proposal "will become more and more evident, and that ultimately [it] will be adopted." The purpose of his book, he tells us, "is to expedite that process and to avoid future crises before they occur."

Hacking at the Roots—
the Call for a Constitutional Convention

Lawrence Lessig—atop he is Harvard-suited, though beneath the tweed of privilege beats a populist heart. Fed on conservative stock—he was an ardent Young Republican who later served as a law clerk to a pair of highly renowned conservative jurists, Judge Richard Posner and Justice Antonin Scalia— Larry Lessig relishes radical departures from conservatism. And though there is a libertarian streak in him—he frowns on certain kinds of government intervention in the marketplace—he nonetheless abhors the corrupting influence of self-serving manipulative wealth. That is where his views, at once informed and drastic, on financing political campaigns come in.

Though legal, our system of financing campaigns is corrupt. It is not so much a quid pro quo form of corruption as a "dependence corruption." With alarming frequency, lawmakers are always in need of (and in search of) that next financial fix from this or that special interest group, be it banks or pharmaceuticals or oil lobbyists. "So long as wealth *can be* used to leverage political power, wealth *will be* used to leverage political power to protect itself" is how he put it in his book *Republic, Lost*. Money in politics is the problem; it distorts the democratic ideal. "Practically every important issue in American politics today is tied to this 'one issue,'" says Lessig. The disease, as he sees it, is systemic and irreversible. Hence, he seeks to attack "the root, the thing that feeds the other ills, and the thing that we must kill first." To that end, he proposes radical constitutional surgery, if only because "sometimes an institution becomes too sick to fix itself." Or as Lessig charged in other terms, "The insiders are not going to fix this mess. We need a movement from the outside."

In Lessig's opinion, what America needs to end the capture of the legislative process by big money is an insurgent citizen movement. That movement, born and bred at the state level, would venture to convince two-thirds of the state legislatures to petition Congress to call a *constitutional convention*. The ostensible objective would be to propose *amendments* to the Constitution that would fundamentally transform the economics of our current electoral process; such amendments could also revise the First Amendment as it has been interpreted in cases such as *Buckley v. Valeo*, *Citizens United v. FEC*, and most recently *McCutcheon v. FEC*. Once such a convention was organized, any constitutional amendments it proposed would have to be ratified by three-fourths of the states.

Lessig's idea, among others, has garnered support from groups such as ArticleV.org, an activist organization with a diverse membership. As it describes itself, it "is the legal expression of the Inter-Occupy Article V Work Group, which includes various Occupy chapters, former military, former 99 Percent Declaration members, and many other individual efforts, etc." The group's mission is to "educate Americans on the reasons to bring about an Article V convention," and to apply its "energy to pressure Congress to call for a Convention to propose amendments to the United States Constitution as described in Article V of the Constitution." Dan Marks, president of the group, was inspired to activism by Justice John Paul Stevens' dissent in *Citizens United*. Marks claims to have submitted "standing legal applications" from forty-two states to the House parliamentarian calling for a constitutional convention. He also contends that the purported applications have been forwarded to the "House Judiciary Committee for review." Though Victor Tiffany of the *Amendment Gazette* supports calls for amending the Constitution in order to overrule the Supreme Court's campaign finance rulings, he told Marks that he thought that the convention approach could open a "Pandora's Box" of problems. Marks conceded the point. Even so, Marks felt the need to proceed: "We do not have the luxury of time. I think there are a lot of people who are afraid of this but what they need to realize is that this is not the tool to be used against the people. Rather, it is the tool that the people need to refresh their government peacefully."

Mind you, such a convention has never been created since the Constitution became the law of our land. True, there were a few close calls, most recently the call for a convention to consider a balanced budget amendment. It took thirty-eight states to call that convention, but only thirty-two petitioned Congress. Of course, the specter of a constitutional convention is a source of considerable anxiety for many, especially those of the political Left. Once such a movement got underway, what might be on the constitutional table and up for grabs?—separation of church and state, fetal personhood, elected Supreme Court justices, national referenda, or greater gun rights? While Lessig believes it possible for there to be a "limited call for a convention" and for Congress to establish rules for how such a limited convention would be conducted, there remains much uncertainty. The prospect of a runaway convention is a real possibility, though he thinks it unlikely given all of the constitutional barriers to surmount in order to do anything.

Dissident Speech in the Supreme Court Chamber

Not all reformists were satisfied with politically orthodox or legally established ways of challenging current realities. Some felt compelled to take their calls for reform "to the streets." One intrepid dissenter, galled by the current constitutional regime governing campaign finance regulation, was driven to protest in the very chamber in which a majority of the Supreme Court justices announced the First Amendment rulings he abhorred.

During oral arguments in a patent case heard by the Court on Wednesday, February 26, 2014, a young man—handsome, clean-cut, and respectably attired in a black suit—stood up in the spectators' galley to address the justices. Clearly and calmly, he declared, "I rise on behalf of the vast majority of the American people who believe that money is not speech, corporations are not people, and our democracy should not be for sale to the highest bidder. Overturn Citizens United. Keep the cap in McCutcheon. The people demand democracy." As he spoke his last words, the dissident was hustled out of the chambers, arrested, and charged with violating a federal statute forbidding "a harangue or oration" or "loud, threatening, or abusive language" in the Supreme Court building.

If the unexpected intrusion were not surprise enough, the incident was captured on video—two minutes of shaky and low-quality footage made on an electronic recording device that had been smuggled into the chamber by one of his colleagues. By the next day, a YouTube posting of the video was all the rage. What fed the public's interest, among other things, was the fact that the Supreme Court never permitted cameras, including traditional news media recordings, in its courtroom. This secretive video—a brief strike of political "guerilla warfare"—was the first time in history that the high court's proceedings were viewed on video by the general public.

On February 28, the daring dissenter—Noah Kai Newkirk, the thirty-three-year-old founding member of 99Rise, which grew out of the Occupy movement—appeared in a Huffington Post "live segment" interview to describe his defiant act and explain his organization's purposes. Fostering activism of many stripes, including diverse experience in social justice groups, the mission statement of 99Rise proclaims: "We are the 99 percent...sick of seeing [our] democracy serve only the interests of the 1 percent."

In keeping with this faith, Newkirk argued that "courageous action" was required to stem "the corruption of our democracy," and that he "stood up" before the justices "to try to set an example." He continued: "We have a government of, by, and for the worst of the 1 percent. And if we don't act to change that, we are facing dark days as a country.... [99Rise] wanted to show the Court and the people in our country that we are not just going to sit silently while [the justices] make these [campaign finance] decisions behind closed doors and assault our democracy."

Toward the end of his interview, Newkirk invoked the "long and proud American tradition" of nonviolent civil disobedience to speak out powerfully and passionately, like a true and honorable dissenter. "Sometimes," he professed, "you have to put your body on the line and disrupt business as usual to get democratic change." There was, of course, a certain irony in it all: a political dissenter took a leaf from the First Amendment (albeit beyond the legal pale) to protest a series of rulings sustaining First Amendment claims.

All of the reformers—the self-regulators, the promoters of tightened disclosure or enhanced public financing, the advocates of corporate transparency, and the champions of constitutional amendments or conventions, and the defiant dissenters—are struggling heavily against the tide of the Supreme Court's modern First Amendment handiwork. Its ruling in *McCutcheon v. FEC* demonstrated that not even *Buckley*'s framework for ideological compromise (i.e., regulating contributions while deregulating expenditures) could fully satisfy Chief Justice Roberts and his conservative colleagues. And what of the foreseeable future? Given what is looming on the horizon, forecasts for progressive reformers do not look sunny.

9. The Next Case?

FOLLOWING SHAUN McCUTCHEON'S victory in the Supreme Court, one thing seemed certain: more such cases would follow. For one thing, various groups, mostly conservative ones, were lining up cases in the state and federal courts. For another thing, the Roberts Court was inclined to become ever more involved in this area of the law—a body of First Amendment jurisprudence likely to be the constitutional hallmark of this Court. And for yet another thing, two other campaign finance cases were in the proverbial pipeline while the *McCutcheon* case was before the Court.

The first, *Iowa Right to Life Committee, Inc. v. Tooker*, was then pending with the justices by way of a petition for certiorari. The second, *Wagner v. Federal Election Commission*, was being held in abeyance pending the outcome in *McCutcheon*. James Bopp, a conservative, brought *Tooker*, whereas Alan Morrison and Arthur Spitzer, two liberals, brought *Wagner*. Both cases, which involved equal protection and First Amendment claims, seemed likely candidates for review in the Supreme Court, difficult as review is to obtain.

Beyond these two cases, there is also a move afoot to contest, on First Amendment grounds, laws that compel campaign finance disclosure. Up to now, such measures have been largely immune from any serious constitutional challenge. But that might also change as the landscape of First Amendment doctrine evolves.

Bopp's Back

Though Erin Murphy and Bobby Burchfield were in the limelight for their victory in *McCutcheon*, James Bopp was hardly out of the picture.

He had, after all, another campaign finance case up his sleeve, and a good one at that.

The claims in *Iowa Right to Life Committee, Inc. v. Tooker* were twofold: 1) that an Iowa ban on political contributions by corporations (and certain business entities), but not by unions, violates the equal protection provision of the Fourteenth Amendment, and 2) that such a corporate-contribution ban runs afoul of the First Amendment. The facts of the controversy involved an attempt by the Iowa Right to Life Committee (a nonprofit corporation) to contribute $100 to Brenna Findley, a candidate for Iowa attorney general. Iowa law, however, prohibits such corporate contributions, but does *not* bar unions from making political contributions. This disparity in treatment notwithstanding, the U.S. Court of Appeals for the Eighth Circuit upheld the law and later declined to rehear the case *en banc*, whereupon James Bopp petitioned the Supreme Court to hear the case.

After suggesting that there was a conflict of law in several lower courts and that the Supreme Court should grant review to reconcile them, Bopp argued that "corporations and unions are similarly situated regarding their interest in making political contributions. Yet in Iowa, corporations, but not unions, are banned from making political contributions. Iowa must justify this disparate treatment. And Iowa must do so under strict scrutiny, both because fundamental rights are involved and because the corporate-contribution ban is content-based." On the First Amendment side of the constitutional ledger, Bopp had to work around a hostile 2003 precedent, *Federal Election Commission v. Beaumont*, a case which he argued and lost to none other than Paul Clement (the co-counsel in *McCutcheon*). That ruling, decided before the advent of the Roberts Court, established that a direct contribution prohibition to nonprofit advocacy corporations is consistent with the First Amendment. For his part, Bopp argued forcefully that "*Beaumont* is on shaky precedential ground in the light of *Citizens United.*"

But alas, it all proved for naught. On April 7, 2014, less than a week after *McCutcheon* was decided, the Supreme Court declined to review *Iowa Right to Life Committee, Inc. v. Tooker*. James Bopp had been foiled yet again.

Liberals Challenge Campaign Finance Law

Alan Morrison, a seasoned appellate advocate and law professor, is nothing if not liberal—in 1971, for example, he worked with Ralph Nader to cofound the Public Citizen Litigation Group, the litigation arm of the famed consumer advocacy organization. In that capacity, he was the lawyer who successfully argued *Virginia Pharmacy Bd. v. Virginia Consumer Council* (1976), which recognized First Amendment protection for certain kinds of commercial speech (in that case for a nonprofit corporate advocacy group).

Now he was co-counsel with Arthur B. Spitzer of the ACLU in *Wagner v. Federal Election Commission*, challenging a little known section of the Federal Election Campaign Act that provided: "[A]ny person who is negotiating for, or performing under, a contract with the federal government is banned from making a contribution to a political party, committee, or candidate for federal office." Accordingly, in their brief to the U.S. Court of Appeals for the District of Columbia, Morrison and Spitzer argued that the three plaintiffs were prevented from making their intended campaign contributions. "One of the plaintiffs," they noted, "is a law professor who had a contract to do a study for the Administrative Conference of the United States; the other two are retired federal employees who continue to work for their former agency on a contract basis. Unlike every other U.S. citizen who does not have a federal contract, they are forbidden by [federal law] from making a contribution of even $1 to any federal candidate, political party, or political committee." Such a law, Morrison and Spitzer maintained, violated both the equal protection component of the Fifth Amendment and the First Amendment. A lower court denied these claims, whereupon review was sought in the court of appeals.

Morrison and Spitzer received some help by way of an amicus brief submitted on their clients' behalf by the Cato Institute. "This case presents an unusual question," wrote Allen Dickerson for the Institute. "While suits challenging limits on political contributions are familiar, the statute at issue here *completely* prohibits a broad group of private, individual citizens from making any contribution. Such sweeping prohibitions are seldom enacted, and courts have rarely assessed their constitutionality. Nevertheless, the limited pronouncements made by the Supreme Court on the subject suggest that strict scrutiny is the appropriate standard of review in this instance" and that the appellants should, therefore, prevail.

Though the case was to be argued before the Court of Appeals on September 30, 2013, at 9:30 A.M., the judges changed their minds beforehand on September 11: "It is ordered, on the Court's own motion, that this case be removed from the oral argument calendar…and held in abeyance pending the Supreme Court's disposition of *McCutcheon v. Federal Election Commission*." Per that order, once *McCutcheon* came down, the parties had thirty days within which to file supplemental briefs "addressing the effect of the Supreme Court's decision in *McCutcheon* on this case."

The clock now began to tick as Alan Morrison and Arthur Spitzer prepared their briefs.

The Next Wave?—Attacks on Disclosure Laws

"Everywhere you look," says Richard Hasen, "campaign finance disclosure laws are under attack." Disclosure has been strongly opposed by a number of groups operating on different fronts. Following the controversial *Citizens United* ruling, Congress declined to buttress disclosure laws to comport with the newfound strength of corporations and labor unions to spend big money on political races. Attempts to pass the DISCLOSE Act have been forcefully defeated thanks to the efforts of Republican leader Mitch McConnell. Meanwhile, adds Hasen, "Republican commissioners on the Federal Election Commission worsened things by embracing an interpretation of existing federal disclosure law making it child's play for political groups to shield the identity of their donors." Moreover, President Obama's efforts to use executive orders to require campaign disclosure by federal contractors ran into a storm of opposition from the Chamber of Commerce. All in all, Professor Hasen opines, "[W]e face the first presidential election since Watergate with the prospect that a significant portion of the money spent on the election will remain secret to the public, though not necessarily to the beneficiaries of the spending."

Generally speaking, the Supreme Court has upheld most of the campaign disclosure laws that have come before it. Even the *Citizens United* Court, save for Justice Clarence Thomas, lent its constitutional stamp of approval to the disclosure and reporting requirements then before it, although the Court did hold out the possibility of considering certain "as applied" challenges in the future. In principle, the Court's deference to public disclosure laws bore out five months after *Citizens United* in their 8–1 ruling in *Doe v. Reed*, again with Justice Thomas dissenting. That case upheld the disclosure of signatures to a controversial referendum concerning same-sex domestic partnerships.

By Justice Thomas' constitutional lights, however, the Court's handiwork was most problematic. In his *Citizens United* dissent, he wrote: "Congress may not abridge the right to anonymous speech based on the 'simple interest in providing voters with additional relevant information.' In continuing to hold otherwise, the Court misapprehends the import of 'recent events' that some *amici* describe [e.g., the Institute for Justice and the U.S. Chamber of Commerce] 'in which donors to certain causes were blacklisted, threatened, or otherwise targeted for retaliation.' The Court properly recognizes these events as 'cause for concern' but fails to acknowledge their constitutional significance." And then to further emphasize the severity of the purported problem, Justice Thomas closed by declaring: "I cannot endorse a view of the First Amendment that subjects citizens of this Nation to death threats, ruined careers, damaged or defaced property, or pre-emptive and threatening warning letters as the price for engaging in core political speech, the 'primary object of First Amendment protection.'"

Lest liberals take immediate and complete exception to Justice Thomas' claims, it would be well for them to remember Justice Thurgood Marshall's opinion in *Brown v. Socialist Workers '74 Committee*(1982), wherein the Court struck down the Ohio Campaign Expense Reporting Law as applied to the Socialist Workers Party (SWP). In that opinion, Justice Marshall advanced arguments somewhat similar to those just mentioned by his successor on the Court, Justice Thomas. Marshall ended his opinion by declaring, "The First Amendment prohibits a State from compelling disclosures by a minor party that will subject those persons identified to the reasonable probability of threats, harassment, or reprisals. Such disclosures," he stressed, "would infringe the First Amendment rights of the party and its members and supporters. In light of the substantial evidence of past and present hostility from private persons and Government officials against the SWP, Ohio's campaign disclosure requirements cannot be constitutionally applied to the Ohio SWP."

In retrospect, it is not surprising that the former NAACP lawyer wrote what he did given the case of *NAACP v. Alabama* (1958), a precedent to which he referred several times in the course of his opinion. Alabama had a law that required certain out-of-state corporations to file a corporate charter along with other reporting requirements. Since the NAACP was a nonprofit corporation organized in New York with affiliates in Alabama, the law applied to it. The statute obligated the group to reveal to the state's attorney general the names and addresses of all its Alabama members and agents. A unanimous Supreme Court set the law aside on First Amendment grounds.

It is against that backdrop—of a general deference to disclosure laws combined with a certain skepticism—that future cases in this area will be judged. As political strife continues, claims of hostility and harassment will likely surface as ever more attention is focused on those who support controversial causes and candidates. When such attention is the fruit of federal or state campaign disclosure laws, we may see a new wave of election law cases that either make the electoral process more covert or more transparent.

Epilogue

Unhappy with who is speaking these days and how much they are speaking, liberals are promiscuously signing on to a variety of positions that simply ignore the core of First Amendment jurisprudence.
—Floyd Abrams (July 21, 1997)

A system of unrestricted free speech markets can easily become a bizarre caricature of democratic goals. In these circumstances, well-designed reforms should be understood not as unconstitutional abridgements of the free speech principle but as consistent with the highest aspirations of that principle.
—Cass R. Sunstein (July 21, 1997)

FOR DECADES, Floyd Abrams was the darling of liberals. He was, after all, the man who, among other things, helped to secure a landmark victory in the 1971 *Pentagon Papers* case, the case that severely curbed the power of Richard Nixon and like-minded presidents to silence the press. In times past, to be liberal meant being a strong (nearly absolutist) defender of First Amendment rights. The *Nation* was on board; the ACLU was on board; progressive lawyers and activists were on board, and most liberal groups were on board. But over time things changed. With increasing frequency, the Left moved to the right on this issue, while the Right moved to the left on it.

Sixteen years ago the *Nation* ran a cover story entitled "Speech and Power." In the symposium issue, some prominent liberals questioned what was once sacred—out-and-out protection of First Amendment freedoms. In the preface to the symposium, the editors complained that "some of the most powerful actors in our society... are wielding the First Amendment in ways that often seem counter to [or] thwart progressive reforms." Several liberal contributors to the symposium agreed, including such notable First Amendment scholars as Owen Fiss, C. Edwin Baker, and Cass Sunstein. Other distinguished First Amendment personae took a strikingly different view: "The First Amendment is not broken," wrote Steven R. Shapiro of the ACLU, "but it may break if we keep trying to fix it." Kathleen Sullivan, Wendy Kaminer, and, of course, Floyd Abrams agreed.

The July 21, 1997, issue of the *Nation* marks as good as any point in time when the liberal community had become openly schizophrenic about its stance on the First Amendment. No longer was being liberal synonymous with being pro–First Amendment. That ambivalence, which later translated into a sort of antipathy, was largely due to the campaign finance and commercial speech rulings of the Burger and Rehnquist Courts. By that measure, the ideological strife can be traced back to Friday, January 30, 1976—the day the Court handed down *Buckley v. Valeo*. Thus, it took two decades for the transformation to develop. And when *Citizens United v. Federal Election Commission* was decided thirteen years after the *Nation's* symposium, that transformation from "liberal–First Amendment" to "neo-liberal–First Amendment" was all but complete, at least as to cases involving free speech claims related to money or corporations or to both.

"In no First Amendment case that I have been involved in has the position I have articulated been more the subject of more condemnation by most of the press, let alone denounced by a sitting president, than the *Citizens United* ruling." That is how Floyd Abrams put it in his book *Friend of the Court* (2013). This eminent free-speech lawyer, whose career spans nearly a half century, was taken aback by how people, especially liberals, responded in vitriolic ways to the idea that the First Amendment should be invoked to defend the idea that money is speech. "People who would enthusiastically defend the free speech rights of Nazis, pornographers, and distributors of videos of animals being tortured or killed," he wrote, "were appalled that corporations and unions should be permitted to weigh in on who should be elected president." Despite the fierce condemnation of his views on the subject, Abrams believes that the *Buckley* and *Citizens United* rulings should be "celebrated, not mocked."

The late legal philosopher Ronald Dworkin saw things differently: "Floyd Abrams has had a distinguished career protecting an invaluable constitutional right. But we must take care not to convert the First Amendment from a matter of principle to a pointless mantra that subverts rather than sustains democracy." Abrams disagreed. "My view," he said in a 2013 SCOTUSblog interview, "is that suppression of speech, particularly but not exclusively political speech, is inconsistent with what the First Amendment is most clearly and importantly about. That does not make the First Amendment a 'pointless mantra'; it is the point of the First Amendment to prevent government from determining who can speak and what is worth saying."

Was Dworkin right? Had Abrams' fervent fidelity to the First Amendment become something akin to a mindless mantra? Or was Dworkin the quintessential example of a liberal who had lost faith in his own liberality, and for whom the ever-bothersome First Amendment had become ideologically intolerable?

However one answers those questions, one thing is clear: defending the First Amendment can prove to be an unpopular vocation. Whether it is invoked to protect the rights of anarchists, communists, pornographers, flag burners, hate groups, corporations, or the super rich, defending free speech is a good way to win enemies. From the vantage point of those who are skeptical about such an undertaking, the problem with First Amendment devotees such as Floyd Abrams is that they are too doctrinaire. Or as Richard Kuh, the prosecutor of the ribald comedian Lenny Bruce, liked to say: their secular "religion demands that [free speech] freedoms exist in pristine, uncompromised condition." Then again, it is precisely that mindset that allowed for the prosecution and conviction of Lenny Bruce, one of America's most famous comedians.

If the Supreme Court's campaign finance rulings have divided the Left, they have just as surely unified the Right when it comes to devotion to the First Amendment. Who would have imagined that the likes of bona fide conservatives such as Rush Limbaugh and George Will would rally behind First Amendment absolutism, at least when in the service of striking down electoral reform laws? Conservative think tanks such as the Heritage Foundation and the libertarian Cato Institute are just as committed in their allegiance to that First Amendment gospel.

Consider this: beyond the back-and-forth of such liberal claims and conservative counterclaims, perhaps it all comes down to whose message is being banned and whether we (liberals or conservatives) disagree with it enough to silence it. In that respect, Nat Hentoff may well have hit the proverbial nail on the head when he said, "free speech for me—but not for thee." That attitude, however unstated, may inform much when it comes to censorship—"the strongest drive in human nature," as Hentoff tagged it.

In light of the above, cases like *McCutcheon* portend the perpetuation of a divide within the liberal community, with one segment siding with the conservative Right and the other with the more reformist Left. Meanwhile, will the newfound conservative allegiance to the First Amendment extend beyond the money and power cases to those involving radical political dissidents and unsavory cultural dissidents?

Liberty vs. Equality

At the very time when the justices were working on drafts of their opinions in *McCutcheon*, a new documentary by Professor Robert Reich (secretary of labor in the Clinton Administration) debuted in movie theaters. It was titled *Inequality for All*. The Weinstein Company distributed the eighty-five-minute movie nationwide. At the outset, Reich sounded the alarm: "Of all developed nations, the United States has the most unequal distribution of income. We're surging toward even greater inequality." Later on in the documentary, he was even more passionate: "We are losing equal opportunity in America." It was more than a movie; it was the start of a movement. The command to "get big money out of politics" was part and parcel of that movement's liberal agenda.

Five years earlier another documentary competed for the American mind. It was the small-budget ninety-minute film titled *Hillary: The*

Movie. The film, produced by a conservative nonprofit group, focused on the alleged scandals that were said to be associated with the presidential candidate. As much as anything else, political corruption was its theme. It was that documentary and the attempt to air and distribute it that gave rise to the *Citizens United* case.

Two documentaries, two views of America, and two radically different notions of what is fair or unfair when it comes to politics and money. It was yet another example of the liberal-conservative divide that has become a regular part of our current political landscape. Still, what is fundamentally at stake here is more than a battle over a liberal or conservative agenda. And it is more than a battle over the meaning of the First Amendment, at least as offered up by black-robed jurists. That something more pointed back in time to the founding of our Republic.

The Constitution of 1787 had no charter of liberty and no guarantee of equality. Both had to be added by amendments to the Constitution, and it took decades before those amendments were given any real meaning by the Supreme Court. On many occasions since then, there has been a battle between liberty, on the one hand, and equality on the other. That battle, it must be remembered, occurs within the context of our culture, which is a highly capitalistic one. That fact alone informs much, though it is seldom, if ever, mentioned on the pages of a judicial opinion.

Unfettered liberty is, in important measure, the cousin of unfettered capitalism. Though none in socialist circles would ever venture to say it, money is freedom. For all of the excesses of capitalism (and there are many), it is hard to deny that any society in the history of humankind has ever enjoyed a greater measure of liberty than what is taken as the standard in contemporary America. *Buckley, Citizens United*, and now *McCutcheon* are an integral part of our modern liberty.

When liberty is mixed into the cauldron of capitalism, however, one of the inevitable byproducts is inequality in the distribution of goods and rights. The idea behind the liberal-equality principle is that laws need to level out the playing field so as to give the less fortunate a meaningful voice in government, one largely equal to that of the powerful. If that is the governing principle, then *Buckley, Citizens United*, and now *McCutcheon* foster rule by plutocracy.

Where one stands on money, politics, and the First Amendment depends largely on whether one leans more to the liberty or equality principle. If we treat political contributions and expenditures as pristine examples of political speech, it is because we value liberty over equality. Then again, if we view such "speech" as corruptive of fundamental principles of democratic government, it is because we value equality over liberty.

And then there is this, our conceptual adieu. Just as the deprivations of liberty committed in the name of reform must never be discounted, so, too, the denials of equality committed in the name of self-determination must never be disregarded.

Acknowledgments

THIS BOOK would have been impossible but for the incredible efforts of our publisher and longtime editor and friend, Alex Lubertozzi. His sober, illuminating, and careful edits have been of considerable help to us, and we are much in his debt for his invaluable assistance.

Much gratitude goes to two federal election campaign finance experts who graciously agreed to review our manuscript: Jeffrey Bowman (executive assistant to former FEC chairman Scott Thomas) and Joel Gora (ACLU counsel in *Buckley v. Valeo* and Brooklyn Law School professor). Their careful reading and wise suggestions provided us with welcome counsel and prevented us from making embarrassing mistakes.

Professor Alan Morrison also lent a helping hand, alerting us to things that we might have missed.

We also extend our sincere appreciation to James Bopp Jr., Bobby Burchfield, Dan Backer, Shaun McCutcheon, and Heather Purcel for kindly agreeing to be interviewed.

The works of several scholars have been vital to this enterprise. They include: Paula Baker, Paul Blumenthal, Elizabeth Drew, Rick Hasen, Lawrence Lessig, Adam Liptak, Robert Mutch, John Nichols and Robert McChesney, Bradley Smith, Rodney Smith, Crank Sorauf, Geoffrey Stone, Jeffrey Toobin, Melvin Urofsky, and Adam Winkler.

Our research assistant, Tricia Wolf, provided able assistance in tracking down many sources that helped to buttress the credibility of this project.

As in the past, Susan A. Cohen offered her own special contributions, which made it possible to complete this work.

The lion's share of this book was written in Bethesda, Maryland and in Seattle, Washington. Some of the near final touches, however, were done in the sunny winter of a wondrous home atop a cliff in Rancho Palos Verdes, California. It was a delightful opportunity made possible by the hospitality of two kind friends.

Appendixes

List of Supreme Court Amicus Briefs in McCutcheon*

Briefs Challenging Federal Law
1. Wisconsin Institute for Law and Liberty
2. Senator Mitch McConnell
3. CATO Institute
4. Center for Competitive Politics
5. National Republican Senatorial Committee, jointly with the Republican Congressional Committee
6. American Civil Rights Union
7. Committee for Justice
8. Institute for Justice
9. Cause of Action
10. Thomas Jefferson Center
11. Combined brief on behalf of the Tea Party Leadership Fund, the National Defense PAC, Combat Veterans for Congress PAC, Conservative Melting Pot PAC, and Freedom's Defense Fund
12. Combined brief on behalf of the Libertarian National Committee, the Constitution Party National Committee, the Free Speech Coalition, the U.S. Justice Foundation, Gun Owners Foundation, English First, Abraham Lincoln Foundation, Institute on the Constitution, Western Center for Journalism, Policy Analysis Center, Conservative Legal Defense & Education Fund

---

* The information set out above came from the Ballot Access News website edited by Richard Winger.

Briefs Supporting Federal Law

1. Brennan Center for Justice
2. Americans for Campaign Finance Reform
3. Representatives Chris Van Hollen and David Price
4. Professor Lawrence Lessig
5. 85 Democratic Members of the United States House of Representatives
6. Combined brief for the Campaign Legal Center, AARP, Asian Americans Advancing Justice, Asian American Legal Defense and Education Fund, Common Cause, Citizens for Responsibility and Ethics in Washington, the League of Women Voters, Progressives United, and Public Campaign
7. Combined brief for the Communications Workers of America, Greenpeace, NAACP, Sierra Club, American Federation of Teachers, Main Street Alliance, Ourtime.org, People for the American Way, Rock the Vote, U.S. PIRG, Working Families Organization, and Demos
8. National Education Association

Justices Who Wrote for the Court in First Amendment Campaign Finance Cases

Cases such as McIntyre v. Ohio Elections Commission *(1995), which involved elections and the First Amendment but no money or money-related campaign issues, are not included in this list. Similarly, cases such as* Caperton v. A.T. Massey Coal Co. *(2009), which involved money and elections but were not decided on First Amendment grounds, are not included. Likewise excluded are cases such as* United States v. Gradwell *(1917), involving election fraud laws.*

Chief Justice John Roberts
Arizona Free Enterprise Club v. Bennett
Federal Election Commission v. Wisconsin Right to Life
McCutcheon v. Federal Election Commission

Justice Anthony Kennedy
Citizens United v. Federal Election Commission

Justice Stephen Breyer
Randall v. Sorrell
Federal Election Commission v. Colorado Republican Federal Campaign Committee (plurality)

Justice Samuel Alito
Davis v. Federal Election Commission

Justice David Souter

Colorado Republican Federal Campaign Committee v. Federal Election
Commission

Nixon v. Shrink Missouri Government

Federal Election Commission v. Beaumont

Justice John Paul Stevens

McConnell v. Federal Election Commission

Chief Justice Warren Burger

Citizens Against Rent Control v. Berkeley

Chief Justice William Rehnquist

Federal Election Commission v. National Right to Work Committee

Federal Election Commission v. National Conservative Political Action
Committee

Justice William Brennan

Pipefitters v. United States

Federal Election Commission v. Massachusetts Citizens for Life

Justice Byron White

Broadrick v. Oklahoma

Justice Lewis Powell

First National Bank v. Bellotti

Justice Thurgood Marshall

California Medical Association v. Federal Election Commission (plurality)

Brown v. Socialist Workers

Austin v. Michigan Chamber of Commerce

Justice Felix Frankfurter

United States v. Auto Workers

Justice Stanley Reed
United States v. Congress of Industrial Organizations

Justice James McReynolds
Newberry v. United States

Per Curiams & Summary Rulings without an Opinion
Buckley v. Valeo
Common Cause v. Schmitt (judgment affirmed by an equally divided Court)
Republican National Committee v. Federal Election Commission
Wisconsin Right to Life v. Federal Election Commission
Bluman v. Federal Election Commission
American Tradition Partnership, Inc. v. Bullock

Lawyers Who Argued First Amendment Campaign Finance Cases

Far too often, very little attention is paid to the lawyers who argued campaign finance cases before the Supreme Court. Since their arguments—both in their briefs and in their oral exchanges with the justices—sometimes influenced the direction the Court ultimately took, we have elected to set out their names below.

The names listed are only those of the lawyers who actually presented their cases in oral arguments with the justices. In the following appendix, we have included a tally of the lawyers who argued most of the modern-era campaign finance cases heard thus far by the Supreme Court. (As for earlier cases, the first one in this area was Newberry v. United States, *decided in 1921. It was argued by Charles Evans Hughes [later to be chief justice] for the plaintiff in error and by William L. Frierson for the government.)*

Cases such as Caperton v. A.T. Massey Coal Co. *(2009), which involved money and elections but were not decided on First Amendment grounds, are not included. Likewise excluded are cases such as* United States v. Gradwell *(1917), involving election fraud laws, and cases such as* Bluman v. Federal Election Commission *(2012), which was summarily affirmed without argument. Finally, cases such as* McIntyre v. Ohio Elections Commission *(1995), which involved elections and the First Amendment but no money or money-related campaign issues, do not appear in this list.*

United States v. Auto Workers
Appellant: J. Lee Rankin
Appellee: Joseph L. Rauh Jr.

United States v. Congress of Industrial Organizations
Appellant: Jesse Climenko
Appellees: Charles J. Margiotti, Lee Pressman

Pipefitters v. United States
Petitioners: Morris A. Shenker
Respondent: Lawrence G. Wallace

Broadrick v. Oklahoma
Appellant: John C. Buckingham
Appellee: Mike D. Martin

Buckley v. Valeo
Appellant: Brice M. Clagett, Joel Gora, Ralph K. Winter
Appellee: Loyd N. Cutler, Archibald Cox, Daniel Freedman, Ralph Spritzer

First National Bank v. Bellotti
Appellant: Francis H. Fox
Appellee: Thomas R. Kiley

California Medical Association v. Federal Election Commission
Appellant: Rick C. Zimmerman
Appellee: Charles N. Steele

Citizens Against Rent Control v. Berkeley
Appellants: James R. Parrinello
Appellee: Natalie E. West

Brown v. Socialist Workers
Appellants: Gary Elson Brown
Appellee: Thomas D. Buckley Jr.

Common Cause v. Schmitt
  Appellants: Archibald Cox
  Appellee: Charles N. Steele

Federal Election Commission v. National Right to Work Committee
  Petitioners: Charles N. Steele
  Respondents: Richard H. Mansfield, III

Federal Election Commission v. National Conservative Political Action Committee
  Petitioners: Charles N. Steele and Robert R. Sparks
  Respondent: Steven B. Feirson

Federal Election Commission v. Massachusetts Citizens for Life
  Appellant: Charles N. Steele
  Appellee: Francis H. Fox

Austin v. Michigan Chamber of Commerce
  Appellants: Louis J. Caruso
  Respondent: Richard D. McLellan

Colorado Republican Federal Campaign Committee v. Federal Election Commission
  Petitioners: [Mr.] Jan W. Baran
  Respondent: Drew S. Days, III

Nixon v. Shrink Missouri Government PAC
  Petitioners: Jeremiah W. Nixon
  Respondent: D. Bruce La Pierre
  S.G.'s Office: Seth P. Waxman (in support of Petitioners)

Federal Election Commission v. Colorado Republican Federal Campaign Committee
  Petitioners: Barbara D Underwood
  Respondent: [Mr.] Jan W. Baran

Federal Election Commission v. Beaumont
> Petitioner: Paul D. Clement
> Respondent: James Bopp Jr.

McConnell v. Federal Election Commission
> Plaintiffs: Floyd Abrams, Bobby R. Burchfield, Kenneth Starr, Jay A. Sekulow, and Laurence Gold
> Defendant: Paul D. Clement, Theodore Olson, and Seth P. Waxman

Wisconsin Right to Life v. Federal Election Commission
> Appellant: James Bopp Jr.
> Appellee: Paul D. Clement

Randall v. Sorrell
> Petitioners: James Bopp Jr. and William H. Sorrell
> Respondent: Brenda Wright

Federal Election Commission v. Wisconsin Right to Life
> Petitioner: Paul D. Clement and Seth P. Waxman
> Respondent: James Bopp Jr.

Davis v. Federal Election Commission
> Appellant: Andrew D. Herman
> Appellee: Paul D. Clement

Citizens United v. Federal Election Commission
> Appellant: Theodore Olson and Floyd Abrams
> Appellee: Seth P. Waxman
> S.G.'s Office: Elena Kagan

Arizona Free Enterprise Club v. Bennett
> Petitioner: William R. Maurer
> Respondent: Bradley S. Phillips
> S.G.'s Office: William M. Jay

McCutcheon v. Federal Election Commission

Petitioner: Erin Murphy (McCutcheon & RNC) and Bobby R. Burchfield (McConnell)

Respondent: Donald Verrilli Jr.

Lawyers Who Argued the Most First Amendment Campaign Finance Cases

- Charles N. Steele (5)
- James Bopp Jr. (4)*
- Paul Clement (4)
- Seth Waxman (3)†
- Floyd Abrams (2)
- Paul Clement (2)
- Archibald Cox (2)
- Theodore Olson (2)
- Bobby R. Burchfield (2)‡
- [Mr.] Jan W. Baran (2)§

---

*As noted in chapter 5, Mr. Bopp authored the merits brief for the RNC in the *McCutcheon* case. He likewise represented the petitioner in *American Tradition Partnership, Inc. v. Bullock* (2012), in which the Court, without oral arguments, issued a per curiam opinion (5–4) reversing the lower court ruling. Bopp successfully argued *Republican Party of Minnesota v. White* (2002), in which the Court (with another 5–4 split) struck down a state law that prohibited candidates for judicial election from announcing their views on disputed legal and political issues. Bopp has likewise filed amicus briefs in other Supreme Court campaign finances cases, such as *Nixon v. Shrink* (2000) and *Citizens United v. Federal Election Commission* (2010).

† Mr. Waxman also filed an amicus brief in *McCutcheon* on behalf of Representatives Chris Van Hollen and David Price.

‡ Mr. Burchfield also filed amicus briefs for Senator McConnell in *Nixon v. Shrink* (2000) and in *Arizona Free Enterprise Club PAC v. Bennett* (2011).

§ Mr. Baran has often represented the U.S. Chamber of Commerce in briefs filed in Supreme Court cases, such as Wisconsin Right to Life, Inc. v. Federal Election Commission, Citizens United v. Federal Election Commission, McConnell v. Federal Election Commission, American Tradition Partnership, Inc. v. Bullock, and Chamber of Commerce v. Federal Election Commission (2003, cert. denied).

Supreme Court Briefs Filed by the National ACLU

The list below refers to briefs (merits and amicus) filed by the national ACLU in First Amendment campaign finance cases in which the Court accepted review and rendered an opinion. Hence, briefs filed by local ACLU chapters (such as the one filed by the Cleveland chapter in Brown v. Socialist Workers*) are not included. Likewise, national ACLU briefs in support of review but which were denied (e.g.,* Republican National Committee v. Federal Election Commission, 1980*) are not included. Also excluded are cases such as* McIntyre v. Ohio Elections Commission *(1995), which involved elections and the First Amendment but no money or money-related campaign issue. The list does, however, reference "former" national ACLU officials who filed amicus briefs, sometimes in direct opposition to briefs filed by the National ACLU.*

United States v. Congress of Industrial Organizations
[none filed]

United States v. Auto Workers
[none filed]

Pipefitters v. United States
[none filed]

Broadrick v. Oklahoma
[none filed]

Buckley v. Valeo
Joel M. Gora and Melvin L. Wulf on behalf of the Appellants.

First National Bank v. Bellotti
[none filed]

California Medical Association v. Federal Election Commission
Amicus brief urging reversal: Bruce J. Ennis Jr.

Citizens Against Rent Control v. Berkeley
[none filed]

Brown v. Socialist Workers
[none filed]

Common Cause v. Schmitt
Amicus brief urging affirmance: Phillip A. Lacovara, Gerald Goldman, Ronald A. Stern, Charles S. Sims, and Arthur B. Spitzer.

Federal Election Commission v. National Right to Work Committee
[none filed]

Federal Election Commission v. National Conservative Political Action Committee
Amicus brief urging affirmance: Philip A. Lacovara, Ronald A. Stern, Charles S. Sims, and Arthur B. Spitzer.

Federal Election Commission v. Massachusetts Citizens for Life
Amicus brief urging affirmance: Marjorie Heins, Burt Neuborne, and Jack Novik.

Austin v. Michigan Chamber of Commerce
Amicus brief urging affirmance: Arthur B. Spitzer, John A. Powell, and Joel M. Gora.

Colorado Republican Federal Campaign Committee v. Federal Election Commission

Amicus brief supporting petitioners: Steven R. Shapiro, Joel M. Gora, and Arthur N. Eisenberg.

Nixon v. Shrink Missouri Government PAC

Amicus brief in support of respondents: Joel M. Gora and Steven R. Shapiro.

Amicus brief in support of petitioners: Norman Dorsen, Bruce J. Ennis, Charles Morgan Jr., Aryeh Neier, John Pemberton, John Powell, and Melvin Wulf. (The following is taken from the afore-mentioned brief: "With the exception of Burt Neuborne, who is counsel for respondent Joan Bray supporting petitioners in this case, and two other persons currently in government service and therefore not free to participate in this brief, every living person to have served as ACLU President, ACLU Executive Director, ACLU Legal Director, or ACLU Legislative Director during the past 30 years, with the exception of the current leadership, has joined this brief supporting the validity of the Missouri limitations at issue. Each has previously signed a statement 'supporting the constitu-tionality of efforts to enact reasonable campaign finance reform.'")

Federal Election Commission v. Colorado Republican Federal Cam-paign Committee

Amicus brief supporting respondents: Steven R. Shapiro, Joel M. Gora, and Arthur N. Eisenberg.

Federal Election Commission v. Beaumont

[none filed]

McConnell v. Federal Election Commission

Brief on behalf of ACLU appellant: Joel M. Gora, Steven R. Shapiro, and Mark L. Lopez.

Amicus brief in support of appellees by Former Leaders of the ACLU: Norman Dorsen, John Pemberton, and Morton Halperin.

Wisconsin Right to Life v. Federal Election Commission

Amicus brief in support of appellant: Joel Gora, Steven R. Shapiro, and Mark L. Lopez.

Amicus brief in support of appellee: Burt Neuborne, Norman Dorsen, Aryeh Neier, and John Shattuck

Randall v. Sorrell

Brief in support of petitioner: Mark J. Lopez, Steven R. Shapiro, and Joel M. Gora.

Amicus brief in support of respondents by Former Officials of the ACLU: Norman Dorsen, Aryeh Neier, Burt Neuborne, John Shattuck, Helen Hershkoff, and Charles S. Sims.

Federal Election Commission v. Wisconsin Right to Life

Amicus brief in support of appellee: Joel M. Gora, Steven R. Shapiro, and Mark J. Lopez.

Amicus brief in support of appellant: Burt Neuborne on behalf of the Brennan Center for Justice, along with Norman Dorsen, Aryeh Neier, and John Shattuck. (The following is taken from the aforementioned brief: "Amici are former officials of the American Civil Liberties Union, who are committed both to a robust First Amendment and to the effective restriction of corporate treasury funds in electoral campaigns.")

Davis v. Federal Election Commission

[none filed]

Citizens United v. Federal Election Commission

Amicus brief in support of appellant: Mark J. Lopez, Steven R. Shapiro, and Joel M. Gora.

Amicus brief of former ACLU officials on behalf of neither party: Norman Dorsen and Burt Neuborne

Arizona Free Enterprise Club v. Bennett

[none filed]

Amicus brief of former ACLU officials in support of respondent:
Norman Dorsen and Burt Neuron

Bluman v. Federal Election Commission
[none filed]

American Tradition Partnership, Inc. v. Bullock
[none filed]
Amicus brief of former ACLU officials in support of neither party:
Burt Neuborne, Norman Dorsen, Aryeh Neier, John Shattuck, and
Morton Halperin.

McCutcheon v. Federal Election Commission
[none filed]

Total Briefs Filed by National ACLU: 14
Total National ACLU Briefs Supporting 1-A Claim: 14
Total Briefs Filed by "Former" ACLU Officials: 8
Total Briefs filed by ACLU and Former ACLU Officials on Different Sides in Same Case: 6
Total Cases with No National ACLU filings: 14

Timeline

1757 In his bid for the Virginia House of Burgesses, George Washington spends £39 to treat voters to 160 gallons of rum and other alcoholic beverages.

1837 First bill to ban campaign-related political assessments from government employees is introduced by Congressman and former Speaker of the House, John Bell of Tennessee. In relevant part, the bill provided that no one shall be appointed to any government position "upon any agreement that such person or persons…shall exert his or their influence in any election." The bill, however, did not reach the House floor until 1840, and then failed.

1839 House of Representatives appoints committee to investigate the practices of Samuel Swartout, the collector of the Port of New York, regarding raising campaign funds by way of political assessments on employees at the New York Customs House.

1860 Abraham Lincoln purchases German-language newspaper, the *Illinois Staats-Anzeiger*, and demands that it endorse the Republican Party.

1867 First campaign finance law, which prohibited federal officials from soliciting contributions from navy yard workers.

1874 *Trist v. Child*: the Supreme Court invalidates contingency contracts for lobbyists.

1877 By way of a state constitutional prohibition, Georgia bans the lobbying of state legislators.

1883 Passage of the Pendleton Civil Service Reform Act, which prohibited political contributions in exchange for appointment to any federal government position and barred the solicitation of campaign donations on federal government property.

1888 John Wannamaker, a department store magnate, contributes $50,000 to Benjamin Harrison's presidential candidate.

1891 Kentucky becomes the first state to ban corporate political election contributions.

1892 Carter H. Harrison, a Chicago mayoral candidate, spends $500,000 on his election.

1894 During New York State's constitutional convention, reformer Elihu Root unsuccessfully attempts to ban corporate contributions to elections.

1897 Nebraska, Missouri, Tennessee, and Florida ban corporate contributions.

1900 Isaac Stephenson, a wealthy lumber business tycoon, purchases *Milwaukee Free Press* to assure positive coverage for Robert LaFollett's bid for governor.

1901 Senator William E. Chandler of New Hampshire introduces the first federal bill to bar corporations from giving money to political committees. Measure fails.

1907 Passage of Tillman Act, the first federal statute to prohibit corporations and national banks from making monetary contributions to federal candidates.

1910 The Federal Corrupt Practices Act (aka the Publicity Act), which established campaign spending limits for political parties in general elections for the House of Representatives and required post-election disclosure in House races for contributions of $100 or more.

    June 1910: Senate conducts investigation of bribery charges against Senator William Lorimer of Illinois, who was exonerated.

1911 Amendments to Federal Corrupt Practices Act limit amounts to be spent in House races to $5,000 and Senate races to $10,000.

June 1911: At Robert M. LaFollette's urging, the Senate reopens the case against Lorimer on the basis of new charges of bribery. Lorimer again exonerated.

August 1911: Senate investigates Senator Isaac Stephenson of Wisconsin on charges of electoral bribery. Stephenson exonerated by a 9–5 vote of the Privileges and Elections Committee.

1912   U.S. Senate adopts a resolution declaring "that corrupt methods and practices were employed in [Lorimer's 1909] election, and that the election, therefore, was invalid."

1918   U.S. Senate race between Henry Ford and Truman Newberry.

1920–1923   Teapot Dome Scandal.

1921   *Newberry v. United States:* Supreme Court holds that primary elections cannot be regulated under Congress's Article I, Sec. 4 powers. A divided Court strikes down the 1911 amendments to the Federal Corrupt Practices Act, which placed spending limits on candidate and political election committee spending in primaries or other nomination processes for federal office.

Senators William Borah and Hiram Johnson call for a constitutional amendment in response to *Newberry* ruling. Proposal fails.

1925   Amendments to the Federal Corrupt Practices Act, which included disclosure requirements and certain limits on campaign contributions and spending, made it a crime for a candidate to accept corporate contributions.

1929   Albert Fall found guilty of bribery, fined $100,000, and sentenced to one year in prison in connection with his role in the Teapot Dome Scandal.

1934   *Burroughs v. United States*: Supreme Court upholds the financial disclosure and reporting requirements of the Federal Corrupt Practices Act.

1941   *United States v. Classic*: Supreme Court holds that Congress has some powers, although qualified, to regulate primary elections and political party nominations procedures. Opinion effectively overrules *Newberry v. U.S.*

1935   Publication of Spencer Ervin's *Henry Ford vs. Truman Newberry: The Famous Senate Election Contest.*

1943   The Congress of Industrial Organizations forms the first political action committee (PAC) in support of Democratic candidates.

Passage of the Smith-Connally Act, which places limits on union spending in federal elections.

1947   Passage of the Taft-Hartley Act, which placed additional limits on union spending in federal elections, along with restrictions on direct campaign contributions by corporations and interstate banks. The law also barred all of them from expending money to influence federal elections.

1948   *United States v. Congress of Industrial Organizations*

1957   *United States v. Auto Workers*

1970   Common Cause, a nonprofit advocacy group interested in electoral reforms related to transparency and political corruption, is formed by Republican John W. Gardner, who had served in the Johnson Administration.

1971–72   Passage of Federal Election Campaign Act (FECA). Signed into law by President Richard Nixon. Among other things, the new law repealed the Federal Corrupt Practices Act and created a new system of campaign finance regulation.

Ralph Nader's Public Citizen Group, the Federation of Homemakers, and the D.C. Consumer's Association file a lawsuit alleging that President Richard Nixon had accepted money from milk co-ops in return for favorable treatment from the Department of Agriculture for lowering milk prices. Public Citizen also files a suit against the Department of Justice for failure to enforce FECA. Additionally, Public Citizen and the National Committee for an Effective Congress petition the SEC to compel corporations to disclose their election-related transactions. In response, President Nixon voluntarily discloses sources of $5 million in

donations. Subsequently, Nixon is ordered by a federal court to disclose the sources of the remaining donations.
Pipefitters v. United States

1973 *Broadrick v. Oklahoma*

1974 Federal Election Campaign Act is amended, establishing a comprehensive system of election regulation and enforcement, as well as creating the Federal Election Commission (FEC).

1975 *Cort v. Ash*: Supreme Court holds that FECA's contribution ban created no private cause of action for corporate shareholders.

1976 *Buckley v. Valeo*

1978 *First National Bank v. Bellotti*

1981 *California Medical Association v. FEC*
     Citizens Against Rent Control v. Berkeley

1982 *Brown v. Socialist Workers*
     FEC v. National Right to Work Committee
     Common Cause v. Schmitt

1985 *FEC v. National Conservative Political Action Committee*

1986 *FEC v. Massachusetts Citizens for Life*

1990 *Austin v. Michigan Chamber of Commerce*

1996 *Colorado Republican Federal Campaign Committee v. FEC*

2000 *Nixon v. Shrink Missouri Government PAC*

2001 *FEC v. Colorado Republic Federal Campaign Committee*

2002 Passage of Bipartisan Campaign Reform Act (BCRA). The law's chief sponsors were Senators Russ Feingold (D-WI) and John McCain (R-AZ).

2003 *FEC v. Beaumont*

McConnell v. FEC

2006 *Randall v. Sorrell*
Wisconsin Right to Life v. FEC

2007 *FEC v. Wisconsin Right to Life*

2008 *Davis v. FEC*

2010 *Citizens United v. FEC*
National Republican Committee v. FEC (summarily affirmed)
January 27: In his State of the Union Address, President Barack Obama criticizes the Supreme Court's *Citizens United* opinion. In response, Justice Samuel Alito frowns and appears to say "not true."

The DISCLOSE Act of 2010 fails to pass in Congress. The proposed law would have amended the Federal Election Campaign Act of 1971 to prohibit foreign influence in federal elections, forbid government contractors from making expenditures with respect to such elections, and establish additional disclosure requirements with respect to spending in such elections.

Formation of Move to Amend Coalition, an activist group organized to amend the Constitution to prevent corporations from having constitutional rights and to overrule the Supreme Court's ruling that "money is speech."

2011 *Arizona Free Enterprise Club v. Bennett*
Occupy Wall Street movement begins in New York. One of the activist group's goals is to reduce corporate influence on elections and politics.

Congressman Theodore "Ted" Deutch (D-FL) introduces "Outlawing Corporate Cash Undermining the Public Interest in our Elections and Democracy" (OCCUPIED) constitutional amendment.

Harvard law professor and Creative Commons board member Lawrence Lessig calls for a constitutional convention during a September 24–25, 2011, Harvard Law School conference cochaired with Mark Meckler, cofounder and national coordinator for Tea Party Patriots.

2012 January 9: *Bluman v. FEC*

March 9: Dan Backer, Jerad Najvar, and Steve Hoersting file advisory opinion request to FEC on behalf of Shaun McCutcheon.

June 22: Five-count complaint filed in three-judge District Court in the District of Columbia on behalf of Shaun McCutcheon.

June 25: *American Tradition Partnership, Inc. v. Bullock*

September 28: Three-judge District Court opinion handed down in *McCutcheon v. FEC*.

October 9: Petition filed in Supreme Court on behalf of Shaun McCutcheon and RNC.

2013 January 15: The Fair Elections Now Act (H.R. 269) is reintroduced in the House of Representatives by Congressman John Yarmuth (D-KY), along with 52 original co-sponsors.

February 14: House Joint Resolution 29 introduced to amend the Constitution. *Section 1 title*: "Artificial Entities Such as Corporations Do Not Have Constitutional Rights." *Section 2 title*: "Money Is Not Free Speech."

February 19: Supreme Court agrees to hear *McCutcheon* case.

May 6: Brief of appellant RNC filed (James Bopp Jr., counsel of record).

Brief of appellant Shaun McCutcheon filed (Michael T. Morley, counsel of record with Dan Backer on brief).

July 18: FEC files its reply brief in *McCutcheon* case.

July 23: *McCutcheon* case set for oral argument in Supreme Court.

August 16: Reply brief of appellant Republican National Committee filed (James Bopp Jr., counsel of record).

August 19: Reply brief of appellant Shaun McCutcheon filed (Michael T. Morley, counsel of record with Erin. E. Murphy on brief).

August 30: Motion of Senator Mitch McConnell for leave to participate in oral argument as amicus curiae and for divided argument is granted.

September 11: U.S. Court of Appeals orders *Wagner v. FEC* case to be held over until Supreme Court decides *McCutcheon* case.

September 17: FEC Chairman Donald F. McGahn resigns after Senate Rules Committee unanimously approves Lee E. Goodman and

Ann Ravel to fill vacancies on the Commission.

Former Massachusetts Governor Mitt Romney's presidential campaign pressed by the FEC as to 23 contributions from possible foreign nationals.

September: By a 2–1 vote, a Texas appellate court reverses the criminal conviction of former U.S. Majority Leader Tom DeLay, who had been charged with conspiracy and money laundering in the 2002 elections.

September 27: James Bopp Jr. files petition for certiorari in *Iowa Right to Life Committee v. Tooker.*

October 8: Supreme Court hears oral arguments in *McCutcheon v. FEC.*

October 16: Senator Ted Cruz (R-TX) blocks the confirmation of Tom Wheeler, nominee for Federal Communications Commission (FCC) chairman, until he states his position on the possibility of the FCC's requiring disclosure of the funders of TV political ads.

October 29: Senator Cruz lifts his hold on the confirmation of Tom Wheeler, the nominee for FCC chairman.

November 25: The Treasury Department and the Internal Revenue Service propose new rules to clarify qualification requirements for tax-exempt status concerning how the IRS defines political activity and how much nonprofits are allowed to spend on it.

December 4: Despite calls from the Corporate Reform Coalition and other transparency groups, the Securities and Exchange Commission (SEC), in announcing its 2014 "Priorities," elected to take no action to compel disclosure of corporate political spending. Other groups, such as the Chamber of Commerce and the Center for Competitive Politics, applaud the SEC's inaction.

2014 April 2: *McCutcheon v. FEC*

Sources & Bibliography

Books & Articles

Abrams, Floyd. *Friend of the Court.* New Haven, CT: Yale University Press, 2013.

————. *Speaking Freely: Trials of the First Amendment.* New York: Viking, 2005.

————. Email to Ronald Collins, 2 April 2014.

Abrams, Floyd & Burt Neuborne. "Debating *Citizens United.*" *Nation*, 13 January 2011.

Abrams, Floyd, Ira Glasser & Joel Gora. "The ACLU Approves Limits on Speech," Wall Street Journal, 30 April 2010 (at http://online.wsj.com/news/articles/SB10001424052748704423504575212152820875486).

Ackerman, Bruce. *The Decline and Fall of the American Republic.* Cambridge, MA: Harvard University Press, 2010.

ACLU Press Release. "ACLU Board Addresses Campaign Finance Policy." 19 April 2010 (at https://www.aclu.org/free-speech/aclu-board-addresses-campaign-finance-policy).

Alexander, Herbert E. *Financing Politics: Money, Elections, and Political Reform.* Washington, DC: Congressional Quarterly Press, 1980.

Alexander, Herbert E. & Monica Bauer. *Financing the 1988 Election.* Boulder, CO: Westview Press, 1991.

Anastaplo, George. *The Constitution of 1787: A Commentary.* Baltimore, MD: Johns Hopkins University Press, 1989.

————. *The Constitutionalist: Notes on the First Amendment.* Dallas, TX: Southern Methodist University Press, 1971.

Anderson, R. Reeves & Anthony J. Franz. "Commentary: The Court's Increasing Reliance on Amicus Curiae in the Past Term." *National Law Journal*, 24 August 2011.

Ashbrook, Tom. "Shaun McCutcheon on *McCutcheon vs. FEC.*" *On Point* Radio, 9 October 2013.

Bai, Matt. "How Much Has *Citizens United* Changed the Political Game?" *New York Times*, 17 July 2012.

Banks, Christopher & John C. Green, editors. *Superintending Democracy: The Courts and the Political Process*. Akron, OH: University of Akron Press, 2001.

Baker, Jean H. *Mary Todd Lincoln: A Biography*. New York: W.W. Norton & Co., 1987.

Baker, Marge. "Commentary—*Citizens United*, the Sequel." *Holland Sentinel* (Michigan), 30 September 2013.

Baker, Paula C., editor. *Money and Politics*. University Park, PA: Pennsylvania State University Press, 2002.

————. *Curbing Campaign Cash: Henry Ford, Truman Newberry, and the Politics of Progressive Reform*. Wichita: KS: University Press of Kansas, 2012.

Barnes, Robert & Matea Gold. "Supreme Court Weighs Campaign Contribution Limits." *Washington Post*, 4 October 2013.

Baude, William. "New Talent for October Oral Arguments," *Volokh Conspiracy* blog, 26 September 2013.

Beckel, Michael. "GOP Super PAC Men Seek to Overturn Donation Limits." *Center for Public Integrity*, 27 March 2012.

————. "Mystery Firm is Election's Top Corporate Donor at $5.3 Million." *Center for Public Integrity*, 5 November 2012.

————. "Nonprofits Outspent Super PACs in 2010, Trend May Continue." *Center for Public Integrity*, 11 July 2012.

————. "Supreme Court Plaintiff McCutcheon Exceeded Campaign Contribution Limit." *Center for Public Integrity*, 3 October 2013.

Beckel, Michael, and Dave Levinthal. "Shaun McCutcheon Hopes Donation in S. Carolina Election Will Be First of Many Nationwide." *Center for Public Integrity*, 3 April 2013.

Bellantoni, Christina. "White House Pushes Back against Chief Justice's Criticism: *Citizens United* Decision Was 'Troubling.'" *Newscom*, 10 March 2010.

BeVier, Lillian. "Campaign Finance Reform: Specious Arguments, Intractable Dilemmas." 94 *Columbia Law Review* 1258 (1994).

————. "Money and Politics: The First Amendment and Campaign Finance Reform." 73 *California Law Review* 1045 (1985).

Bickel, Alexander M. *The Least Dangerous Branch: The Supreme Court at the Bar of Politics*. New York: Bobbs-Merrill Co., 1962.

————. *The Supreme Court and the Idea of Progress*. New York: Harper & Row, 1970.

Biersack, Bob. "Why Campaign Contribution Limits Matter." *Moyers & Company,* 19 September 2013.

Birnbaum, Jeffrey H. *The Money Men: The Real Story of Fundraising's Influence on Political Power in America.* New York: Crown Publishers, 2000.

Biskupic, Joan. "Kagan, Now in a Robe, Argues Again for Campaign Finance Limits." *Reuters,* 9 October 9 2013.

Blumenthal, Paul. "Next *Citizens United? McCutcheon* Supreme Court Case Targets Campaign Contribution Limits."*Huffington Post,* 31 July 31 2013.

————. "Elizabeth Warren: 'We Face A Clear Danger' in Campaign Finance Supreme Court Case." *Huffington Post,* 26 September 2013.

————. "Supreme Court Case Could Spark Dramatic Rise in Campaign Contributions from Wealthy Donors."*Huffington Post,* 4 October 2013.

————. "Mitch McConnell Will Ask Supreme Court to Scrap Campaign Contribution Limits Entirely." *Huffington Post,* 3 October 2013.

"Book Discussion on *Buckley v. Valeo,*" *C-SPAN Video Library,* 22 December 1997.

Bopp, James Jr. Telephone Interviews, 15 October 2013 and 24 January 2014, and email, 20 November 2013.

Brammer, Jack. "Groups Take Aim at Mitch McConnell over Stance on Campaign Contribution Laws." *Kentucky Com,* 3 October 2013.

Breyer, Stephen. *Active Liberty: Interpreting Our Democratic Constitution.* New York: Knopf, 2005.

Briffault, Richard. "*McCutcheon* and the Future of Campaign Finance." *Jurist,* 4 November 2013.

————. "*Davis v. FEC:* The Roberts Court's Continuing Attack on Campaign Finance Reform." 44 *Tulsa Law Review* 475 (2009).

Brudney, Victor. "Business Corporations & Stockholders' Rights under the First Amendment." 91 *Yale Law Journal*235 (1981).

Buckley, James L. *Gleanings from an Unplanned Life: An Annotated Oral History.* Claremont, CA: Intercollegiate Studies Institute, 2006.

————. "Bucks and *Buckley*: The Plaintiff Makes His Case." 27 *National Review,* 27 September 1999.

Burchfield, Bobby. "Enemies of the First Amendment." *The Weekly Standard,* 11 October 1999.

————. Telephone Interview, 4 November 2013.

Burner, David. "James C. McReynolds." In Friedman, Leon, & Fred L. Israel, editors. *The Justices of the United States Supreme Court 1789-1969: Their Lives and Major Opinions.* New York: Chelsea House Publishers, 1969.

Califano, Joseph A. Jr. "Run for the Money." *Washington Times*, 7 May 1998.

Caplan, Lincoln. "The Stealthy Solicitor General." *New York Times*, 22 March 2013.

Chandler, Kim. "Hoover Businessman at Center of U.S. Supreme Court Case on Contribution Limits." *AL.com*, 9 August 2013.

Chemerinsky, Erwin. "The Distinction between Contribution Limits and Expenditure Limits." *SCOTUSblog*, 12 August 12 2013.

Chen, David W. "Lhota Backers Challenge Cap on Spending." *New York Times*, 25 September 2013.

Cillizza, Chris. "Winners and Losers from the McCutcheon v. FEC Ruling." *Washington Post*, 2 April 2014.

"Citizens United 2.0?" *The Cycle*, 8 October 2013 (video clip of Pete Williams from MSNBC).

Clements, Jeffrey D. "The Realistic Solution to *Citizens United*," *Daily Kos*, October 5, 2011.

————. *Corporations Are Not People: Why They Have More Rights than You Do and What You Can Do about It.* San Francisco: Berrett-Koehler Publishers, 2012.

Cline, Seth. "12 Biggest Donors of the 2012 Election." *US News Weekly*, 26 October 2012.

Coburn, Tom. "Just Say No to Earmarks." *Wall Street Journal*, 10 February 2006.

Cole, David. "The Roberts Court's Free Speech Problem." *New York Review of Books*, 28 January 2010.

Collins, Ronald. "Ask the Author: Floyd Abrams & His Fighting Faith." *SCOTUSblog*, May 17, 2013.

————. Interview with Shaun McCutcheon and Dan Backer. Levick Agency, Washington, DC, 30 September 2013.

Confessore, Nicholas. "Big Money Flows in New Jersey Races to Thwart Christie Agenda." *New York Times*, 5 November 2013.

————. "New Rules Would Rein In Nonprofits' Political Role." *New York Times*, 26 November 2013.

Confirmation Hearing on the Nomination of John Roberts to Be Chief Justice of the Supreme Court of the United States, 12 September 2005.

Confirmation Hearing on the Nomination of Samuel Alito Jr. to Be an Associate Justice of the Supreme Court of the United States, 9–13 January 2006.

Copelin, Laylan. "Court Reverses DeLay Conviction." *The Statesman*, 19 September 2013.

Corrado, Anthony, et al. *The New Campaign Finance Sourcebook.* Washington, DC: Brookings Institution Press, 2005.

Coyle, Marcia. "High Court Wary of Another Campaign Contribution Barrier." *National Law Journal,* 8 October 2013.

Democracy 2. Press Release, 2 April 2014.

Denniston, Lyle. "Argument Preview: Campaign Finance— Again." *SCOTUSblog,* 5 October 2013.

————. "Argument Recap: How Is Political Influence Bought?" *SCOTUSblog,* 8 October 2013.

————. "Opinion Analysis: Freeing More Political Money." SCOTUSblog, 2 April 2014.

Dickson, Del, editor. *The Supreme Court in Conference (1940-1985): The Private Discussions Behind Nearly 300 Supreme Court Decisions.* New York: Oxford University Press, 2001.

Dionne, E.J. "Politics as Public Auction." *Washington Post,* 19 June 19 1998.

"Donald B. Verrilli Jr." *SCOTUSblog on Camera,* 21 October 2013.

Dowling, Conor M. & Michael G. Miller. *Super PAC!: Unregulated Money in American Politics.* New York: Routledge, 2014.

Drew, Elizabeth. *Politics and Money: The New Road to Corruption.* New York: Macmillan Co., 1984.

————. "Let's Force Politicians to Reform Campaign Finance." *Salt Lake Tribune,* 10 November 10 1996.

————. "Can We Have a Democratic Election?" *New York Review of Books,* 23 February 2012.

Dworkin, Ronald. "The 'Devastating' Decision." *New York Review of Books,* 25 February 2010.

————. "The Decision That Threatens Democracy." *New York Review of Books,* 13 May 2010.

————. "Free Speech & the Dimensions of Democracy." In Rosenkranz, E. Joshua, editor. *If* Buckley *Fell: A First Amendment Blueprint for Regulating Money in Politics.* New York: The Century Foundation Press, 1999.

Emison, John Lincoln. *Uber Alles: Dictatorship Comes to America.* Gretna, LA: Pelican Publishing Co., 2011.

Epstein, Richard. "*Citizens United v. FEC:* The Constitutional Right That Big Corporations Should Have But Do Not Want." 34 *Harvard Journal of Law & Policy* 639 (2011).

Ervin, Spencer. *Henry Ford vs. Truman H. Newberry: The Famous Senate Election*

Contest. New York: R.R. Smith, 1935.

Franz, Michael. "Campaign Finance Law: The Changing Role of Parties and Interest Groups." In Streb, Michael J., editor. *Law and Election Politics: The Rules of the Game*. New York: Routledge, 2013.

Freund, Paul. "Storms over the Supreme Court." *American Bar Association Journal*, October, 1983.

Fried, Charles. "It's Not *Citizens United*." *New York Times*, 1 October 2013.

Friedman, Barry. "The Wages of Stealth Overruling (with Particular Attention to *Miranda v. Arizona*)." 99 *Georgetown Law Journal* 1 (2010).

Friendly, Fred W. and Martha J. H. Elliott. "Does Money Talk? Elections, Contributions, and Speech." In *The Constitution, That Delicate Balance: Landmark Cases That Shaped the Constitution*. New York: Random House, 1984.

Fuchs, Erin. "The Supreme Court Will Consider Making It Even Easier for Rich People to Buy Elections." *Business Insider*, 23 September 2013.

Garrett, Sam R. *The State of Campaign Finance Policy: Recent Developments and Issues for Congress*. Washington, DC: Congressional Research Services, 29 April 2011.

Gertz, Elmer. *Gertz v. Robert Welch, Inc.: The Story of a Landmark Libel Case*. Carbondale, IL: Southern Illinois University Press, 1992.

Gierzynski, Anthony. *Money Rules: Financing Elections in America*. Boulder, CO: Westview Press, 1999.

Gillon, Steven M. *That's Not What We Meant to Do: Reform and Its Unintended Consequences in Twentieth Century America*. New York: Norton, 2000.

Goodman, Amy & Juan Gonzales. "'500 People Will Control American Democracy' If Supreme Court Overturns Campaign Finance Law." *Democracy Now*, 11 October 2013.

Gora, Joel M. "Campaign Finance Reform: Still Searching Today for a Better Way." 6 *Journal of Law and Policy* 137 (1997-1998).

Greenhouse, Linda. "Precedents Begin to Fall for Roberts Court." *New York Times*, 21 June 2007.

Greenwald, Glenn. *With Liberty and Justice for Some: How the Law Is Used to Destroy Equality and Protect the Powerful*. New York: Metropolitan Books, 2011.

Gross, Terry. "Understanding the Impact of *Citizens United*." *National Public Radio*, 23 February 2012.

Gunther, Gerald. "Foreword: In Search of Evolving Doctrine on a Changing

Court, A Model for a New Equal Protection." 86 *Harvard Law Review* 1 (1972).

Hacker, Jacob S. & Paul Pierson. *Winner-Take-All Politics: How Washington Made the Rich Richer—and Turned Its Back on the Middle Class.* New York: Simon & Schuster, 2011.

Hall, Kermit L. "James Clark McReynolds." In *The Oxford Companion to the Supreme Court of the United States.* New York: Oxford University Press, 2005.

Hasen, Richard L. *The Supreme Court and Election Law: Judging Equality from Baker v. Carr to Bush v. Gore.* New York: New York University Press, 2006.

————. "The Nine Lives of *Buckley v. Valeo.*" In Garnett, Richard & Andrew Koppelman, editors. *First Amendment Stories.* New York: Thompson Reuters / Foundation Press, 2011.

————. "*Citizens United* and the Illusion of Coherence." 109 *Michigan Law Review* 581 (2011).

————. "Beyond Incoherence: The Roberts Court's Deregulatory Turn in *FEC v. Wisconsin Right to Life.*" 92 *Minnesota Law Review* 1064 (2008).

————. "Chill Out: A Qualified Defense of Campaign Finance Disclosure Laws in the Internet Age," 27 *The Journal of Law & Politics* 557 (2012).

————. "*Buckley* is Dead, Long Live Buckley: The New Campaign Finance Incoherence of *McConnell v. Federal Election Commission.*" 153 *University of Pennsylvania Law Review* 31 (2004).

————. "The Untold Drafting History of *Buckley v. Valeo.*" 2 *Elections Law Journal* 241 (2003).

————. "Fixing Washington." 126 *Harvard Law Review* 550 (2012).

————. "RNC Names Bopp Special Counsel." *Election Law Blog,* 8 April 2013.

————. "The Campaign Finance Case at the Supreme Court Next Week Will Be Big—or Huge." *Slate,* 30 September 2013.

Helderman, Rosalind. "DISCLOSE Act, New Donor Transparency Law, Blocked in Senate." *Washington Post,* 16 July 2012.

Henderson, Harry. *Campaign and Election Reform.* New York: Facts on File, 2004.

Hentoff, Nat. *Free Speech for Me—But Not for Thee.* New York: HarperCollins, 1992.

Herman, Susan. "ACLU Backs the First Amendment," *Wall Street Journal,* 6 May 2010 (letter to the editor).

Howe, Amy. "The Chief Justice Looks for a Compromise on Contribution Caps?" *SCOTUSblog*, 8 October 2013.

Huffington, Arianna. *Third World America*. New York: Crown Publishers, 2010.

Humphrey, Hubert. "Minutes of the Senate Democratic Conference, May 9, 1973." In Zelizer, Julian E. "Seeds of Cynicism: The Struggle over Campaign Finance, 1956–1974." 14 *Journal of Policy History* 73 (2002).

Hurley, Lawrence & Joan Biskupic. "Unauthorized Video of U.S. Supreme Court Protest Posted Online." Reuters.com, 27 February 2014.

"Inside the Great Campaign Finance Case of 1976: A Conversation with Ira Glasser." 4 *Civil Liberties Review* 8 (Sept.-Oct. 1977).

Izadi, Elahe. "The Supreme Court Takes Another Step to Advance Money in Politics." *National Journal*, 2 April 2014.

Jacobs, Ben. "Meet Shaun McCutcheon, the Republican Activist Trying to Make History at the Supreme Court." *The Daily Beast*, 8 October 2013.

James Madison Center for Free Speech. Press Release, 2 April 2014.

Jaworski, Leon. *The Right and the Power: The Prosecution of Watergate*. New York: Pocket Books, 1977.

Kaiser, Robert G. *So Damn Much Money: The Triumph of Lobbying and the Corrosion of American Government.*New York: Vintage, 2010.

Kaminer, Wendy. "America Needs Fewer Campaign-Finance Laws." *The Atlantic*, 28 February 2013.

Kang, Cecilia. "Sen. Cruz Blocks Nominee for FCC Chairman." *Washington Post*, 18 October 2013.

Kaplan, Thomas. "Court Lifts Limit on Contributing to Pro-Lhota PAC." *New York Times*, 24 October 2013.

Kirkpatrick, David. "A Quest to End Spending Rules for Campaigns." *New York Times*, 24 January 2010.

Klein, Ezra. "Our Corrupt Politics: It's Not All Money." *New York Review of Books*, 22 March 2012.

Kuh, Richard H. *Foolish Figleaves? Pornography In-and-Out of Court*. New York: Macmillan Co., 1967.

Kurland, Phillip B. & Gerhard Casper. *Landmark Briefs and Arguments of the Supreme Court of the United States: Constitutional Law 1975 Term Supplement.* Volume 85 (*Buckley v. Valeo* (1976), Part 2). Washington, DC: University Publications of America, 1977.

LaRaja, Raymond J. *Small Change: Money, Political Parties, and Campaign Finance Reform*. Ann Arbor, MI: University of Michigan Press, 2008.

Lessig, Lawrence. *Republic, Lost: How Money Corrupts Congress—and a Plan to Stop It.* New York: Twelve, 2011.

Leventhal, Harold. "Courts and Political Thickets," 77 *Columbia Law Review* 345 (1977).

Levitt, Justin. "Confronting the Impact of *Citizens United.*" 29 *Yale Journal of Law and Policy Review* 217 (2010).

Lewis, Anthony. *Freedom for the Thought We Hate: A Biography of the First Amendment.* New York: Basic Books, 2007.

————. "The Court on Politics." *New York Times,* 5 February 1976.

Little, Morgan. "For Government Lawyer Verrilli, Tough Week on Healthcare Case." *Los Angeles Times,* 3 March 2012.

Liptak, Adam. "Justices, 5-4, Reject Corporate Spending Limit." *New York Times,* 21 January 2010.

————. "Justice Defends Ruling on Finance." *New York Times,* 4 February 2010.

————. "Justices to Weigh Key Limit on Political Donors." *New York Times,* 1 October 2013.

————. "Supreme Court Again Weighs Spending Limits in Campaigns." *New York Times,* 8 October 2013.

————. "Supreme Court Strikes Down Aggregate Limits on Federal Campaign Contributions." *New York Times,* 2 April 2014.

Lithwick, Dahlia. "Poor Little Rich Guys." *Slate,* 8 October 2013.

Lowenstein, Daniel Hays, Richard L. Hasen & Daniel P. Tokaji. *Election Law: Cases and Materials.* Durham, NC: Carolina Academic Press, 5th ed. 2012.

Magelby, David, & Anthony Corrado, editors. *Financing the 2008 Election: Assessing Reform.* Washington, DC: The Brookings Institution, 2011.

Mason, George. In "Notes of Robert Yates." *The Records of the Federal Convention of 1787,* vol. 1.

Mauro, Tony. "Republicans Tap New Talent to Argue Key Campaign Case." *The Blog of Legal Times,* 26 September 2013.

————. "The Unsung Associate at Paul Clement's Side." *National Law Journal,* 2 April 2012.

McCloskey, Sharon. "Amicus Briefs Filed by the Right Help Shape the Supreme Court Docket." *The Progressive Pulse,* 5 April 2013.

"McCutcheon Money: The Projected Impact of Striking Aggregate Contribution Limits." *Demos,* 4 October 2013.

McCutcheon, Shaun. "Donation Caps Hurt Democracy." *Politico,* 7 October 2013.

————. *Outsider Inside the Supreme Court: A Decisive First Amendment Battle.* April 2014 (ebook).

————. Email to Ronald Collins, 22 October 2013.

————. Telephone interview with Ronald Collins, 2 April 2014.

McGuire, Kevin T. *The Supreme Court Bar: Legal Elites in the Washington Community.* Charlottesville, VA: University of Virginia Press, 1993.

McGahn, Donald. "Reject the FEC's Activist Overreach." *Politico,* 14 July 14 2009.

Mencimer, Stephanie. "The Man behind *Citizens United* Is Just Getting Started." *Mother Jones,* May-June, 2011.

Mitchell, Alison. "Deadlock in Senate Blocks Campaign Finance Reform, All but Killing It for Year." *New York Times,*27 February 1998.

Morrison, Alan, B. "Watch What You Wish For: The Perils of Reversing *Buckley v. Valeo.*" *American Prospect,* January-February, 1998.

Moyers, Bill. "The End Game for American Democracy?" *Moyers & Company,* 4 September 2013.

————. "How Money Rules Washington—Interview with Sheila Krumholz & Danielle Brian." *Moyers & Company,* 17 May 2013.

Murphy, Laura W. "'Fixing' *Citizens United* Will Break the Constitution." *ACLU. org,* 28 June 2012.

Mutch, Robert E. *Campaigns, Congress, and the Courts: The Making of Federal Campaign Finance Law.* New York: Praeger, 1988.

————. "The First Federal Campaign Finance Bills." In Paula Baker, editor. *Money and Politics.* University Park, PA: Pennsylvania State University Press, 2002.

Nawaz, Farah. "Campaign Finance Reform 'Dollar for Votes'—The American Democracy."14 *Journal of Civil Rights and Economic Development* 155 (1999).

Neuborne, Burt. Op-ed. SCOTUSblog, 3 April 2014.

————. "Soft Landings." In Rosenkranz, E. Joshua, editor. *If Buckley Fell: A First Amendment Blueprint for Regulating Money in Politics.* New York: The Century Foundation Press, 1999.

————. "Why the ACLU Is Wrong About *Citizens United.*" *Nation,* 21 March 2012.

Nichols, John & Robert W. McChesney. *Dollarocracy: How the Money and Media Election Complex Is Destroying America.* New York: Nation Books, 2013.

Overby, Peter. "The 'Country Lawyer' Shaping Campaign Finance Law." *National Public Radio,* 22 June 2011.

Pacchia, Lee. "Interview: Strossen Discusses *Citizens United*, Federal Election." *Bloomberg Law Podcast*, 22 January 2010.

PBS NewsHour, 2 April 2014, 6:00 P.M. EST.

Pizzigati, Sam. "Worse than Watergate." *The Bemidji Pioneer*, 18 October 2013.

Polsby, Nelson B. "*Buckley v. Valeo*: The Special Nature of Political Speech." 1976 *Supreme Court Review* 1.

Post, Robert. "Campaign Finance Reform and the First Amendment." *Tanner Lectures on Human Values*, Harvard Law School, 2 May 2013.

Potter, Trevor. "The Supreme Court Needs More Politics." *Washington Post*, 13 October 2013.

Rakove, Jack N., editor. *The Annotated U.S. Constitution and Declaration of Independence*. Cambridge, MA: Harvard University Press, 2009.

Redish, Martin. Email to authors, 1 March 2014.

————. *Money Talks*. New York: NYU Press, 2001.

Rosen, Jeffrey, moderator. "Gans, Shapiro Debate the *McCutcheon* Campaign Finance Case." *National Constitution Center*, 10 October 2013.

Rosen, Jeffrey. "Packing the Courts." *New York Times*, 10 May 2013.

Rosenkranz, E. Joshua, editor. *If Buckley Fell: A First Amendment Blueprint for Regulating Money in Politics*. New York: The Century Foundation Press, 1999.

Rucker, Philip. "The Film That Cracked the Case." *Washington Post*, 22 January 2010.

Sabato, Larry J. *PAC Power: Inside the World of Political Action Committees*. New York: W.W. Norton & Co., 1984.

Sacks, Mike. "Group Behind SCOTUS Video Speaks Out." HuffPost Live segment, 28 February 2014 (at http://live.huffingtonpost.com/r/archive/segment/5310aa8978c90a1a7300048c).

Samples, John. *The Fallacy of Campaign Finance Reform*. Chicago: University of Chicago Press, 2006.

Savage, David G. "Supreme Court May Strike New Blow to Campaign Funding Laws." *Los Angeles Times*, 21 September 2013.

Schauer, Frederick & Richard H. Pildes. "Electoral Exceptionalism." In Rosenkranz, E. Joshua, editor. *If Buckley Fell: A First Amendment Blueprint for Regulating Money in Politics*. New York: The Century Foundation Press, 1999.

Scheuer, Jeffrey. "Against the Commercial Impulse." *Nieman Reports*, Summer 2000.

Schiff, Adam. "Only a Constitutional Amendment Can Overturn *Citizens United.*" *San Gabriel Valley Tribune*, 20 July 20 2012.

Schoenberg, Shira. "Conservative Lawyer in *Citizens United* Case Endorses Mitt Romney for President." *Boston Globe*, 7 February 2012.

Schreiner, Bruce. "Mitch McConnell Criticized for Involvement in Campaign-Finance Case." *Courier-Journal*, 4 October 2013.

Schwinn, Steven D. "FEC Denies Disclosure Exemption for Tea Party." *Constitutional Law Prof blog*, 22 November 2013.

Segal, Jeffrey A. & Harold J. Spaeth. "The Influence of *Stare Decisis* on the Votes of United States Supreme Court Justices." 40 *American Journal of Political Science* 971 (1996).

Senate Confirmation Hearings of Elena Kagan, 28-30 June and 1 July 2010.

Serwer, Adam. "Obamacare's Supreme Court Disaster." *Mother Jones*, 27 March 2012.

Shapiro, Andrew. "Controversy: Should *Buckley* Be Overturned?" *American Prospect*, 16 November 2001 (with reply by Alan Morrison).

Shapiro, Ilya. Email to Ronald Collins, 2 April 2014.

Shapiro, Ilya and Trevor Burrus. "Federal Contractors Shouldn't Lose First Amendment Rights." *Cato at Liberty*, 16 July 2013.

Shapiro, Steven, R. "Remarks." Washington, DC: ACLU National Office, 25 September 2013.

Sherman, Paul. "It's Time to End Our Failed Affair with Campaign Finance Laws." *Forbes*, 15 September 2013.

Shiffrin, Steven. Email to authors, 1 March 2014.

Sitkoff, Robert. "Corporate Political Speech, Political Extortion, and the Competition for Corporate Charters." 69*University of Chicago Law Review* 1103 (2002).

Slaback, Frederick G., editor. *The Constitution and Campaign Finance Reform: An Anthology*. Durham, NC: Carolina Academic Press, 1998.

Smith, Bradley A. *Unfree Speech: The Folly of Campaign Finance Reform*. Princeton, NJ: Princeton University Press, 2001.

—————. "Interview." *The Sound of Ideas*, WCPN, 29 March 2011.

Smith, Donald V. "The Influence of the Foreign-Born of the Northwest in the Election of 1860." 19 *Mississippi Valley Historical Journal* 192 (September, 1932).

Smith, Rodney A. *Money, Power, & Elections: How Campaign Finance Reform Subverts American Democracy*. Baton Rouge: LA: Louisiana State University Press, 2006.

Snowe, Olympia. *Fighting for Common Ground: How We Can Fix the Stalemate in Congress.* New York: Weinstein Books, 2013.

Somin, Ilya. "Commentary: Alito's Libertarian Streak." *Cato Institute Website.*

Sorauf, Frank J. *Inside Campaign Finance: Myths and Realities.* New Haven, CT: Yale University Press, 1992.

————. "Politics, Experience, and the First Amendment: The Case of American Campaign Finance." 94 *Columbia Law Review* 1348 (1994).

"Speech & Power" Symposium, *Nation,* 21 July 1997.

Steele, Charles N. and Jeffrey H. Bowman. "The Constitutionality of Independent Regulatory Agencies Under the Necessary and Proper Clause: The Case of the Federal Election Commission." 4 *Yale Journal on Regulation* 363 (1987).

Stevens, John Paul. Five Chiefs: A Supreme Court Memoir. New York: Little, Brown & Co., 2011.

————. Six Amendments: How and Why We Should Change the Constitution. New York: Little, Brown & Co., 2014.

Stohr, Greg. "Campaign-Money Limits at Risk in New Court Term." *Bloomberg News,* 4 October 2013.

Stone, Geoffrey R. "Is Money Speech?" *Huffington Post,* 5 February 2012.

————. "Fixing *Citizens United.*" *Huffington Post,* 12 June 2012.

————. "Roberts, Alito, and The Rule of Law." *Huffington Post,* 28 June 2007.

Story, Joseph. *Commentaries on the Constitution of the United States.* Edited by Ronald Rotunda and John Nowak. Durham, NC: Carolina Academic Press, 1987 (original publication, 1833).

Strauss, David H. "Corruption, Equality and Campaign Finance." 94 *Columbia Law Review* 1369 (1994).

Sullivan, Kathleen M. "Political Money and Freedom of Speech." 30 *University of California Davis Law Review* 663 (1997).

Sullivan, Sean. "Everything You Need to Know About *McCutcheon v. FEC.*" *Washington Post,* 8 October 2013.

Sunstein, Cass R. "Exchange: Speech in the Welfare State: Free Speech Now." 59 *University of Chicago Law Review* 255 (1992).

————. "Speech and Power." *Nation,* 21 July 1997.

Superville, Darlene. "Obama Weekly Address VIDEO: President Blasts Supreme Court over *Citizens United*Decision." *Huffington Post,* 23 January 2010.

Tau, Byron. "Supreme Court Set to Consider Donor Limits." *Politico,* 7 October 2013.

Teachout, Zephyr. "The Anti-Corruption Principle." 94 *Cornell Law Review* 341 (2009).

Thayer, George. *Who Shakes the Money Tree? American Campaign Financing from 1789 to the Present.* New York: Simon & Schuster, 1973.

Thomas, Scott E. and Jeffrey H. Bowman. "Is Soft Money Here to Stay Under the 'Magic Words' Doctrine?" 10*Stanford Law & Policy Review* 33 (1998).

————."Obstacles to Effective Enforcement of the Federal Election Campaign Act." 52 *Administrative Law Review*575 (2000).

Thompson, Margaret Susan. *The "Spider Web": Congress and Lobbying in the Age of Grant.* Ithaca, NY: Cornell University Press, 1986.

Tiffany, Victor. "Article V.org's Dan Marks Sees Risky Convention as Necessity." *The Amendment Gazette*, 21 August 2013 (video interview with Dan Marks).

Tillman, Seth Barrett. "*Citizens United* and the Scope of Professor Teachout's Anti-Corruption Principle." 107*Northwestern University Law Review* 399 (2012).

————. "Why Professor Lessig's 'Dependence Corruption' Is Not a Founding-Era Concept." 13 *Election Law Journal* (forthcoming 2014).

"Time to Rethink *Buckley v. Valeo.*" *New York Times*, 12 November 1998.

Toobin, Jeffrey. "Another Citizens United—But Worse." *The New Yorker*, 30 July 2013.

————. "Money Unlimited: How Chief Justice John Roberts Orchestrated the *Citizens United* Decision." *The New Yorker*, 21 May 2012.

————. *The Oath: The Obama White House and The Supreme Court.* New York: Doubleday, 2012.

Totenberg, Nina. "Supreme Court Weighs Easing Limits on Campaign Contributions." *National Public Radio*, 8 October 2013.

Tribe, Laurence. "The Once-and-for-All Solution to Our Campaign Finance Problems." *Slate*, 13 June 2012.

Troyan, Mary Ordorff. "Alabama GOP Donor Challenges Limits." *USA Today*, 9 August 2013.

Tummarello, Kate. "Cruz Lifts Hold on Obama's Nominee to Lead FCC." *The Hill*, 29 October 2013.

Turow, Scott. "The High Court's Twenty-Year-Old Mistake." *New York Times*, 12 October 1997.

Tushnet, Mark. *In the Balance: Law and Politics on the Roberts Court.* New York: W.W. Norton, 2013.

Unger, Nancy C. *Fighting Bob La Follette: The Righteous Reformer.* Chapel Hill, NC: University of North Carolina Press, 2000.

Urofsky, Melvin I. *Money & Free Speech: Campaign Finance Reform and the Courts.* Oletha, KS: Kansas University Press, 2005.

VictorMTA [pseud.]. "Article V.org's Dan Marks Sees Risky Convention as Necessity." *The Amendment Gazette,* 21 August 21 2013.

Volokh, Eugene. "Why *Buckley v. Valeo* Is Basically Right." 34 *Arizona State Law Journal* 1095 (2013).

Walsh, Mark. "A Civil Day on the Bench for Opinions on the Impolite World of Campaign Finance." SCOTUSblog, 2 April 2014.

————. "It Was Another Big Term for Amicus Curiae Briefs at the High Court." *American Bar Association Journal,* 1 September 2013.

Warren, James. "Richard Posner Bashes Supreme Court's *Citizens United* Ruling." *The Daily Beast,* 14 July 2012.

Wertheimer, Fred. "A Campaign Finance Reform Agenda for 2013 Statement by Democracy 21 President Fred Wertheimer." *Democracy 21,* 6 November 2012.

————. "Democracy 21's Fred Wertheimer Explains." *USA Today* video, 2013.

————. "Supreme Court Could Create System of Legalized Bribery in Washington Depending on Its Decision in*McCutcheon* Case." *Huffington Post,* 21 February 2013.

————. "The Supreme Court's Democracy Test." *Politico,* 12 September 2013.

Wertheimer, Fred and Susan Weiss Manes. "Campaign Finance Reform: A Key to Restoring the Health of our Democracy." 94 *Columbia Law Review* 1126 (1994).

White, Theodore H. *Breach of Faith: The Fall of Richard Nixon.* New York: Atheneum, 1975.

Wilson, Reid. "Former FEC Chairman McGahn to Return to Private Practice." *Washington Post,* 18 September 2013.

Winkler, Adam. "The Coming of the Kagan Court." *Slate,* 6 October 2013.

————. "Other People's Money: Corporations, Agency Costs, and Campaign Finance Law." 92 *Georgetown Law Journal* 571 (2004).

————. "Political Corporate Contributions Won't Be Aired in Daylight." *The Daily Beast,* 5 December 2013.

Winter, Ralph K. *Watergate and the Law: Political Campaigns and Presidential Power.* Washington, DC: American Enterprise Institute, 1974.

————. "The History and Theory of *Buckley v. Valeo*." 6 *Journal of Law and Policy* 93 (1997–1998).

Wolf, Richard. "Chief Justice Roberts Holds Key in Campaign-Finance Case." *USA Today*, 12 September 2013.

———. "Everyday Heroes Etched in Supreme Court History." *USA Today*, 19 September 2013.

Wright, Skelly. "Money and the Pollutions of Politics: Is the First Amendment an Obstacle to Political Equality?" 82 *Columbia Law Review* 609 (1982).

———. "Politics and the Constitution: Is Money Speech?" 85 *Yale Law Journal* 1001 (1976).

Youn, Monica, editor. *Money, Politics, and the Constitution: Beyond Citizens United*. New York: The Century Foundation, 2011.

Zeleny, Jeff. "Top Donors to Republicans Seek More Say in Senate Races." *New York Times*, 2 February 2013.

Zelizer, Julian E. "Seeds of Cynicism: The Struggle over Campaign Finance, 1956-1974." 14 *Journal of Policy History* 73 (2002). Reprinted in Paula Baker, editor. *Money and Politics*. University Park, PA: Pennsylvania State University Press, 2002.

Zinn, Howard. *A People's History of the United States*. New York: Harcourt Brace Jovanovich, 1980.

Select Blogs & Websites

ALGOP.org

ArticleV.org

Center for Competitive Politics

Center for Responsive Politics

Common Cause ("Money in Politics")

DB Capitol Strategies

Democracy 21

Election Law Blog

Federal Election Commission

McCutcheon v. Federal Election Commission (Shaun McCutcheon's site)

OpenSecrets.org

Public Campaign Action Fund

SCOTUSblog

Symposium: McCutcheon v. Federal Election Commission (SCOTUSblog, August 2013) (contributors: Erwin Chemerinsky, Ronald Collins, Robert Corn-Revere, Joel Gora, Justin Levitt, Tamara Piety, and Adam Winkler)

Select Federal Election Laws

Bipartisan Campaign Reform Act ("BCRA"), Pub. L. No. 107-155, 116 Stat. 81 (2002).

FECA Amendments of 1976, Pub. L. No. 94-283, 90 Stat. 475 (1976).

Federal Election Campaign Act of 1971 ("FECA"), 2 U.S.C. §§ 441(c) *et seq.*

Supreme Court Cases

Trist v. Child, 88 U.S. 441 (1874)

Lochner v. New York, 198 U.S. 45 (1905)

United States v. Gradwell, 243 U.S. 476 (1917)

Newberry v. United States, 256 U.S. 232 (1921)

United States v. Classic, 313 U.S. 299 (1941)

United States v. Congress of Industrial Organizations, 335 U.S. 106 (1948)

United States v. Auto Workers, 352 U.S. 567 (1957)

Pipefitters v. United States, 407 U.S. 385 (1972)

Broadrick v. Oklahoma, 413 U.S. 601 (1973)

Buckley v. Valeo, 424 U.S. 1 (1976)

First National Bank v. Bellotti, 435 U.S. 765 (1978)

Republican National Committee v. Federal Election Commission, 445 U.S. 955 (1980)

California Medical Association v. FEC, 453 U.S. 182 (1981)

Citizens Against Rent Control v. Berkeley, 454 U.S. 290 (1981)

Brown v Socialist Workers, 459 U.S. 87 (1982)

FEC v. National Right to Work Committee, 459 U.S. 197 (1982)

Common Cause v. Schmitt, 455 U.S. 129 (1982)

FEC v. National Conservative Political Action Committee, 470 U.S. 480 (1985)

FEC v. Massachusetts Citizens for Life, 479 U.S. 238 (1986)

Austin v. Michigan Chamber of Commerce, 494 U.S. 652 (1990)

Colorado Republican Federal Campaign Committee v. FEC, 518 U.S. 604 (1996)

Nixon v. Shrink Missouri Government PAC, 528 U.S. 377 (2000)

FEC v. Colorado Republican Federal Campaign Committee, 533 U.S. 431 (2001)

FEC v. Beaumont, 539 U.S. 146 (2003)

McConnell v. FEC, 540 U.S. 93 (2003)

Randall v. Sorrell, 548 U.S. 230 (2006)

Wisconsin Right to Life v. FEC, 546 U.S. 410 (2006)

FEC v. Wisconsin Right to Life, 551 U.S. 449 (2007)

Davis v. FEC, 554 U.S. 724 (2008)

Citizens United v. FEC, 558 U.S. 310 (2010)

Doe v. Reed, 130 S.Ct. 2811 (2010)

Arizona Free Enterprise Club v. Bennett, 131 S. Ct. 2806, 564 U.S. ___ (2011)

American Tradition Partnership, Inc. v. Bullock, 123 S. Ct. 2490 (2012)

Bluman v. Federal Election Commission, 132 S.C. 1087 (2012)

McCutcheon v. Federal Election Commission, 572 U.S. ___ (2014)

Iowa Right to Life Committee, Inc. v. Tooker (cert. petition: doc. # 13-407)

Select Lower Court Cases

United States v. Nat'l Comm. for Impeachment, 469 F.2d 1135 (2d. Cir. 1972)

ACLU v. Jennings, 366 F. Supp. 1041 (D.D.C. 1973), vacated sub nom., *Staats v. ACLU*, 422 U.S. 1030 (1975)

Buckley v. Valeo, 519 F.2d 821 (D.C. Cir. 1975)

Sistrunk v. City of Strongsville, 99 F.3d 194 (1996)

Bush-Quayle '92 Primary Committee v. Federal Election Commission, 104 F.3d 448 (D.C. Cir. 1997)

Kasky v. Nike, Inc., 45 P.3d 243 (Cal., 2002), cert. denied, *Nike, Inc. v. Kasky*, 123 S. Ct. 2554 (2003)

EMILY's List v. FEC, 581 F.3d 1 (D.C. Cir. 2009)

SpeechNow.org v. Federal Election Commission, 599 F.3d 686 (D.C. Cir. 2010), cert. denied, *Keating v. Federal Election Commission*, 131 S. Ct. 553 (2010)

Preston v. Leake, 660 F.3d 726 (4th Cir. 2011)

McCutcheon v. Federal Election Commission, 893 F. Supp. 2d 133 (D.D.C. 2012)

United States v. Ring, 706 F.3d 460 (D.C. Cir. 2013)

New York Progress and Protection PAC v. Walsh, ____ F.3d ____ (2nd Cir. 2013)

Wagner v. Federal Election Commission, ____ F.3d ____ (D.C. Cir., pending 2014)

About the Authors

Ronald K.L. Collins is the Harold S. Shefelman Scholar at the University of Washington Law School. Before coming to the Law School, Collins served as a law clerk to Justice Hans A. Linde on the Oregon Supreme Court, a Supreme Court Fellow under Chief Justice Warren Burger, and a scholar at the Washington, D.C., office of the First Amendment Center, where he wrote and lectured on freedom of expression and oversaw the online library component of the First Amendment Center's website. In 2010 he was a fellow in residence at the Norman Mailer Writers Colony.

Collins has taught constitutional and contract law at Temple Law School, George Washington Law School, Seattle University School of Law, and the University of Washington Law School. He has written constitutional briefs that were submitted to the Supreme Court and various other federal and state high courts. His journalistic writings on the First Amendment have appeared in the *Columbia Journalism Review, New York Times, Los Angeles Times,* and *Washington Post,* among other publications. He is the book editor of SCOTUSblog. In addition to the books that he coauthored with David Skover, he is the editor of *The Fundamental Holmes: A Free Speech Chronicle and Reader* (Cambridge University Press, 2010) and coauthor with Sam Chaltain of *We Must Not Be Afraid to Be Free* (Oxford University Press, 2011). His latest book is *Nuanced Absolutism: Floyd Abrams and the First Amendment* (2013).

David M. Skover is the Fredric C. Tausend Professor of Law at Seattle University School of Law. He teaches, writes, and lectures in the fields of federal constitutional law, federal jurisdiction, mass communications theory, and the First Amendment.

Skover graduated from the Woodrow Wilson School of International and Domestic Affairs at Princeton University. He received his law degree from Yale Law School, where he was an editor of the *Yale Law Journal.* Thereafter, he served as a law clerk for Judge Jon O. Newman of the U.S. Court of Appeals for the Second Circuit. In addition to the books that he coauthored with Ronald Collins, David is the coauthor with Pierre Schlag of *Tactics of Legal Reasoning* (Carolina Academic Press, 1986).

Together, Collins and Skover have authored *The Death of Discourse* (1996, 2005), *The Trials of Lenny Bruce: The Fall and Rise of an American Icon* (2002, 2012), *Mania: The Outraged & Outrageous Lives That Launched a Cultural Revolution* (2013), and *On Dissent: Its Meaning in America* (2013). They have also authored numerous scholarly articles in various journals including the *Harvard Law Review, Stanford Law Review, Michigan Law Review,* and the *Supreme Court Review,* among other publications.

The *Trials of Lenny Bruce* (updated & enhanced) and *Mania* are available as ebooks from Top Five Books.

About SCOTUS Books-in-Brief

The SCOTUS Books-in-Brief series is designed to provide readers—lay and scholarly alike—with a reliable, informative, and engaging narrative account of significant Supreme Court rulings shortly after they are rendered. Provided in ebook format, each work is economically priced and accessible on multiple platforms, including Kindle (Amazon), iPad (Apple iBooks), Nook (Barnes & Noble), Android devices (Google Play), and Kobo. Each ebook will be available within a week of the decision and will consist of:

- a historical account of the case
- a statement of its facts
- profiles of the parties
- analyses of the lower court judgments
- descriptions of briefs filed & oral arguments in the Supreme Court
- a discussion of the larger issues raised by the case, and
- a comprehensive timeline

Each SCOTUS Books-in-Brief title will be researched and written by a noted legal authority in the field. To further enhance the reading experience, every ebook will have photographs and hyperlinks (including links to court opinions and audio files).

Editorial Board
- **Ronald K.L. Collins**, University of Washington School of Law
- **David M. Skover**, Seattle University, School of Law

Advisory Board
- **Erwin Chemerinsky**, University of California at Irvine, School of Law
- **Robert Corn-Revere**, Davis Wright Tremaine

- **David M. O'Brien**, University of Virginia, Department of Politics
- **Geoffrey Stone**, University of Chicago, School of Law
- **Nadine Strossen**, New York Law School
- **Stephen Vladeck**, American University, School of Law
- **Kathryn Watts**, University of Washington, School of Law
- **Adam Winkler**, UCLA School of Law

CPSIA information can be obtained at www.ICGtesting.com
Printed in the USA
BVOW03s1704290414

351678BV00004B/19/P

À Lisa.
B. C.

Pour mon frère Nabil Saadi.
D. L.

© 2006, Albin Michel Jeunesse

22, rue Huyghens – 75014 Paris

www.albin-michel.fr

Loi 49–956 du 16 juillet 1949 sur les publications destinées à la jeunesse

Dépôt légal : premier semestre 2006 - Numéro d'édition : 13273 - ISBN : 2 226 16861 3

Imprimé en Italie

Didier Lévy

Benjamin Chaud

La fée Coquillette
aime les histoires d'amour

Albin Michel Jeunesse

La fée Coquillette plane dans les airs.
Comme c'est bon de se laisser porter par le vent,
sans effort, sans souci, sans but…

La voilà au-dessus d'un merveilleux château.
– Mais c'est la demeure du prince Mike ! s'exclame
Coquillette. Je me demande si le prince est aussi
beau en vrai qu'en photo ?

La petite fée se remet du rouge à lèvres et fonce !

Le prince Mike est assis au bord
de sa merveilleuse piscine.
– Il est encore plus beau qu'à la télé,
soupire Coquillette. Mais ce qu'il a l'air
grognon !

La fée se pose sur son nez.

– Va-t'en ! s'énerve le prince.

– Du calme, prince Mike. C'est moi, la fée Coquillette !

Je suis là pour exaucer ton vœu le plus cher,

poil au dromadaire !

– Un vœu ? s'étonne le prince Mike.

Vite, il sort une photo de sa poche.

– Je veux cette fille ! Elle s'appelle Norma,

c'est une vendeuse de bonbons ! Je veux qu'elle m'aime !

La fée observe la photo.

– Tu es amoureux d'elle ? demande Coquillette.

Tu es allé la voir ? Tu lui as dit ce que tu ressentais ?

Les yeux brillants de colère, le prince Mike hoche la tête.

– Évidemment ! Et tu sais ce qu'elle a osé me répondre ? Elle a dit qu'elle n'était pas du tout amoureuse de moi.

Le prince se lève :
– Je ne comprends pas, je suis beau, je suis riche, je suis célèbre, toutes les filles sont amoureuses de moi. Et pas elle !!!

Je veux cette fille !

– Prince Mike, répond Coquillette, une fée peut accomplir bien des miracles, mais ce que tu demandes est tout simplement impossible. L'amour, ça ne se commande pas, poil au bras !
Le prince l'attrape dans sa grosse paluche. Il bout de colère.
– Qu'est-ce que tu me racontes là ?! Réalise mon vœu immédiatement ou je te réduis en purée. Allez !…

Le prince se met à serrer Coquillette, la petite fée va étouffer…

Coquillette arrive tout juste à prononcer une formule magique. D'un seul coup, le prince n'a plus la moindre force, et ses doigts s'ouvrent comme les pétales d'une fleur.

– Tu commences à m'énerver, prince Mike ! s'écrie Coquillette. Je vais préparer une petite infusion pour nous calmer, et on va discuter un peu tous les deux.

De rage, il écrabouille les tasses
d'infusion et se met à hurler.
Un cri terrible, sans fin,
plein de colère et de chagrin.
Ahhhhhhh…

Mais, peu à peu, le cri se transforme.
Il devient une plainte, un chant.
Ahhhhhhhh…

Soudain, **Coquillette a une idée !**
D'un nouveau coup de baguette magique,
elle fait apparaître une guitare, et elle accompagne
le pauvre prince Mike.

Il est malheureux, le prince Mike, mais il trouve ça joli, ces petites
notes de guitare qui se mêlent à sa voix. Et puis, ça lui fait du bien
de chanter pour exprimer sa peine.
Ahhhhhhhh...

À la fin de la chanson, Coquillette applaudit.
Le prince Mike sourit. Il a encore l'air
un peu triste, mais il est calme, détendu.
— Tu chantes drôlement bien, dit Coquillette.
— Et toi, tu joues drôlement bien de la guitare,
répond Mike.
— Je peux t'apprendre, propose Coquillette
(qui suit sa petite idée…).

Coquillette fait apparaître un deuxième instrument.
Et elle enseigne les secrets de la guitare au prince Mike
qui se découvre, jour après jour, une véritable passion
pour la musique.

Il chante le matin, le midi, le soir…
Les vaches et les moutons du pré voisin l'applaudissent !

Au fil des semaines, le caractère du prince Mike se transforme.
Lui qui était colérique et égoïste, le voilà qui distribue
ses couronnes, ses habits, ses voitures, ses maisons…
Il garde juste sa guitare et part, seul, chanter dans les villes
et les campagnes.

De concert en concert, la fée Coquillette le suit discrètement.
Un soir que le prince Mike chante sur la place d'un village,
Coquillette repère quelqu'un dans la foule. Incroyable !
C'est Norma, la vendeuse de bonbons dont le prince
était amoureux !
« Et si Norma tombait amoureuse de lui maintenant
qu'il a changé ? » se demande soudain Coquillette,
le cœur battant.

À la fin du concert, Norma et deux de ses amis viennent saluer le chanteur. Coquillette s'approche, elle veut absolument savoir ce qui va se dire…

– Bonjour prince Mike, vous vous souvenez de moi ?
Je suis Norma, la vendeuse de bonbons.
– Bien sûr, sourit Mike.
Norma se tourne vers ses amis, et fait les présentations :
– Prince Mike, voilà Albert, mon fiancé, et sa sœur Capucine.
Coquillette est horriblement déçue,
Norma a déjà un amoureux !

Mike, lui, n'a pas du tout l'air déçu. Au contraire, il semble de très bonne humeur. Il invite Norma et ses amis à boire une grenadine à la terrasse d'un bar proche. Comme il est tard, la terrasse se vide peu à peu, mais Mike ne s'en rend pas compte car il est en grande discussion avec Capucine, la sœur d'Albert.

Norma et Albert sont partis se coucher,
tout le monde est parti se coucher.
À la terrasse du bar, il ne reste plus que Mike et Capucine
qui discutent toujours. Et Coquillette qui les observe de loin.
« Mais que peuvent-ils bien se raconter ?! » se demande
Coquillette.
Soudain, ça alors ?! Mike et Capucine se penchent
l'un vers l'autre. Et s'embrassent sur la bouche.

Oui, sur la bouche !

– Youpi ! hurle coquillette, folle de joie.
Le prince Mike a enfin trouvé l'amour !
Youpi ! Hourra !!!
Mike voit la petite fée qui tourbillonne dans la nuit.
Alors, tout sourire, il prend sa guitare,
et improvise une chanson très douce :

Coquillette, Coquillette,
C'est la fée, Poil au nez !
Coquillette, Coquillette,
C'est la toute petite fée
Qu'il me faut remercier !